50 HIKES
IN THE SIERRA NEVADA

OTHER BOOKS IN THE 50 HIKES SERIES

50 Hikes in Michigan & Wisconsin's North Country Trail

50 Hikes in the North Georgia Mountains

50 Hikes in Northern New Mexico

50 Hikes in Ohio

50 Hikes in Orange County

50 Hikes in the Ozarks

50 Hikes in South Carolina

50 Hikes in the Upper Hudson Valley

50 Hikes in Wisconsin

50 Hikes in the Berkshire Hills

50 Hikes in Alaska's Kenai Peninsula

50 Hikes in Coastal and Inland Maine

50 Hikes in Kentucky

50 Hikes in the Catskills

50 HIKES
IN THE SIERRA NEVADA

SECOND EDITION

Julie Smith

THE COUNTRYMAN PRESS

A division of W. W. Norton & Company

Independent Publishers Since 1923

Copyright © 2009, 2019 by The Countryman Press

For information about special discounts for bulk purchases, please contact W. W. Norton Special Sales at specialsales@wwnorton.com or 800-233-4830

Manufacturing by Versa Press
Book design by Chris Welch
Production manager: Lauren Abbate

The Countryman Press
www.countrymanpress.com

A division of W. W. Norton & Company, Inc.
500 Fifth Avenue, New York, NY 10110
www.wwnorton.com

978-1-68268-293-7 (pbk.)

10 9 8 7 6 5 4 3 2 1

For my mom and dad, for showing me that some
of the best paths in life are dirt.

Climb the mountains and get their good tidings. Nature's peace
will flow into you as sunshine flows into trees. The winds will blow
their own freshness into you, and the storms their energy,
while cares will drop off like autumn leaves.
—John Muir

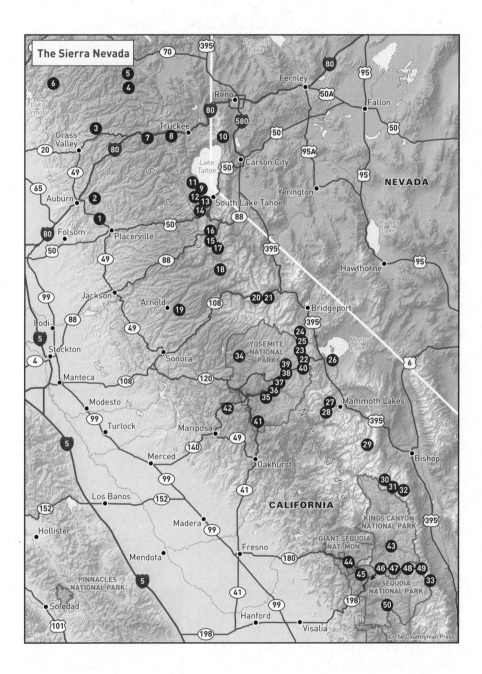

Contents

Hikes at a Glance | 10
Acknowledgments | 14
Introduction | 15

I. GOLD COUNTRY | 25

1. MONROE RIDGE AND MONUMENT TRAIL LOOP | 26
2. AMERICAN CANYON TRAIL | 31
3. HUMBUG TRAIL | 36
4. SIERRA BUTTES | 40
5. ROUND LAKE LOOP | 44
6. FEATHER FALLS | 48

II. LAKE TAHOE | 53

7. LOCH LEVEN LAKES | 54
8. MOUNT JUDAH LOOP | 58
9. RUBICON TRAIL | 62
10. TAHOE MEADOWS | 66
11. CRAG LAKE | 70
12. CASCADE FALLS AND GRANITE LAKE | 74
13. MOUNT TALLAC | 78
14. ECHO LAKE TO LAKE ALOHA | 82

III. TRANS-SIERRA PASSES | 87

15. ROUND TOP LAKE LOOP | 88
16. MEISS MEADOW TO ROUND LAKE | 92
17. GRANITE LAKE | 96
18. BULL RUN LAKE | 100
19. CALAVERAS BIG TREES STATE PARK—SOUTH GROVE | 104
20. SONORA PASS | 108
21. LEAVITT MEADOW TO LANE LAKE | 112
22. BENNETTVILLE TRAIL | 116
23. TWENTY LAKES BASIN | 120

IV. EASTERN SIERRA | 125

24. GREEN LAKE | 126
25. VIRGINIA LAKES BASIN | 130
26. MONO LAKE | 134
27. SAN JOAQUIN RIDGE | 138
28. DEVILS POSTPILE TO RAINBOW FALLS | 142
29. LITTLE LAKES VALLEY TO GEM LAKES | 146
30. BLUE LAKE | 150
31. LONG LAKE | 154
32. BIG PINE LAKES BASIN TO SECOND LAKE | 159
33. LONE PINE LAKE | 164

V. YOSEMITE NATIONAL PARK AREA | 169

34. WAPAMA FALLS | 170
35. PANORAMA TRAIL | 175
36. HALF DOME | 180
37. CLOUDS REST | 185
38. CATHEDRAL LAKES | 190
39. WATERWHEEL FALLS | 195
40. GAYLOR LAKES | 200
41. CHILNUALNA FALLS | 204
42. HITE COVE | 208

VI. SEQUOIA AND KINGS CANYON NATIONAL PARKS | 213

43. MIST FALLS | 214
44. REDWOOD MOUNTAIN GROVE | 218
45. LITTLE BALDY | 223
46. TOKOPAH FALLS | 227
47. LAKES TRAIL TO HEATHER LAKE | 231
48. CIRCLE MEADOW | 236
49. CRESCENT AND LOG MEADOWS LOOP | 240
50. EAGLE LAKE | 244

Hikes at a Glance

Hike	Area
1. Monroe Ridge and Monument Trail Loop	Marshall Gold Discovery SHP
2. American Canyon Trail	Auburn State Recreation Area
3. Humbug Trail	Malakoff Diggins SHP
4. Sierra Buttes	Tahoe National Forest
5. Round Lake Loop	Lakes Basin Recreation Area
6. Feather Falls	Plumas National Forest
7. Loch Leven Lakes	Tahoe National Forest
8. Mount Judah Loop	Tahoe National Forest
9. Rubicon Trail	DL Bliss and Emerald Bay State Parks
10. Tahoe Meadows	Humboldt-Toiyabe National Forest
11. Crag Lake	Desolation Wilderness
12. Cascade Falls and Granite Lake	Desolation Wilderness
13. Mount Tallac	Desolation Wilderness
14. Echo Lake to Lake Aloha	Desolation Wilderness
15. Round Top Lake Loop	Mokelumne Wilderness (Carson Pass)
16. Meiss Meadow to Round Lake	Eldorado National Forest (Carson Pass)
17. Granite Lake	Mokelumne Wilderness (Carson Pass)
18. Bull Run Lake	Carson-Iceberg Wilderness (Ebbetts Pass)
19. Calaveras Big Trees State Park—South Grove	Calaveras Big Trees State Park (Ebbetts Pass)
20. Sonora Pass	Emigrant Wilderness (Sonora Pass)
21. Leavitt Meadow to Lane Lake	Humboldt-Toiyabe National Forest (Sonora Pass)
22. Bennettville Trail	Inyo National Forest (Tioga Pass)
23. Twenty Lakes Basin	Hoover Wilderness (Tioga Pass)
24. Green Lake	Hoover Wilderness
25. Virginia Lakes Basin	Hoover Wilderness
26. Mono Lake	Mono Basin National Forest Scenic Area
27. San Joaquin Ridge	Inyo National Forest
28. Devils Postpile to Rainbow Falls	Devils Postpile National Monument
29. Little Lakes Valley to Gem Lakes	John Muir Wilderness
30. Blue Lake	John Muir Wilderness
31. Long Lake	John Muir Wilderness
32. Big Pine Lakes Basin to Second Lake	John Muir Wilderness
33. Lone Pine Lake	John Muir Wilderness

Region	Type	RT Distance	Rating	Elevation
Gold Country	D	3.0	E–M	+620'/-620'
Gold Country	D	4.8	M	+2'/-1,058'
Gold Country	D	5.4	M	+145'/-947'
Gold Country	D	5.0	M–S	+1,556'/-57'
Gold Country	D	4.0	E	+470'/-470'
Gold Country	D	8.4	M–S	+2,228'/-2,228'
Lake Tahoe	D	6.0	M	+1,199'/-223'
Lake Tahoe	D	5.0	M	+1,445'/-1,445'
Lake Tahoe	D	5.4	E	+765'/-511'
Lake Tahoe	D	1.3; 3.4	E; E	+74'/-74'; +286'/-247'
Lake Tahoe	D/O	10.0	M	+1,290'/-27'
Lake Tahoe	D	1.4; 2.2	E; M	+111'/-211'; +776'/-33'
Lake Tahoe	D	9.2	S	+3,295'/-0'
Lake Tahoe	D/O	6.8	M	+914'/-174'
Trans-Sierra Passes	D	5.0	M	+1,214'/-1,214'
Trans-Sierra Passes	D	10.0	M	+464'/-1,012'
Trans-Sierra Passes	D/O	4.0	E	+597'/-44'
Trans-Sierra Passes	D/O	7.4	M	+1,023'/-521'
Trans-Sierra Passes	D	5.4	E	+800'/-800'
Trans-Sierra Passes	D	8.6	M–S	+1,640'/-502'
Trans-Sierra Passes	D/O	6.6	M	+686'/-505'
Trans-Sierra Passes	D	3.9	E	+359'/-0'
Trans-Sierra Passes	D/O	4.5	E–M	+600'/-600'
Eastern Sierra	D/O	6.2	M	+1,004'/-63'
Eastern Sierra	D	6.0	M–S	+1,282'/-1'
Eastern Sierra	D	2.0; 0.75	E; E	+357'/-357'; +31'/-31'
Eastern Sierra	D	4.5	M	+1,044'/-51'
Eastern Sierra	D	3.5	E	+455'/-347'
Eastern Sierra	D/O	7.1	M	+760'/-73'
Eastern Sierra	D/O	6.3	M–S	+1,383'/-76'
Eastern Sierra	D/O	4.2	M	+955'/-43'
Eastern Sierra	D/O	9.0	M–S	+2,314'/-22'
Eastern Sierra	D	5.5	M–S	+1,852'/-195'

Hike	Area
34. Wapama Falls	Yosemite National Park Area
35. Panorama Trail	Yosemite National Park Area
36. Half Dome	Yosemite National Park Area
37. Clouds Rest	Yosemite National Park Area
38. Cathedral Lakes	Yosemite National Park Area
39. Waterwheel Falls	Yosemite National Park Area
40. Gaylor Lakes	Yosemite National Park Area
41. Chilnualna Falls	Yosemite National Park Area
42. Hite Cove	Sierra National Forest
43. Mist Falls	Kings Canyon National Park
44. Redwood Mountain Grove	Kings Canyon National Park
45. Little Baldy	Sequoia National Park
46. Tokopah Falls	Sequoia National Park
47. Lakes Trail to Heather Lake	Sequoia National Park
48. Circle Meadow	Sequoia National Park
49. Crescent and Log Meadows Loop	Sequoia National Park
50. Eagle Lake	Sequoia National Park

HIKE RATING KEY

E: Easy
M: Medium
S: Strenuous

Region	Type	RT Distance	Rating	Elevation
Yosemite NP	D	5.0	E	+581'/-515'
Yosemite NP	D	8.2	M–S	+900'/-4,000'
Yosemite NP	D/O	14.0; 16.4	S++; S++	+4,953'/-216'
Yosemite NP	D	14.4	S'	+2,355'/-696'
Yosemite NP	D	6.5	M	+1,010'/-294'
Yosemite NP	O	16.4	M–S	+592'/-2,375'
Yosemite NP	D	3.5	M–S	+1,039'/-198'
Yosemite NP	D	8.0	S	+2,257'/-165'
Yosemite NP	D	7.4	M	+524'/-341'
Sequoia/Kings Cyn NP	D	8.0	E–M	+638'/-0'
Sequoia/Kings Cyn NP	D/O	7.2	M	+1,465'/-1,465'
Sequoia/Kings Cyn NP	D	3.4	M	+764'/-110'
Sequoia/Kings Cyn NP	D	3.8	E	+683'/-3'
Sequoia/Kings Cyn NP	D/O	8.2	M–S	+2,210'/-229'
Sequoia/Kings Cyn NP	D	4.0	E	+694'/-694'
Sequoia/Kings Cyn NP	D	2.5	E	+570'/-570'
Sequoia/Kings Cyn NP	D/O	6.8	S	+2,202'/-11'

Acknowledgments

Thanks to everyone that helped make the second edition of this guide a reality. Thanks to all the park rangers who offered their insight, answered my endless questions, and pointed me in the right direction. Thanks to my Cardno family for allowing me to escape the insanity for a bit to focus on this revision and for helping me identify some tricky flora and fauna. A big thanks to W. W. Norton for inviting me to work on a second edition and to the editorial staff that truly do all the heavy lifting. Thank you to my parents for introducing me to nature's magnificence and for their constant support along all the trails of my life. Last, but most certainly not least, thanks to my husband Richard for supporting me in this endeavor and being my companion on practically every hike in this book. Some of my most treasured memories were born on these hikes. Hopefully, readers will make a few of their own.

Introduction

From a skyline of serrated granite to a delicate carpet of spring wildflowers, the Sierra Nevada is a range of sensory extremes. It is a dramatic medley of sharp edges, rough textures, and fragile biota that forms some of the most sublime landscapes in the world.

The Sierra is a perpetually evolving natural masterpiece filled with boundless perspectives. Whether you're perched atop Mount Whitney with an ocean of snow-capped spires lapping against your feet or spying a black bear and her cub saunter across a blossoming meadow, each vantage has its own intoxicating panorama.

The Sierra Nevada is the longest single mountain range in the contiguous United States. This prominent geographic feature runs almost entirely within the eastern portion of California, briefly spilling into Nevada near Lake Tahoe. The range contains the deepest lake, the tallest waterfall, the largest living tree, the deepest gorge, and the highest mountain in the continental United States.

The oak woodland-covered foothills of the western Sierra, beginning around 1,000 feet in elevation, give way to mixed conifer forests and pine stands, ultimately culminating at stark, treeless mountaintops above 14,000 feet, where little will grow but lichen and moss. This wide range of elevation, climate, and topography results in a remarkable diversity of flora and fauna. Climbing the Sierra Nevada is comparable to making a trip from the deserts of the southwestern United States to arctic Canada—each 1,000 feet of elevation gain roughly corresponding to traveling 300 miles northward. Each dramatic shift in elevation includes a different set of denizens, all adapted to their specific niches.

The cultural history of the Sierra Nevada has transitioned from peaceful coexistence with early Native American inhabitants, to deleterious mining, logging, and grazing by European-American settlers, to a conservation movement spearheaded by naturalist John Muir. Through his writing and political activism, he became a pivotal figure in preserving the integrity of the Sierra and the creation of our national parks system.

Today, much of the Sierra Nevada is maintained as a patchwork of federal- or state-designated parks, forests, monuments, and wilderness areas. Most notably, Yosemite, Sequoia, and Kings Canyon National Parks are found tucked amid the range's rock outcroppings and forested slopes.

The most intimate way to experience this vast range is under your own power. The Sierra is crisscrossed by an extensive trail network—from sections of the rugged, 2,650-mile Pacific Crest Trail (PCT) to paved interpretive nature walks and everything in between. Choosing 50 hikes was challenging, but I think you will find this book includes a pleasant mix of classic Sierra treks and lesser-known, less-frequented gems just waiting for you to explore.

As you roam the Sierra trails, whether you find yourself on a remote ridge of the Mokelumne Wilderness or on a bustling trail in Yosemite Valley, be in awe—listen to the trees, touch the polished granite, fill your lungs with sweet mountain air, watch a butterfly dance. Most important, be present in that moment amid Nature's brilliance and know what it means to be home.

GEOGRAPHY

The Sierra Nevada, Spanish for "snowy mountain range," stretches more than 400 miles from the southern edge of the Cascade Range in northern California to Tehachapi Pass. Spanning between 40 and 80 miles wide, the Sierra is bounded by the Central Valley to the west and the Great Basin to the east.

The beauty and unique geography of the Sierra are the results of a complex combination of volcanic activity, tectonic processes, and glacial erosion. When dinosaurs roamed the Earth, an arc-shaped chain of volcanoes erupted where the present-day Sierra Nevada stands. During repeated volcanic episodes that occurred over millions of years, some molten rock erupted at the surface as lava, but most solidified deep below the Earth's crust, forming granite. Over time, the volcanoes eroded, exposing the deep-seated granitic rock that forms the backbone of the range.

Less than 5 million years ago, through a combination of uplift of the Sierran block along its eastern margin and down-dropping of the Great Basin to the east, the Sierra Nevada began to rise. The range is a massive tilted block of Earth's crust that rises abruptly in the east and slopes gently westward toward the Central Valley.

This asymmetrical structure makes for two vastly different sides. The mild gradient of the western Sierra lends itself to densely wooded slopes with broad meadows, meandering rivers, and countless lakes. Conversely, the steep eastern side is much drier because it lies in the rain shadow effect of the range. It is characterized by deep, rugged canyons, sheer rock faces, and sawtooth pinnacles that seem to pierce the sky.

During the most recent Ice Age, the Earth cooled and glaciers grew in the higher elevations. As these moving masses of ice made their way down former river channels, they carved impressive U-shaped valleys and left in their wake precipitous hanging valleys, amphitheater-shaped cirques, and milky turquoise tarns.

Though the geologic forces molding the Sierra Nevada—faulting, uplift, earthquakes, erosion, volcanism, and glaciation—have varied in intensity throughout the millions of years it took to shape the range, these powerful processes remain with us, bending, building, and carving.

HAZARDS

This section provides a cursory introduction to the potential hazards lurking in the Sierra. Preparation is key to avoiding these hazards or knowing what to do in an emergency situation. I encourage you to seek out resources on the Internet and in print which provide more detailed information on mastering backcountry skills, including first aid, safety, and trip planning.

ALTITUDE SICKNESS

Altitude sickness occurs when you cannot get enough oxygen from the air at high altitudes. When you go too high too fast, your body can have trouble adapting to the new altitude. Each individual's susceptibility to altitude sickness is different—however, it happens most often when people who are not used to high altitudes go quickly from lower elevations to 8,000 feet or higher. Symptoms include headache, loss of appetite, nausea, insomnia, shortness of breath, and fatigue. Considering most of the hikes in this guidebook are in the 6,500- to 11,000-foot range, understanding the symptoms of altitude sickness and how to avoid them is essential for a safe trip into the Sierra high country. If you believe someone in your party is suffering from altitude sickness the best remedy is to descend to a lower elevation as soon as possible.

HYPOTHERMIA

In the Sierra Nevada, weather can change rapidly, especially during the summer months, which are notorious for afternoon thunderstorms, making hypothermia a very real threat for hikers. Hypothermia is a condition in which the body's core temperature drops below normal levels. It occurs when the body loses heat at a rate faster than it can be replaced by metabolic and muscular activity. Left untreated, hypothermia can lead to death.

Wet clothing and windy weather are the primary hypothermia-inducing culprits, the combination of which can quickly strip the body of heat even when the air temperature is above freezing. Symptoms of hypothermia include shivering, confusion, loss of coordination, slurred speech, and lethargy. As the condition progresses, a person may become unable to walk, suffer from a slow or irregular heart rate, exhibit irrational and/or incoherent behavior, and the skin may appear blue or puffy.

If you suspect someone in your party is a victim of hypothermia, seek a dry, warm place out of the elements, remove wet clothing, and replace it with dry clothing or blankets. Have the victim drink warm liquids, ingest high-caloric foods, and, if possible, get them moving to generate body heat by doing jumping jacks or running in place.

To improve your odds of staying dry and warm on the trail, dress in layers and wear a hat to easily regulate body temperature. Avoid wearing cotton, which dries slowly, and instead opt for a synthetic inner layer that wicks moisture and perspiration away from the body. Wear a wind- and waterproof outer shell that keeps your inner layers dry. Eat small amounts of high-caloric food at frequent intervals to keep your body fueled, drink plenty of water, and avoid alcohol and caffeine. If you anticipate inclement weather—or even if you don't—it doesn't hurt to carry dry clothes in a waterproof bag, just in case.

LIGHTNING

Mountain thunderstorms are a hazard that shouldn't be taken lightly, especially for hikers above the tree line. Even though—during the summer months—thunderstorms generally form in early to mid-afternoon in the Sierra, the reality is they are unpredictable and can move quickly into an area at any time. Hiking early so that you have descended from high-risk areas before the lightning threat is greatest and continuously monitoring the sky for changing weather conditions are important methods to reduce vulnerability.

If you are in the backcountry and hear thunder, immediately move to safer terrain, such as a dense stand of even-height trees, a significant depression, or a dry ravine. Avoid peaks, ridges, wide open areas where presumably you would be the tallest object, bodies of water, lone trees or trees of uneven height, caves, rock overhangs, and electrical conductors.

By timing the interval between seeing the lightning and hearing the accompanying thunder, it is possible to estimate the distance to the lightning (five seconds equals a mile). If at risk, distance yourself from any metal objects like ice axes, crampons, hiking poles, and backpacks. If available, place an insulated object like a foam pad or a soft bag full of clothing between you and the ground. Squat, curl up in a ball, wrap your arms around your legs, and put your feet together. Make yourself as low as possible without lying prone and have the least possible amount of bodily contact with the ground. Stay in this position, sometimes called the "lightning position," until the storm passes. If you are in a group, spread out at least 50 feet apart to reduce the chance of multiple injuries. You do not have to be hit directly by lightning to be affected. Lightning can travel along the ground from a nearby strike to you, or jump from nearby objects that are struck.

If someone in your group is struck by lightning and is not breathing, you should immediately administer cardiopulmonary resuscitation (CPR) and send for help. People struck by lightning do not retain the electrical charge and are safe to touch. Use basic first aid principles to treat other injuries due to lightning, like burns or shock, and get victims to medical professionals as quickly as possible.

POISON OAK

Western poison oak (*Toxicodendron diversilobum*) is one of the West's most notorious natural villains. This widespread deciduous shrub or climbing vine is found throughout the mountains and valleys of California, generally below 5,000 feet of elevation. Because of its extremely variable growth habitat and leaf appearance, recognizing this outdoor nemesis can be difficult.

Normally, leaves are divided into three leaflets, with the middle leaflet having a much longer stalk than those of the other two, hence the adage, "leaves of three, let it be;" however, occasionally leaves are composed of five, seven, or nine leaflets. Each leaflet ranges from 1 to 4 inches in length and can have smooth, toothed, or lobed edges. Leaves are generally green and sometimes light red in early spring, bright green during the summer, and various shades of yellow, orange, and red in the fall. White flowers form in the spring and, if fertilized, develop into greenish-white or tan berries.

All parts of the poison oak plant, including the roots, stems, leaves, flowers, and berries, contain the poisonous, oily substance urushiol, which causes allergic contact dermatitis in most people. Contamination can occur by direct contact with bruised or broken plants that have released their deleterious oily resin; contact with contaminated objects, such as shoes, clothing, tools, and animals; and even by inhaling smoke particles from the burned poison oak plant.

If you have an unfortunate run in with poison oak, wash the affected area immediately with soap and copious amounts of cold water. Then, as soon as possible, wash again with a mild solvent such as isopropyl alcohol, followed by more cold water. If these steps are performed within the first few minutes of contact, a reaction may be prevented. Missing this small window of opportunity can lead to a blistery rash, oozing sores, and severe itching within 24 to 48 hours of exposure. If an outbreak occurs, hydrocortisone cream, antihistamines, and products like Tecnu®, which removes the urushiol from the skin, can provide some relief.

WATERBORNE PARASITES

The water of America's backcountry has been invaded by microscopic parasites, namely *Giardia lamblia* and *Cryptosporidium*, which would like nothing better than to set up shop in your intestines and wreak havoc. Both *Giardia* and *Cryptosporidium* live in the intestines of infected humans or animals. They are found in soil, food, water, and on surfaces that have been contaminated with the feces from infected individuals.

Both parasites cause a variety of intestinal maladies, including diarrhea, stomach cramps, gas, nausea, and vomiting. No matter how clear, cool, and free-running a stream may appear, dipping your Nalgene® bottle for a swig simply isn't worth the risk of ingesting the microorganisms, bacteria, and chemical toxins lurking in the water of the world's wild places, including the Sierra.

If it's impractical to carry enough water with you for a trip, treating your backcountry water is imperative. The Centers for Disease Control and Prevention (CDC) recommends heating water to a rolling boil for at least one minute, or using either a filter that has an absolute pore size of 1 micron or smaller, or one that has been rated by the National Sanitation Foundation (NSF) for "cyst removal." Chemically treating water by chlorination or iodine will remove *Giardia*; however, *Cryptosporidium* is resistant to these disinfectants due to its thick outer shell. My advice: boil or filter and stay cootie-free.

SUN EXPOSURE

Protecting our skin and eyes from the sun should be a priority every day, but even more so when we spend time at altitude. Ultraviolet (UV) radiation is greater at higher elevations, where the atmosphere is thinner and less able to filter harmful rays. Add to this the reflection of light from snow, water, and rock surfaces and the effect is intensified. Protect yourself by applying sunblock to exposed skin and wearing sunglasses that block 99–100 percent of UV radiation. Wearing a wide-brimmed hat and sun-protective clothing can also shield areas prone to overexposure.

WILDLIFE

The Sierra Nevada is a wild and rugged range full of equally wild and rugged denizens. Observing these beautiful animals in their natural habitat can be exhilarating, but it can also be maddening. Spying a black bear feeding in a meadow can be an amazing experience; a marmot biting a hole in your backpack and raiding your trail mix, not so much.

BEARS

All bears inhabiting the Sierra Nevada are black bears (*Ursus americanus*). Sadly, though California's state flag is emblazoned with a grizzly bear, the last one seen in the wild in California was in 1924. Black bears come in shades of black, brown, and cinnamon and are generally found in the 3,000- to 7,000-foot elevation range, where food is abundant.

The likelihood of seeing a bear while day hiking is slim. Most bear encounters occur in campgrounds or at backpacker campsites where food and other scents lure them. Many drive-in campgrounds in the Sierra, and some trailhead parking areas, now provide bear-proof metal lockers for securing food and other scented items—soap, sunscreen, toothpaste, lotion, lip balm, etc. If you are backpacking, safeguarding food and toiletries in trees or using bear-proof canisters is imperative for both you and the bears.

Bears naturally fear humans. Those that have become habituated to our presence and food-conditioned to scavenge in campsites and trash cans for human vittles become destructive and dangerous. Unfortunately, sometimes the worst offenders have to be killed.

Use common sense. Never leave food unattended outside; don't take food into your tent at night; use a bear-resistant container for grocery storage or lock food in your vehicle and cover it with blankets; and dispose of or store garbage immediately. Remember, proper food storage is required by federal regulations, and feeding wildlife is prohibited.

While on the trail, carry bear pepper spray and make noise to avoid a surprise encounter. Never approach or feed a bear, and never get between a bear and her cub or its food. If an encounter does occur, remain calm and do not run; identify yourself as human by talking in low tones and gently waving your arms; ready your pepper spray; try to appear as large as possible, and back away slowly. If attacked, use your pepper spray according to the manufacturer's instructions. If the bear continues to attack, lay flat on your stomach with hands clasped behind your neck. Spread your legs to make it harder for the bear to turn you over and stay still. If, despite your being passive, the bear continues its aggression, bear experts advise that you fight back.

MOUNTAIN LIONS

Mountain lions (*Felis concolor*), also referred to as cougars or pumas, prowl the Sierra foothills and lower-elevation forests. These powerful cats are quiet, solitary, and elusive. They typically avoid people, although conflicts are increasing as California's urban sprawl encroaches on mountain lion habitat and more people venture into the backcountry.

To prevent an encounter, avoid hiking solo or when mountain lions are most active—dawn, dusk, and at night. As with all wild animals, do not feed mountain lions or approach them for any reason. If you stumble upon one, avoid the overwhelming temptation to run. Face the animal, make noise, and try to look bigger by waving your arms. Throw rocks, sticks, or anything you can get your hands on. If you have small children with you, pick them up. If attacked, do not play dead, but fight back savagely. Many people have successfully fended off an attacking mountain lion.

RATTLESNAKES

Rattlesnakes, the only poisonous snake species inhabiting California, are found throughout the lower elevations of the Sierra—typically below 6,500 feet, but most commonly below 5,000 feet. Though most of the hikes covered in this guidebook are above their preferred range, keep a vigilant eye and a keen ear nonetheless.

The western rattlesnake (*Crotalus viridis*), the species found in the Sierra, has a wide triangular head, narrow neck, and a rattle on its tail. Their bodies are brown with a series of dark brown patches down the back. They are shy creatures that prefer to remain out of sight. Their coloring provides camouflage for their predation of small rodents;

however, it also means that they blend in nicely with the trail and adjacent leaf litter, so watch where you step and place your hands. Listen for the telltale rattle or buzzing noise made when they shake their tails—a courteous warning when we get too close.

If you encounter a snake on the trail, give it a wide berth and move away slowly. Given an escape route, they will generally vacate the area and you can happily continue on.

RODENTS

Of all the creatures living in the Sierra Nevada, rodents are the most irksome, hazardous, and destructive to hikers and backpackers. They may look cute, but let's not forget that these deceptively charming mammals can carry Hantavirus, bubonic plague, and a host of other icky diseases.

Squirrels, mice, chipmunks, and marmots are cunning and relentless. They have one thing and one thing only on their minds—food. Don't leave your backpack or snacks unattended for a moment; these rodents are extremely fast and can scurry off with your baggie of gorp or slice a hole in your pack or tent with their razor-sharp teeth in an instant. In addition, avoid camping in areas with evidence of rodent activity, like burrows and droppings, to decrease your chance of contact with these disease-carrying varmints.

TICKS

Ticks have the unfortunate distinction of being the number one infectious disease carrier in the United States. Though they are generally found in the chaparral and grasslands of the Sierra foothills, it doesn't hurt to keep an eye out for these miniature menaces whenever you're on the trail. Wearing light-colored clothing can make the job of spotting these bitty beasties easier. Wear long-sleeved shirts and long pants tucked into your socks or boots. Most importantly, use an insect repellent. Repellents containing DEET (N, N-diethyl-meta-toluamide) or picaridin (KBR 3023) typically provide the longest-lasting protection. You can also apply repellents containing permethrins to your clothing and gear, but not directly to the skin, for greater protection.

Check for ticks routinely throughout the day in heavily infested areas. If a tick has latched on, the best removal method is to firmly grasp the tick with tweezers as close to the skin as possible. Pull gently until the entire tick comes free. Avoid crushing or squeezing the tick body during removal, as this can increase the chance of disease transmission. Thoroughly cleanse the bite area with soap and water, and apply an antibiotic cream.

MOSQUITOES

Dealing with mosquitoes seems to be a rite of passage of sorts in the Sierra, especially in the spring and early summer. In the United States, these pesky vectors are most notable for their potential transmission of a whole host of diseases, including West Nile and Zika virus.

Protect yourself by wearing long pants, long-sleeved shirts, and using an insect repellent. Repellents containing DEET and picaridin are effective for mosquitoes as well as ticks. In addition, oil of lemon eucalyptus (p-menthane-3,8-diol) appears to be an effectual plant-based deterrent.

If you are bitten, an itchy round pink or red bump will develop. Wash the bite with soap and water and apply an anti-itch cream. Scratching the bite can break the skin and lead to infection.

BEING PREPARED

Venturing into the backcountry, whether it's for a few hours or a few days, comes with some inherent risks—risks that can be tempered with a little foresight and a lot of common sense. Ultimately, you are responsible for yourself on the trail, so be prepared.

The list below includes essential items every hiker should carry for a safe foray into the mountains. Although you may not use all these items on every hike, they can be lifesavers in an emergency.

1. Map
2. Compass
3. Water
4. Water filter
5. Raingear and extra clothing
6. Extra food
7. Food storage device
8. Firestarter and waterproof matches
9. First-aid kit
10. Knife or multipurpose tool
11. Flashlight (with extra bulbs and batteries)
12. Sunglasses and sunscreen
13. Whistle
14. Bear pepper spray

Become self-reliant by educating yourself about the terrain you are venturing into, local weather patterns, and your equipment before ever stepping on the trail. Leave your hiking plans with someone, including where you are going and when you expect to return. Keep your group together and know your limitations.

LEAVE NO TRACE

Leave No Trace is a program designed to educate outdoor enthusiasts about the nature of their recreational impacts and to provide techniques to prevent and minimize them. Practicing the seven principles of Leave No Trace ensures we are all doing our part to leave natural places the way we found them: plan ahead and prepare; travel and camp on durable surfaces; dispose of waste properly; leave what you find; minimize campfire impacts; respect wildlife; and be considerate of other visitors.

HOW TO USE THIS GUIDEBOOK

The 50 hikes included in this guidebook are divided into six regions: Gold Country, Lake Tahoe, Trans-Sierra Passes (Carson, Ebbetts, Sonora, and Tioga Passes), Eastern Sierra, Yosemite National Park, and Sequoia and Kings Canyon National Parks.

Each hike is contained within its own chapter and begins with a quick-reference information box that includes the type of hike, season, total distance, difficulty rating, elevation, location, reference maps, applicable fees and permits, and contact information.

Type: A hike will either be listed as a day hike, overnight, or both.

Season: The season provided will vary from year to year depending on weather conditions and is meant as a guide to when the trail is generally open and free of snow.

Total distance: Distances include the total round-trip mileage.

Rating: Hikes are rated easy, moderate, or strenuous based on trail length, elevation changes, and overall trail conditions and followability for the average hiker. Keep this in mind when deciding whether a hike is appropriate for your skill level.

Elevation: The first number of each

entry is the trailhead elevation. The second set of numbers represents the total elevation gain and loss. The gain and loss data are one-way for out-and-back trips and total for point-to-point, loop, and semi-loop trips. Elevations are given in feet. To convert feet to meters, multiply by 0.3048.

Location: This is the geographic location of the hike.

Maps: In addition to the trail map provided in each chapter, other useful maps are listed, including the USGS 7.5-minute quadrangles, Trails Illustrated Map, and/or local jurisdiction map.

Fees and permits: The Sierra Nevada has multiple jurisdictions, each having its own fee structure and permit requirements. Whether you are embarking on a day hike or overnight journey, it is your responsibility to be aware of local rules and regulations. I recommend securing overnight permits well in advance, as most Sierra wilderness areas have instated peak-season trailhead quotas limiting the number of overnight users entering an area on any given day.

Contacts: Pertinent contact information is provided for your reference.

Following the quick-reference information box is a brief introduction to the hike, followed by directions to the trailhead from a nearby prominent locale. Finally, there is a comprehensive description of the trail and what you can expect to encounter, from its ups and downs, junctions and crossings, to significant points of interest and natural history.

Happy trails!

MAP LEGEND

——	Described trail	═══ Interstate highway
- - - -	Important trail	═══ Secondary highway
←——	Hike direction arrow	—— Minor highway, road, street
——	Perennial stream	- - - - Unpaved road, trail
- - - -	Intermittent stream	+—+—+ Railroad
——	Major contour line	—··— International border
......	Minor contour line	-··—··- State border

▓	National/state park, wilderness	🅿 Parking area
▢	National/state forest, wildlife refuge	🚶 Trailhead
▢	Perennial body of water	• City, town
▢	Intermittent body of water	⋘ Overlook, scenic view
	Swamp, marsh	Λ Campground, campsite
▓	Wooded area	⋔ Shelter
		× Mountain peak
		▪ Place of interest

I.

GOLD COUNTRY

Monroe Ridge and Monument Trail Loop

TYPE: Day hike	

TYPE: Day hike

SEASON: Year-round

TOTAL DISTANCE: 3.0-mile loop

RATING: Easy to moderate due to some steep sections

ELEVATION: 932 feet; +620 feet/-620 feet

LOCATION: Marshall Gold Discovery State Historic Park

MAPS: USGS 7.5' Coloma; Marshall Gold Discovery State Historic Park brochure map

FEES AND PERMITS: A permit is not required for this day hike. There is a $8 day-use fee per vehicle.

CONTACT: Marshall Gold Discovery State Historic Park (530-622-3470; www.parks. ca.gov/?page_id=484).

This loop hike in the heart of California's Gold Country takes you through bucolic oak woodlands and visits a number of historic sites around Coloma, the former hub of the northern mining region. It was here in January 1848 that James Marshall found some flakes of gold in the South Fork of the American River—a portentous discovery that would forever change history. The Monroe Ridge Trail rises gradually but steadily to a ridge overlooking the Coloma Valley before descending toward the river. Explore the site of John Marshall's historic gold discovery, the replica of Sutter's Mill, and the exhibits and displays at the visitor center before joining the Monument Trail, which climbs gently along a shaded path to the lofty John Marshall Monument and completes the loop.

GETTING THERE

From I-80 traveling east in Auburn, take the Elm Avenue exit and turn left, then drive 0.1 mile east and turn left onto CA 49/El Dorado Street/High Street. Almost immediately, veer right to continue on CA 49 for approximately 13 miles to Coloma. Park in the second lot on your left, near the sawmill replica, and pay the admission fee. Visit the Gold Discovery Museum and historic buildings to orient yourself before driving to the trailhead.

To reach the trailhead from Coloma, proceed south along CA 49. At the south end of town, CA 49 bends sharply east, but continue straight onto Cold Springs Road. Continue 0.1 mile, then turn right onto Monument Road and take this 0.3 mile to the parking area on the right.

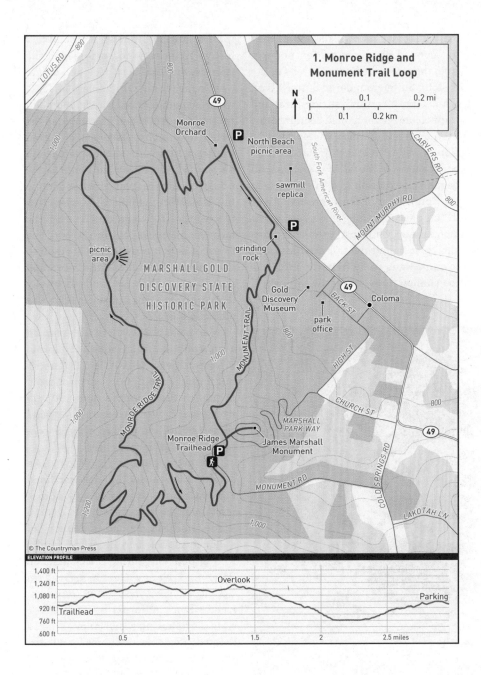

THE HIKE

The Greek word "Eureka" has appeared on the California state seal since 1849 and means "I have found it." This motto presumably refers to the fateful discovery of gold in California's foothills. Archimedes, the ancient Greek scholar, is said to have exclaimed "Eureka!" when he discovered a method of determining the purity of gold (the Archimedes Principle). I wonder if John

Marshall gave his own shout-out when he scooped up a few golden nuggets from the streambed near Sutter's mill.

John Sutter, founder of Sutter's Fort, a nineteenth-century agricultural and trade colony—later named Sacramento—partnered with James W. Marshall, a New Jersey carpenter, to go into the lumber business. In the fall of 1847, Marshall began construction of a sawmill along the South Fork of the American River in the peaceful Coloma Valley. A few months later, while testing the mill, Marshall discovered the tailrace, designed to carry water away from the mill, was too shallow, preventing the mill wheel

from operating properly. Marshall had Native American laborers deepen the tailrace, and the loose rock and debris was washed away. On January 24, 1848, while inspecting the tailrace, Marshall spotted nuggets of gold glistening in the water. He took his discovery to Sutter, who consulted his encyclopedia and performed some tests to confirm the find. Concerned about their economic investment in the mill, they attempted to keep the discovery a secret until the mill was in operation. In the end, the secret was just too good to keep all to themselves. Within months, word had spread to San Francisco and eventually the world. The California Gold Rush was officially on.

Marshall's chance discovery sparked a mass migration of people to California in a scramble to strike it rich. The state's nonnative population soared from 14,000 in 1848 to more than 200,000 by 1852, and over the ensuing 50 years some 125 million ounces of gold were taken from California's hills.

This hike utilizes two trails to make a loop through the foothill oak woodland above Coloma. To begin, walk across Monument Road to the signed Monroe Ridge trailhead, named in memory of a pioneering African American family who settled here during the Gold Rush. Peter and Nancy Gooch arrived in Coloma as slaves in 1849, but were soon freed when California became a free state the following year. Nancy earned a living doing domestic chores for miners, and in 1861 had saved enough money to buy the freedom of her son, Andrew Monroe, who was still enslaved in Missouri. Andrew brought his family to Coloma, where they became respected farmers and landholders.

Begin a 0.75-mile, 350-foot ascent through a thin canopy of digger pines

REPLICA OF SUTTER'S MILL

MONROE RIDGE TRAIL

and interior live oaks as you follow signs to North Beach, the picnic area at the end of this trail. If you're doing this hike in the summer, get an early start and carry plenty of water. The trail meanders in and out of shady sections and can get quite toasty. Scattered along the trail are California toyon, distinctive red-barked manzanita, fragrant California buckeye, and our favorite foothill nemesis, poison oak. At 0.65 mile, come to a spur trail on your right leading up to a vista point—definitely a misnomer as the views are mostly obscured by vegetation. Not to worry, the best view is just up ahead.

A second spur trail leads to a picnic table on your left and marks the summit, but don't stop here. Continue along the ridge as it gently descends past a fire road that veers right to a second picnic area at 1.35 miles that offers the best view of the Coloma Valley and the American River gliding below. From your vantage point, the trail begins a steep descent through a shady forest before crossing an old mining ditch at 1.9 miles. The ditches were originally used by miners to carry the vast amounts of water needed for placer mining and then later, when mining declined, for crop irrigation.

Follow the trail through the old Monroe orchard to CA 49 (the North Beach picnic area is directly across the road). Turn right and follow the highway shoulder 0.1 mile to an opening in the split rail fence with a trail marker. You can proceed through the fence and follow the dirt service road past the oak-shaded picnic area and restrooms or, if you haven't done so already, cross CA 49 and join the riverside path that visits the gold discovery site, the working replica of Sutter's Mill, and various exhibits. After exploring, cross the highway again and join the signed Monument Trail near the park museum.

If you head straight for Monument Trail, stop to check out the bedrock mortar used by the Nisenan tribe to grind acorns. The bowl-shaped holes are, unfortunately, some of the last remaining evidence of their presence here. At 2.5 miles, a trail sign directs you to the Marshall Monument—California's first State Historic Monument. Following a split rail fence, ascend through vine-covered hillsides 0.5 mile farther to the end of the trail. From here a paved road leads to the imposing John Marshall Monument to your left, or proceed straight to reach the parking lot and your vehicle. The gigantic statue atop a granite pedestal marks the grave of John Marshall—his bronze finger intrepidly pointing to the spot where he found the first flecks of gold.

There are so many fascinating human stories that came out of the Gold Rush: the entrepreneurs who never lifted a shovel but made their fortunes by establishing stores, hotels, and banks to support miners who had money to spend; pickax-wielding women who toiled alongside men equally afflicted with gold fever; tales of arduous journeys over land and sea; and the devastating effect a shiny mineral had on Native American populations that once thrived here.

Ironically, neither Sutter nor Marshall ever struck it rich. Sutter's workmen abandoned their jobs to seek fortunes in the gold fields, ultimately leaving him bankrupt. When the sawmill was abandoned in 1850 due to management and legal difficulties, Marshall drifted from place to place, bitterly resenting his misfortune.

American Canyon Trail

TYPE: Day hike	

SEASON: Year-round

TOTAL DISTANCE: 4.8 miles round trip

RATING: Moderate

ELEVATION: 1,722 feet; +2 feet/-1,058 feet

LOCATION: Auburn State Recreation Area (SRA)

MAPS: USGS 7.5' Greenwood; Auburn State Recreation Area brochure map

FEES AND PERMITS: A permit is not required for this day hike.

CONTACT: Auburn SRA (530-885-4527; www.parks.ca.gov/?page_id=502).

This steep but manageable trail descends a narrow mountain canyon and passes through a variety of foothill woodland and riparian vegetation before culminating at Poverty Bar, along the Middle Fork of the American River. With rugged mountain scenery, a burbling creek never far from earshot, Gold Rush–era history, and, if you hit it right, a feast of wild blackberries, this trail has a little something for everyone. Once teeming with gold-hungry prospectors, the 38,000-acre Auburn SRA, which encompasses the North and Middle Forks of the American River, is now a popular outdoor recreation area. Pack your fishing pole, swimsuit, and a picnic and do some recreating of your own.

GETTING THERE

From I-80 traveling east in Auburn, take the Elm Avenue exit and turn left, then drive 0.1 mile east and turn left onto CA 49/El Dorado Street/High Street. Almost immediately, veer right to continue on CA 49 for approximately 5.7 miles to the town of Cool. Turn left onto CA 193/Georgetown Road and drive 5.5 miles east. Turn left onto unsigned Sweetwater Trail (the road on the opposite side of CA 193 is signed Pilgrim Court). Drive 0.2 mile farther to the small trailhead parking area on your right, just before the gated entrance to Auburn Lake Trails residential development. You can also park along Sweetwater Trail in roadside pullouts farther back.

THE HIKE

As you drive to the trailhead, notice the Auburn-Foresthill Bridge that spans the canyon some 720 feet above the confluence of the North and Middle

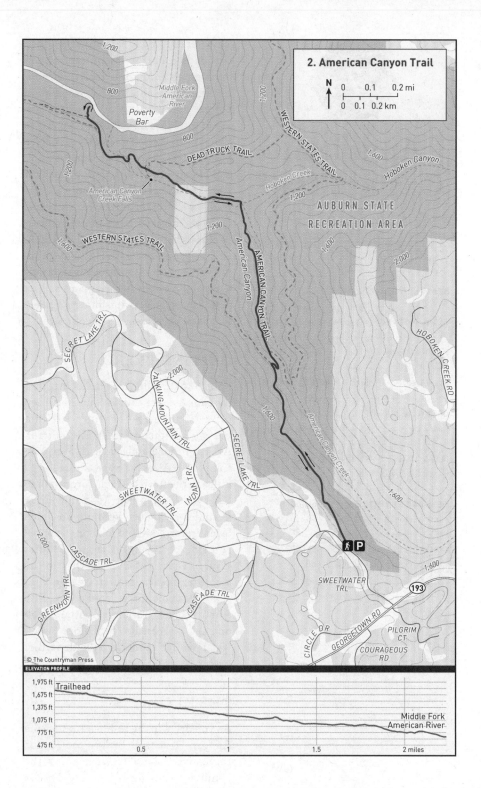

2. American Canyon Trail

N

| 0 | 0.1 | 0.2 mi |
| 0 | 0.1 | 0.2 km |

1,200

Middle Fork
American
River

800

Poverty
Bar

1,200

1,200

800

DEAD TRUCK TRAIL

WESTERN STATES TRAIL

1,600

Hoboken Canyon

Hoboken Creek

American Canyon
Creek Falls

1,200

AUBURN STATE
RECREATION AREA

American Canyon

WESTERN STATES TRAIL

1,600

1,200

1,200

1,600

2,000

American Canyon Trail

1,600

HOBOKEN CREEK RD

SECRET LAKE TRL

TALKING MOUNTAIN TRL

2,000

SECRET LAKE TRL

INDIAN TRL

SWEETWATER TRL

American Canyon Creek

1,600

1,600

2,000

CASCADE TRL

GREENHORN TRL

CASCADE TRL

SWEETWATER
TRL

1,600

193

800

CIRCLE DR

GEORGETOWN RD

PILGRIM
CT

COURAGEOUS
RD

© The Countryman Press

ELEVATION PROFILE

1,975 ft	Trailhead
1,675 ft	
1,375 ft	
1,075 ft	
775 ft	
475 ft	

Middle Fork
American River

0.5   1   1.5   2 miles

Forks of the American River. It is the second highest bridge built by the federal Bureau of Reclamation, surpassed only by the bridge at Glen Canyon. The bridge was completed in 1973 as part of the Central Valley Project, which ultimately intended to construct the Auburn Dam. The bridge would have carried the roadway over a portion of the reservoir that would have been created by the impounded river (the considerably lower CA 49 bridge you drove over would be deep underwater).

The dam was designed to provide flood protection and water to the Sacramento Valley, but due to environmental concerns, economics, and the seismic instability of the proposed dam site, construction was halted and the project abandoned. Since it's still possible, though unlikely, that the highly-contentious project could be revived, no infrastructure has been built and the Bureau of Reclamation has allowed the State of California to use a portion of the river as a recreation area.

The Auburn State Recreation Area contains 40 miles of the North and Middle Forks of the American River and is crisscrossed with over 100 miles of hiking, biking, and equestrian trails. It also includes a designated off-highway vehicle area and spectacular whitewater rafting on both forks of the river, with class II, III, and IV runs. Its proximity to greater Sacramento means the park gets its share of use, but with 38,000 acres it's easy for everyone to spread out.

From the trailhead sign, start descending immediately down a well-defined dirt trail that is densely treed with a variety of oak and foothill pines. At 0.1 mile, an unsigned spur trail climbs to the left. Continue straight along the wide, generally well-graded trail. Runoff has formed ruts along segments of the trail, so watch your footing.

The American Canyon Trail is no different than other Western foothill hikes listed in this book in terms of precarious denizens we would all prefer to avoid, namely poison oak, rattlesnakes, ticks, and mountain lions. It goes without saying, but I'll say it anyway: Keep your guard up and be aware when entering any wilderness area.

The trail winds through several blackberry brambles as you trace along the canyon wall. The berries ripen between July and September and are just waiting to provide nourishment to passing hikers. If you are lucky enough to happen upon them before others have stripped the vines clean, by all means indulge in their wild sweetness.

At 0.7 mile, reach an intersection with the Wendell T. Robie/Western States Trail. In 1955, Robie, in a mission to prove horses could still cover 100 miles in one day, rode from Squaw Valley to Auburn along the rugged Western States Trail. He subsequently founded the Western States Trail Foundation and organized the annual Western States Trail Ride, commonly called the Tevis Cup "100 Miles One Day" ride, which remains the oldest modern-day equestrian endurance ride in the world. This is not to be confused with the Western States Trail Endurance Run, which was born in the mid-1970s when Gordy Ainsleigh joined the horses to see if he could complete the course on foot (what a stud—no pun intended). The Western States Endurance Run Foundation now hosts the annual event that draws athletes from around the globe.

Turn right and switchback down a short distance to another trail junction, where you will stay straight. The trail narrows, and the soothing sound of

MIDDLE FORK AMERICAN RIVER AT POVERTY BAR

tumbling American Canyon Creek can be heard below. At 1.2 miles, the trail drops down to meet American Canyon Creek, followed shortly thereafter by Hoboken Creek, a small tributary of American Canyon. Cross both using strategically placed rocks that provide dry passage much of the year. Crossing may be more difficult during the winter or after storm events when flows are high.

The trail bends sharply west after crossing Hoboken Creek, and the two creeks converge shortly thereafter. The terrain levels out and the canopy opens as you make your way to an intersection with Dead Truck Trail at 1.6 miles. Just before the junction, look for a steep, unmarked side trail branching left that leads down to American Canyon Creek Falls. The falls are only about 20 feet high, but are quite scenic as they drop through a narrow cleft into an inviting pool below.

Stay straight at the intersection with Dead Truck Trail, which rises abruptly to the right. From here the path becomes very steep and rutted as you switchback down the drier southwest-facing slope, where scrub oak, manzanita, and dry grasses dominate. Cross American Canyon Creek again at 1.75 miles using stepping stones and proceed northward as you move up and away from the creek.

As the creek drops sharply toward its confluence with the American River, there are several mini-waterfalls that are obscured by the trees. Without a safe trail to scramble down, we must be satisfied with partial views and allow our imagination to fill in the rest.

An upstream perspective of the American River as it curves beneath French Hill comes into view at 1.9 miles. Just past the viewpoint the trail drops sharply toward the river and gets narrow and overgrown. Steering clear of encroaching poison oak, come to an intersection with the Tevis Cup segment of the Western States Trail at 2.2 miles. Turn right and proceed down to the cobble-strewn southern bank of the Middle Fork.

Directly across the river on the northern bank is Poverty Bar, the location of a bustling mining outpost set up along the river after gold was discovered just upstream on the South Fork near Coloma. Thousands of prospectors panned, sluiced, or dredged every accessible river bar in the gold fever frenzy. Gold panning and rock hounding are allowed in permanent running streambeds in the Auburn SRA, so pack along your pan, but be sure to follow local rules and regulations.

The river is also a great spot to cast a line or take a refreshing dip on a warm summer afternoon. You may, however, be supremely content scouting out a shady spot along the river's edge and spreading out a picnic before retracing your steps to the trailhead.

Humbug Trail

TYPE: Day hike

SEASON: Year-round

TOTAL DISTANCE: 5.4 miles round trip

RATING: Moderate

ELEVATION: 2,950 feet; +145 feet/-947 feet

LOCATION: Malakoff Diggins State Historic Park

MAPS: USGS 7.5' North Bloomfield; Malakoff Diggins State Historic Park brochure map

FEES AND PERMITS: A permit is not required for this day hike. There is a $10 day-use fee Memorial Day weekend through Labor Day, $5 the remainder of the year.

CONTACT: Malakoff Diggins State Historic Park (530-265-2740; www.parks.ca .gov/?page_id=494).

The bad news is this trail has a few precarious sections, is occasionally steep, and poison oak likes to invade the path. The good news is this hike into the canyon carved by Humbug Creek is replete with Gold Rush–era history and colorful springtime wildflowers, and culminates at an inviting swimming hole along the South Yuba River. The lower elevation makes the trail accessible year-round, with spring and fall being the most scenic. The trail ultimately intersects the 20-mile-long South Yuba Trail near its midpoint. The South Yuba Trail is managed by the Bureau of Land Management as part of the South Yuba Recreation Area and includes several campgrounds for hikers looking to extend exploration in the area (www.blm .gov/visit/south-yuba-river).

GETTING THERE

From Nevada City, drive 11 miles north on CA 49 from its intersection with CA 20 and turn right onto Tyler Foote Crossing Road. Drive 16.4 miles, following signs to Malakoff Diggins State Historic Park. The road name will change en route to Cruzon Grade Road and later to Backbone Road. Turn right onto Derbec Road, which becomes North Bloomfield Road, and follow this into the park. Stop at the visitor center to purchase a dayuse pass, and then drive 1.5 miles west to the trailhead and park along the road.

THE HIKE

Malakoff Diggins State Historic Park is the site of what was once the world's largest hydraulic gold mine. When word got out that a prospector had discovered gold by the Yuba River, miners flooded the area. Finding nothing, they declared the site a "humbug," a pejorative name

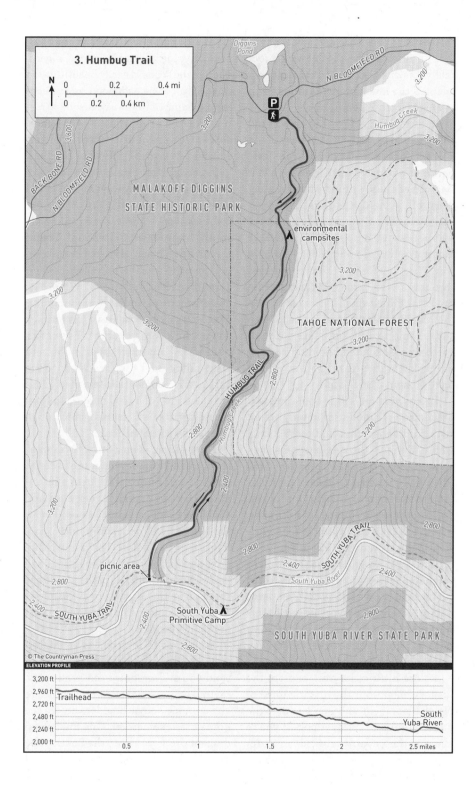

3. Humbug Trail

N

0	0.2	0.4 mi
0	0.2	0.4 km

Diggins Pond

N BLOOMFIELD RD

3,200

3,600

BACK BONE RD

N BLOOMFIELD RD

3,200

Humbug Creek

3,200

MALAKOFF DIGGINS
STATE HISTORIC PARK

environmental
campsites

3,200

TAHOE NATIONAL FOREST

3,200

3,200

HUMBUG TRAIL

2,800

Humbug Creek

2,800

2,400

2,800

SOUTH YUBA TRAIL

2,800

2,400

SOUTH YUBA TRAIL

2,400

South Yuba River

picnic area

2,800

2,400

SOUTH YUBA TRAIL

2,400

South Yuba
Primitive Camp

2,400

SOUTH YUBA RIVER STATE PARK

2,800

2,800

© The Countryman Press

ELEVATION PROFILE

3,200 ft	
2,960 ft	Trailhead
2,720 ft	
2,480 ft	
2,240 ft	South Yuba River
2,000 ft	

0.5   1   1.5   2   2.5 miles

that stuck to the creek and adjacent village until several years later, when gold really was discovered, and the residents adopted the much more dignified town name of North Bloomfield.

It wasn't long before the easy-to-find surface gold played out at Malakoff and a more efficient method to extract finer particles was needed. The 1852 invention of hydraulic mining unfortunately fit the bill. Armed with giant, high-pressure nozzles called monitors, miners sprayed water onto the gold-bearing mountainside, causing the soil to give way. The mud was then channeled through sluice boxes that caught the precious gilded metal. It is estimated that during its operation from 1866 to 1884, some 41 million cubic yards of earth was excavated, yielding several million dollars worth of gold and a hefty environmental price tag.

The byproduct of this operation was an enormous amount of muddy water, rock, and debris that had to go somewhere. So, into the area streams they went. Debris dumped into the Yuba River had a devastating effect on riparian environments, raised riverbeds in the Sacramento Valley (resulting in massive flooding), and hindered navigation on the Sacramento River. This went on until 1884, when, in a hallmark environmental case, Woodruff v. The North Bloomfield Gravel Mining Company, Judge Lorenzo Sawyer issued a permanent injunction against discharging tailings into the Yuba River, effectively bringing an end to the devastation.

Before hitting the trail, explore the visitor center, tour the historic town of North Bloomfield, and wander out to the adjacent mining pit overlook. If you're short on time, a fairly level, 3.5-mile rim trail circles the mine, or you can descend 600 feet along a 3-mile loop into the expansive pit, which looks like a scaled-down version of Utah's Bryce Canyon. Though the scene is eerily beautiful, you can't help but be saddened by the ecological damage that was caused.

From the trailhead, begin a mild descent to a wooden footbridge that crosses a seasonal tributary of Humbug Creek. The channel has a rusty tinge due to the oxidation of iron found in nearby rock deposits. Follow the rivulet downstream before the trail bends south, paralleling Humbug Creek. Douglas firs, black oaks, and dogwoods provide ample shade, and the pine-needle-strewn floor a soft tread. White star flower, wild rose, and an overabundance of poison oak line the trail (oftentimes encroaching on the path). Pass rainwater-filled shafts on your right, and at 0.7 mile a spur trail heads left to the park's "environmental campsites." Join an abandoned dirt road coming in from the right and briefly follow it downhill to its end at a seasonal creek.

After a short ascent, the path resumes its downhill trend, now more steeply. Cross a wooden catwalk near the 1.3-mile mark as Humbug Creek slips and slides between a water-honed slot in the bedrock before leaping into a pool of green water below. The creek offers up a few more watery displays as you pass several unofficial paths bound for small pools that aren't worth the effort. The river is much more inviting and isn't that much farther.

Watch your footing, as a missed step on the single-track trail could send you sliding down the declivitous ravine. Cross a rickety wooden bridge and shimmy across boulders before the grade eases somewhat. One final steep descent drops you onto the South Yuba Trail and a peaceful picnic area on a shady bench overlooking the river at

SOUTH YUBA RIVER

2.7 miles. Hikers wanting to cool trail-worn toes should turn left (east) onto the South Yuba Trail and down to a bridge crossing over Humbug Creek. Find a safe spot to scramble down boulders and rocks to the river's edge or continue 0.3 mile toward South Yuba Primitive Camp where an inviting swimming hole awaits. Linger as long as you like, keeping in mind the elevation you have to regain.

Sierra Buttes

4

This popular climb to a fire lookout crowning the jagged Sierra Buttes will get your heart pumping. From atop the lookout, at 8,587 feet, the northern Sierra panorama is seemingly endless. Pack a good topographic map and knock yourself out identifying the peaks and valleys that emanate from this airy perch.

GETTING THERE

From I-80 in Truckee, drive 22.5 miles north on CA 89 to Sierraville. At the stop sign, turn left onto CA 49 and drive 17.2 miles toward Bassetts. Turn right onto Gold Lake Road (near Bassett's Station) and proceed 1.3 miles to the turnoff for Sardine and Packer Lakes (County Road 621). Turn left over a narrow bridge and drive 0.3 mile to a fork, where you turn right and head toward Packer Lake. Follow paved Packer Lake Road 2.7 miles, past several campgrounds, to a turnoff for Packer Lake Lodge. Stay left (road designation changes to FS 93) and you'll soon pass Tamarack Lakes Trailhead, where the pavement narrows and steepens considerably as you climb toward Packer Lake Saddle. Remain on FS 93 for 0.4 mile past the saddle and veer left onto unpaved FS Road 93-2. Continue 0.1 mile to the parking area and signed trailhead. There are no facilities at the trailhead.

THE HIKE

The Sierra Buttes tower some 5,000 feet above Sierra City, a tiny Gold Rush–era town tucked away in the northern Sierra Nevada. The city was established as a mining town in 1850 and by the late 1800s several mines were operating on or near the Buttes. In the winter of 1852, heavy snow coupled with the region's steep slopes sent a wall of snow

TYPE: Day hike

SEASON: Mid-June through October

TOTAL DISTANCE: 5.0 miles round trip

RATING: Moderate to strenuous

ELEVATION: 7,006 feet; +1,556 feet/-57 feet

LOCATION: Tahoe National Forest

MAPS: USGS 7.5' Sierra City; USFS Lakes Basin, Sierra Buttes, and Plumas-Eureka State Park

FEES AND PERMITS: A permit is not required for this day hike.

CONTACT: Tahoe National Forest, Yuba River Ranger District (530-288-3231; www.fs.usda.gov/tahoe).

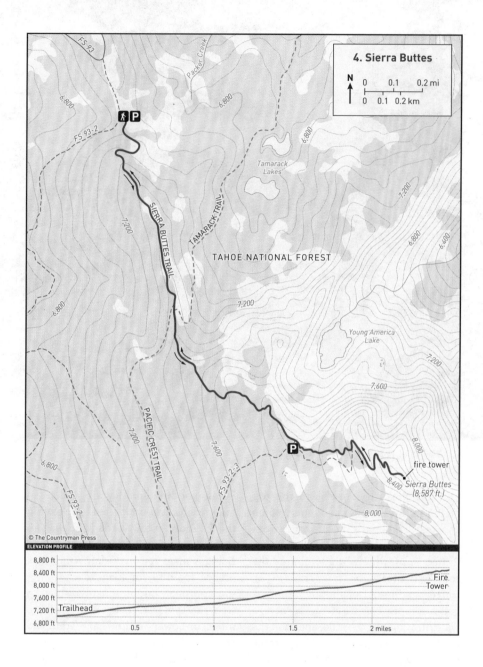

careening down, wiping out the entire town. It was subsequently relocated to a safer site; however, avalanches continued to plague the area. Despite nature's threat, the mines were producing handsomely and the settlement flourished, reaching a population of 10,000 at its peak. The town is much quieter now, with its 225 residents, but the looming specter of Sierra Buttes is still there beckoning you with the promise of stellar panoramas—it doesn't disappoint.

ALONG THE TRAIL TO SIERRA BUTTES FIRE LOOKOUT

There are other routes to the top of Sierra Buttes—some longer, some shorter. This path falls somewhere pleasantly in the middle. The Sierra Buttes Trail, which briefly shares the route with the Pacific Crest Trail (PCT), wastes no time. After slipping around a gate, promptly begin a steep ascent up a wide dirt road. At 0.5 mile, abandon the road and veer right onto a single-track trail and catch your breath as you traverse a level ridgeline scattered with Indian paintbrush, arrow-leaved balsam root, and spreading phlox.

Looking closely, spot the fire lookout to the southeast, perched atop the massive mound of rock forming the buttes.

Begin plodding uphill again, and at 0.9 mile reach a trail fork. Veer left, leaving the PCT, and a few yards later reach a second junction with the Tamarack Trail rising to meet you on the left. Ambitious hikers looking for a more challenging approach might consider starting from the Tamarack Lakes Trailhead (1.8 miles) or Lower Sardine Lake Trailhead (4.6 miles). The trails converge near Tamarack Lakes before ascending to this junction.

Continuing your southeast course, a moderately steep ascent ensues. The forest thickens and you weave through a field of rather large boulders before emerging onto an open ridge where you spy Young America and Sardine lakes below, the hulking Sierra Buttes looming larger than ever.

At 1.8 miles, reach a four-wheel-drive parking area. Yes, I said four-wheel-drive parking area. By continuing about 3.75 miles past our trailhead, the fire road deposits you here, where you can easily make the 0.75-mile jaunt to the top. Granted, this would be easier on the knees, but our path is much more scenic and your lungs and legs are getting a workout to boot.

From the parking area you can either ascend via a slippery slope of switchbacks that snakes through the forest, or follow the much more pleasingly inclined, though slightly longer, fire road. Sticking with the road, go around a locked gate blocking vehicular traffic and continue uphill. Soon you'll reach the junction where the steep trail joins the road. From where the two meet (easy to miss on the return trip) the trail switchbacks up the rocky road.

As you round a bend, the fire lookout appears, isolated atop a cliff of metamorphic rock whose volcanic origins date back some 350 million years. Soon thereafter you spot the precariously exposed stairway that will take you to it. Non-acrophobes can climb the stairs,

SIERRA BUTTES FIRE LOOKOUT

installed by the Forest Service in 1964, to the lookout building. While you cannot go inside, you can walk around its vertigo-inducing, windswept balcony, where the views in every direction are stupendous.

5

Round Lake Loop

The name of this relatively crowd-free corner of Plumas National Forest—Lakes Basin Recreation Area—should give you a pretty good indication of what you can expect to see here: lakes! This pleasant loop visits five picturesque mountain gems that tempt swimmers on hot summer days and lure anglers to their shores. The undulating trail meanders through meadows, forests, and over ridges, one scene as splendid as the next. A network of trails crisscrosses the area, making it easy to adjust the length of your journey.

GETTING THERE

From I-80 in Truckee, drive 22.5 miles north on CA 89 to Sierraville. At the stop sign, turn left onto CA 49 and drive 17.2 miles toward Bassetts. Turn right onto Gold Lake Road (near Bassett's Station) and proceed 7.5 miles to the signed turn-off for Round Lake Trail, which is just before the Plumas/Sierra county line. Turn left and proceed 150 yards to the trailhead parking area equipped with pit toilets.

THE HIKE

From the parking area, follow the wide path, an old mining road, southwest as it skirts behind Gold Lake Lodge. At 0.2 mile, reach a signed fork and bear left toward Round Lake. The path to the right is the return leg of our loop. Western white pines and red firs make up the forest mix while lupine, yampah, and woolly mule ears sprout from sun-drenched grassy clearings.

Breaking out of the forested confines, you traverse a dry hillside blanketed with pinemat manzanita and, at 0.8 mile, spot Big Bear Lake down below. The surrounding mountainside

TYPE: Day hike

SEASON: June through October

TOTAL DISTANCE: 4.0-mile loop

RATING: Easy

ELEVATION: 6,608 feet; +470 feet/-470 feet

LOCATION: Plumas National Forest, Lakes Basin Recreation Area

MAPS: USGS 7.5′ Gold Lake; USFS Lakes Basin, Sierra Buttes, and Plumas-Eureka State Park

FEES AND PERMITS: A permit is not required for this day hike.

CONTACT: Plumas National Forest, Beckwourth Ranger District (530-836-2575; www.fs.usda.gov/plumas).

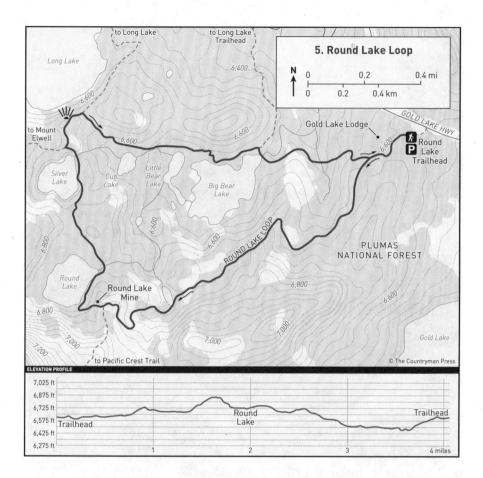

© The Countryman Press

sporadically shows itself through the trees and along open sections of trail. Continue southwest past scattered trees and shrubs and a lovely little unnamed pond at 1.2 miles. Pass through a thicket of water birch occupying the southern shore, its characteristic dark bronze bark highlighted by bright green leaves.

Hidden on the other side of the southern ridge is expansive Gold Lake, named by an expedition of Argonauts (a name chosen to describe Gold Rush immigrants after the mythic Greek tale of Jason and the Argonauts, who searched for the Golden Fleece) who were duped by Thomas Stoddard, a colorful character responsible for what came to be

known as the Gold Lake Fiasco. As the story goes, Stoddard created a flurry of excitement in 1850 when he told tales of a lake ringed with gold nuggets and a few weeks later backed up his claim with a sack full of gold. When he started out with a small expedition to rediscover the lake, nearly a thousand others followed. The group traipsed all over the mountainside visiting lakes, none of which was the one he spoke of, and it quickly became apparent that Stoddard was disoriented and confused. Some believed he was trying to hoard the find for himself and still others that it was a hoax (imagine that). The group eventually came to a large body of water,

SILVER LAKE

larger than what Stoddard had originally described, and he proclaimed it to be the one. Of course it wasn't, but it was dubbed Gold Lake nonetheless. Though Stoddard's fabled lake continued to lure gold seekers to the region, it was never actually found.

Leave the pond and begin a mild rocky ascent to the high point of our journey, from which you have fantastic views of the surrounding terrain. Mount Elwell, the highest point in the Lakes Basin at 7,818 feet, dominates the northwesterly view, while forested ridges and pine-ringed lakes stretch out at your feet. Descend steeply to a signed junction. Ignore a left-branching trail that ultimately meets up with the Pacific Crest Trail (PCT) and turn right toward Round Lake and the remnants of Round Lake Mine, situated on a ledge above the lake.

After exploring the scattered relics, head downhill to Round Lake's shore. Bound for the outlet, pick your way along the narrow single-track trail as it parallels the brushy southeast shoreline. The lake is beautifully backdropped by a granite headwall that's studded with pines and lingering snow early in the season. Easily rock-hop over the outlet at 1.8 miles and begin a northward traverse over a low ridge that confines the clear water. Past a rather pathetic-looking pond, Silver Lake, arguably more scenic than Round Lake, comes into view. Descend and stroll along its eastern shore before crossing its outlet on steppingstones at 2.3 miles.

Not long after, reach a trail junction and turn right. The left course is bound for the summit of Mount Elwell

and the PCT. The trail then makes a sweeping clockwise arc, at about the middle of which you gain a spectacular ridgetop view of Long Lake, the largest on our route, and Mount Elwell rising from its northwest shore. At 2.5 miles, reach another signed intersection and turn right on a downhill course through sun-loving pinemat manzanita and huckleberry oak.

In quick succession pass Cub (2.7 miles), Little Bear (2.9 miles), and Big Bear lakes (3.0 miles), all south of the trail and easily accessed via unofficial paths. Each are popular destinations for swimming and fishing.

At 3.3 miles, pass a left-branching trail leading to Long Lake Trailhead and instead veer right, soon crossing Big Bear Lake's outlet via a flattened log. Pause atop the log and look southwest for a fine, tree-framed vista toward the headwall of this glacier-carved basin. A brief climb becomes a descent as you continue toward Round Lake Trailhead. Cross a seasonal stream in a grassy gully. From this low point, moderately ascend toward the first trail junction and close the loop at 3.8 miles. Then, retrace your steps the final 0.2 mile back to the trailhead.

If you have the luxury of time, Plumas-Eureka State Park, site of Johnsville, an old mining settlement, is just up the road. Replete with Gold Rush–era history and beautiful mountain scenery, it is a worthy destination. There is a museum as well as several historic structures to explore, along with two splendid trails—the Eureka Peak Loop (6.0 miles) and the Grass Lake Trail, which visits a series of lakes (6.5 miles).

6

Feather Falls

TYPE: Day hike

SEASON: Year-round

TOTAL DISTANCE: 8.4-mile semi-loop

RATING: Moderate to strenuous due to some steep sections and the overall elevation change.

ELEVATION: 2,474 feet; +2,228 feet/-2,228 feet

LOCATION: Plumas National Forest

MAPS: USGS 7.5' Forbestown, Brush Creek; USFS Plumas National Forest

FEES AND PERMITS: A permit is not required for this day hike.

CONTACT: Plumas National Forest, Feather River Ranger District (530-534-6500; www .fs.usda.gov/plumas).

Though there is some effort to expend on this hike through the Sierra Nevada foothills, it's well worth it. The trail leads to a wooden overlook perched across from plummeting Feather Falls, arguably one of the most impressive waterfalls in California, outside the confines of Yosemite National Park. This hike can be done year-round, however spring affords the most dramatic water and wildflower displays, and fall is a medley of color as green summer foliage is transformed into an autumnal palette of reds, golds, and oranges. The trail, though well-shaded, can get uncomfortably hot in the summer and has some steep sections that will give your legs and lungs a workout. Go early to avoid the crowds.

GETTING THERE

From CA 70 in Oroville, exit onto CA 162 (Oro Dam Boulevard). Proceed east 1.6 miles and turn right onto Olive Highway. Drive 6.4 miles and turn right onto Forbestown Road (a sign here directs you to Feather Falls). Continue another 6 miles and turn left onto Lumpkin Road and follow it for 10.6 miles. Turn left onto Forest Road 21N35Y just before reaching the town of Feather Falls. Continue along this paved but narrow and bumpy road for 1.5 miles to the trailhead, where you will find ample parking and pit toilets.

THE HIKE

Walk to the northern end of the parking area, where an information placard marks the start of the trail. Enjoy the shade of bigleaf maple, ponderosa pine, pacific madrone, and black oaks along this fairly level segment and arrive at a trail fork at 0.4 mile. Both routes culminate at Feather Falls, so you can't

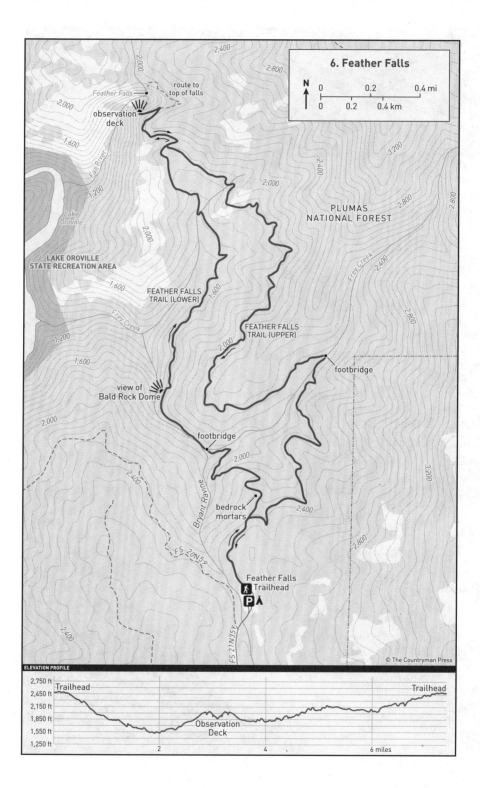

6. Feather Falls

N

| 0 | | 0.2 | | 0.4 mi |
| 0 | 0.2 | | 0.4 km | |

Feather Falls

route to
top of falls

observation
deck

Fall River

2,000

2,000

1,600

1,200

Lake
Oroville

LAKE OROVILLE
STATE RECREATION AREA

1,600

1,200

1,600

2,000

Frey Creek

FEATHER FALLS
TRAIL (LOWER)

2,000

view of
Bald Rock Dome

footbridge

2,400

2,400

Bryant Ravine

FS 20N59

2,400

2,400

2,400

2,800

3,200

2,400

2,000

PLUMAS
NATIONAL FOREST

Frey Creek

2,800

2,800

FEATHER FALLS
TRAIL (UPPER)

footbridge

2,000

bedrock
mortars

2,400

2,800

3,200

Feather Falls
Trailhead

P

FS 21N35Y

© The Countryman Press

ELEVATION PROFILE

2,750 ft	Trailhead					Trailhead
2,450 ft						
2,150 ft						
1,850 ft			Observation			
1,550 ft			Deck			
1,250 ft		2		4		6 miles

FEATHER FALLS

make a wrong choice. The catch is that bearing left (the lower route) gets you there faster (3.6 miles), but is more difficult due to a steeper gradient. Bearing right (the upper route) makes the trip to the falls much more gradual, but is longer (4.5 miles). The trails join again just before the final 0.5-mile climb to the Feather Falls overlook. Enjoy both routes by taking the shorter trail down to the falls, and the longer but easier trail on the way out for a rewarding loop.

Bear left at the junction and, once under the mixed conifer forest, begin descending Bald Rock Canyon. Receiving around 60 inches of rain per year, the area is cool and moist and plays host to a variety of plant and animal species. Spring brings a colorful bounty of wildflowers, like Indian pinks, sticky monkey flower, and red ribbons. Poison oak thrives along much of the trail, so be mindful of its presence. While we're being mindful, also note that rattlesnakes, bloodthirsty mosquitoes and ticks, and mountain lions thrive here too.

Not long after the fork you come to another junction with a short cutoff trail. Bear left and climb a small hill to view bedrock mortars created by the Maidu people, who inhabited this region hundreds of years ago. The Maidu, also known as Foothill Konkow, lived in village communities and practiced a mixed gathering, hunting, and fishing economy. They were incredibly knowledgeable about the distribution and usefulness of plants in their territory. Conscious of harvest times, families would move into areas to gather seasonal foods like greens, tubers and roots, berries, nuts, and seeds, the most important being acorns. They were amassed, dried, and stored for winter use. The bowl-shaped depressions in the bedrock were used by the Konkow to grind acorns and other nuts.

Life for the Konkow changed drastically with colonization. The Gold Rush of 1849, which lured thousands of prospectors to the Feather River and surrounding hills in search of their fortune, was particularly devastating. The miners brought disease, destroyed landscapes with mining techniques, and drove the Konkow people off their land in violent confrontations.

After exploring the mortars, continue along the cutoff to rejoin the main trail. As you approach the first Frey Creek crossing at 1.0 mile, listen for the unmistakable clicking noise of bark beetles and note the appearance of willows, alders, and ferns, which are so characteristic of riparian habitats. One of our most important and most neglected natural resources, they provide food, nesting habitat, cover, and migration corridors for a multitude of birds, reptiles, mammals, invertebrates, and amphibians. Between November and March, the riparian area around Frey Creek becomes a hibernating ground for millions of ladybugs. The vegetation along the trail becomes covered with them until spring, when they take flight and return to the valley floor to feed.

Cross the creek via a wooden footbridge and continue downstream along the east bank for another 0.5 mile before arriving at an unobstructed view of Bald Rock Dome, looming ominously 2,000 feet above the Middle Fork of the Feather River. Bald Rock Dome is part of a 2-mile-wide pluton of granite that formed deep below the earth's surface. As it cooled, part of its coarse-grained granitic rocks became very resistant to weathering, while other parts were highly susceptible to erosion. Over time, powerful erosional processes (wind, water, etc.) removed the weaker rock, exposing the granitic dome we see today. These same processes are responsible for the formation of Feather Falls. The rocks surrounding the falls are very resistant to erosion compared to the rocks in the canyon downstream. Over millions of years, as the Fall River chose its path of least resistance, the weaker rocks were worn away and Feather Falls took shape.

Continue along the shady trail past several seasonal stream crossings and rejoin the upper trail we take on the return at 3.1 miles. From this junction, the trail switchbacks up a rocky, exposed segment dominated by sun-loving vegetation. As you continue on, catch glimpses of the falls through the manzanita- and oak-covered hillside as you follow a steel handrail 0.2 mile farther to a trail junction. Bear left and continue 0.1 mile down to a precipitous wood observation deck directly across from the falls. From your perch, watch the Fall River plunge some 400 feet over a sheer granite ledge to the canyon floor in its rush to meet the Middle Fork of the Feather River and Lake Oroville. Behind you, there is an equally impressive view of the forested slopes of Bald Rock Canyon and the river coursing below.

When you've had your fill, leave the overlook along the same trail and, if you can muster the energy, turn left at the first trail junction and hike 0.25 mile to the granite precipice atop the falls— hardly the best vantage, but a fun side trip nonetheless. Be cautious maneuvering on wet rocks around the top of the falls, as they can be slick and dangerous. Though the water is inviting, keep in mind the deadly drop. Safer swimming holes are found farther upstream and are the perfect energizer for the return trek.

Make your way back to the trail fork 0.5 mile from the overlook, but instead of returning the way you came, turn left and take the longer but less steep upper trail. This trail runs somewhat parallel to, but above, the previous trail. You will see many of the same sights and cross the same creeks and seasonal drainages, but from higher up on the canyon wall. The gentle trail gradient and shade-casting canopy make the uphill back to your car seem, well, almost effortless. When you reach the junction with the lower trail, bear left and retrace your steps back to the trailhead.

II.

LAKE TAHOE

7

Loch Leven Lakes

TYPE: Day hike

SEASON: June through October

TOTAL DISTANCE: 6.0 miles round trip

RATING: Moderate

ELEVATION: 5,805 feet; +1,199 feet/-223 feet

LOCATION: Tahoe National Forest

MAPS: USGS 7.5' Cisco Grove, Soda Springs; USFS Tahoe National Forest

FEES AND PERMITS: A permit is not required for this day hike.

CONTACT: Tahoe National Forest, American River Ranger District (530-367-2224; www.fs.usda.gov/tahoe).

Craving a dose of nature, but don't want to wander too far off the beaten path? This moderately challenging jaunt to Loch Leven Lakes just might be the ticket. Initially, it may not be the most pristine natural setting, as you have to contend with the hum of the all-too-near interstate, but once you slip over a ridge and deeper into the forest, all that becomes a distant memory and you are transported into more peaceful environs with a collection of fantastic glacially carved lakes to explore.

GETTING THERE

From Truckee, drive 19 miles west on I-80 to the Big Bend/Rainbow Road exit. At the end of the ramp, turn left onto Hampshire Rocks Road and proceed under the freeway. Drive 1 mile to the parking area with pit toilets. Find the signed trailhead on the south side of the road, opposite the parking area.

THE HIKE

From the trailhead, begin ascending a rocky, sun-drenched path that snakes through boulders and along granite slabs. Cairns (aka ducks or rock piles), the navigational beacons of the backcountry, guide you along sections where the trail is faint. The terrain is littered with huckleberry oak and dotted with occasional pines. The freeway noise can be a bit unnerving—however, press on; the roar eventually becomes a purr and later disappears altogether.

A short descent takes you into a shady, pocket-sized stand of lodgepole pines. Your brief forest stroll comes to an abrupt end and you ascend the boulder-strewn landscape once again. Reach a murky, grass-filled pond at 0.6 mile. Near the middle point of the pond

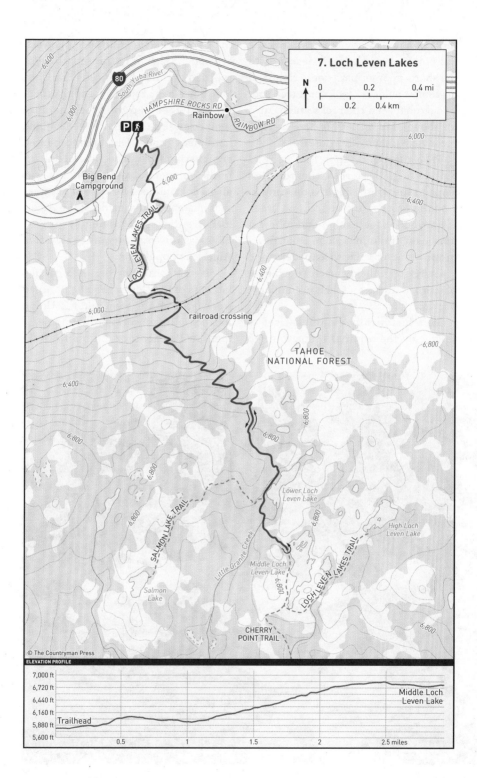

7. Loch Leven Lakes

N

| 0 | | 0.2 | | 0.4 mi |
| 0 | 0.2 | | 0.4 km | |

80

South Yuba River

HAMPSHIRE ROCKS RD

Rainbow

RAINBOW RD

P

Big Bend Campground

LOCH LEVEN LAKES TRAIL

6,400

6,000

6,000

6,000

6,400

6,400

6,800

railroad crossing

TAHOE NATIONAL FOREST

6,800

6,800

6,800

6,800

6,800

6,800

6,800

SALMON LAKE TRAIL

Little Granite Creek

Lower Loch Leven Lake

High Loch Leven Lake

LOCH LEVEN LAKES TRAIL

Middle Loch Leven Lake

Salmon Lake

CHERRY POINT TRAIL

© The Countryman Press

ELEVATION PROFILE

7,000 ft					
6,720 ft					
6,440 ft					Middle Loch
6,160 ft					Leven Lake
5,880 ft	Trailhead				
5,600 ft					
	0.5	1	1.5	2	2.5 miles

there is a not-so-obvious trail fork. At the point where the trail descends to the shore, another path veers right and up some boulders (look for a tree root wedged between the rocks and a cairn up above). Either path is fine, as they reconvene a short while later.

Past the pond, spot the railroad cutting a path across the forested slope to the south. Begin a descent; at 1.0 mile cross a dogwood-lined creek via a wooden footbridge and follow it upstream through a somewhat overgrown area colored with leafy daisy and giant hyssop. Quickly reach a double set of railroad tracks and their accompanying signal lights.

This historically significant set of rails is on the original 1860s route of the Central Pacific Railroad—the western leg of the first transcontinental railroad. While the original rail has long since been replaced, and the roadbed upgraded and repaired, the lines remarkably run on top of the original, handmade grade. This unprecedented engineering feat opened a vital link for trade, commerce, and travel, but was also a portentous milestone of progress that hastened the closing of the American frontier and ultimately proved devastating to the country's Native American population.

Six years after the groundbreaking, laborers of the Central Pacific Railroad working from the west and the Union Pacific Railroad working from the east met at Promontory Summit, Utah.

TRAIL TO LOCH LEVEN LAKES

It was here in May 1869 that Leland Stanford drove the "golden spike" that symbolized the completion of the transcontinental railroad (which at the time actually connected Omaha and Sacramento).

Looking both ways, cross the tracks, and pick up the trail on the opposite side. Bending west at first, the trail eventually resumes it southward tack through a shady mixed conifer forest, and over the ensuing 1.2 miles you ascend 750 vertical feet over a rocky, root-laden path that takes some careful footwork and can be slow going at times.

Cresting a ridge, the gradient significantly eases and you meander through a thinning forest. At 2.5 miles, spot Lower Loch Leven Lake below and descend steeply to its western shore. From here, the trail parallels a bedrock ridge before coming to a right-branching trail at 2.7 miles bound for Salmon Lake. If you are spending the whole day in the area, the 0.9-mile jaunt to Salmon Lake is a worthy side trip—however, only after you've explored the more aesthetically pleasing Loch Leven Lakes and have energy to spare.

From the junction with the Salmon Lake Trail, you soon cross Lower Loch Leven Lake's outlet. Pass through a notch in a low ridge and reach Middle Loch Leven Lake at the 3-mile mark. Take a well-deserved rest atop one of the

ROOT-COVERED SECTION OF LOCH LEVEN LAKES TRAIL

surrounding granite slabs that form the lake's margins (also perfect for sunbathing after a quick dip). This is our turnaround point, although more ambitious hikers can continue on to High Loch Leven Lake, found 0.8 mile farther at the terminus of the trail.

Mount Judah Loop

TYPE: Day hike

SEASON: July to October

TOTAL DISTANCE: 5-mile semi-loop

RATING: Moderate

ELEVATION: 7,054 feet; +1,445 feet/-1,445 feet

LOCATION: Tahoe National Forest

MAPS: USGS 7.5' Norden; Trails Illustrated Lake Tahoe Basin No. 803

FEES AND PERMITS: A permit is not required for this day hike.

CONTACT: Tahoe National Forest, Truckee Ranger District (530-587-3558; www.fs.usda.gov/tahoe).

Following portions of the Pacific Crest Trail, this relatively easy jaunt to the peak of Mount Judah rewards hikers with commanding views of the rugged Sierra crest north of Lake Tahoe. The trail is easily accessible from I-80, and the crowded parking area is a testament to its popularity. Though the solitude factor is low, the arresting views, pioneering history, and palette of vibrant wildflowers more than make up for its lack of seclusion. Be sure to carry a windbreaker, plenty of water, and a good map so you can match names with peaks from your panoramic perch.

GETTING THERE

From I-80 west of Truckee, exit Donner Pass Road and turn left. Travel west 6.7 miles toward Donner Pass (along the way you will pass Donner Memorial State Park and Donner Lake). Just past Donner Summit Bridge, turn left (south) onto an unnamed dirt road next to Sugar Bowl Academy (look for the small Pacific Crest Trail placard). Proceed 0.1 mile to the trailhead on your left. Parking is available along the narrow road.

THE HIKE

This hike is set just south of Donner Pass, named for the hapless party of California-bound American migrants who became stranded here in the winter of 1846–47, just short of their destination. Filled with fabulous stories of the wonders of California and eager to make new lives for themselves, countless wagon trains made the arduous pilgrimage west. The Donner Party's journey started out just like any other, but in Wyoming, a careless decision to follow a shortcut (which turned out to be not so short) and winter's early arrival set the

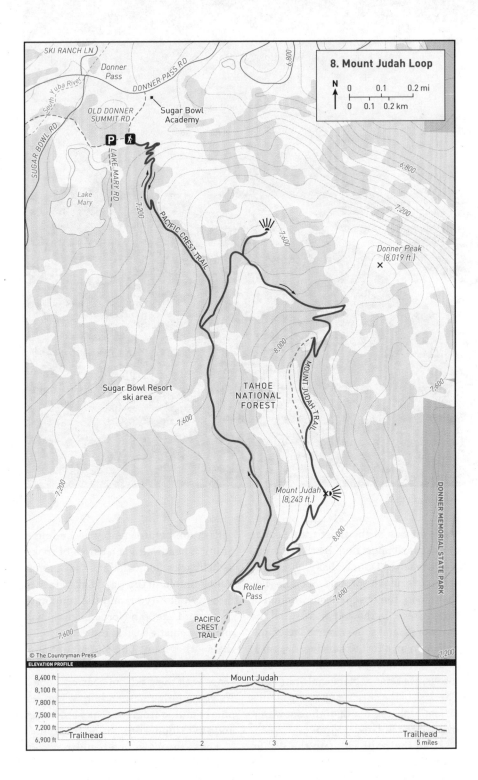

SKI RANCH LN

Donner
Pass

South Yuba River

DONNER PASS RD

OLD DONNER
SUMMIT RD

Sugar Bowl
Academy

SUGAR BOWL RD

P

LAKE MARY RD

Lake
Mary

7,200

PACIFIC CREST TRAIL

8. Mount Judah Loop

N

| 0 | 0.1 | 0.2 mi |

| 0 | 0.1 | 0.2 km |

6,800

6,800

7,200

7,600

Donner Peak
(8,019 ft.)
×

8,000

MOUNT JUDAH TRAIL

7,600

TAHOE
NATIONAL
FOREST

Sugar Bowl Resort
ski area

7,600

7,200

Mount Judah
(8,243 ft.)
×

8,000

Roller
Pass

PACIFIC
CREST
TRAIL

7,600

7,600

DONNER MEMORIAL STATE PARK

7,200

© The Countryman Press

ELEVATION PROFILE

Mount Judah

8,400 ft					
8,100 ft					
7,800 ft					
7,500 ft					
7,200 ft					
6,900 ft Trailhead				Trailhead	
	1	2	3	4	5 miles

MOUNT JUDAH

stage for one of the most tragic sagas of westward migration. By the time the party reached Donner Lake, there was snow covering the ground. Six miles farther along, they became snowbound at Alder Creek. In the end, nearly half the party died, and some resorted to cannibalism in an effort to survive. Just east of our hike along I-80, and well worth the visit, is Donner Memorial State Park. The base of the park's monument stands 22 feet high, the depth of the snow that trapped the ill-fated migrants.

From the trailhead, join the Pacific Crest Trail (PCT) as it heads south through a short swath of moisture-loving vegetation before steeply ascending a granitic headwall via a series of rocky switchbacks. Soon views of the Summit Valley unfold to the west. Lake Mary is directly below you, and the remnants of former Lake Van Norden, now a lush meadow, can be seen in the distance. To the south, Mount Lincoln, Mount Disney, and Crows Nest dominate the landscape with their ski-run-scarred slopes. As you continue ascending, watch for phlox spilling from the rocky crevasses and violet lupine decorating the trail.

Leave the views and boulder-strewn trail behind for the moment as you traverse the now predominantly dirt trail through a shady stand of verdant firs before emerging onto an open ski run. At 0.9 mile, reach the northern junction with the Mount Judah Loop trail. Veer left, leaving the PCT, and climb through slopes seasonally carpeted with fuzzy mule ears, Indian paintbrush, penstemon, and groundsel.

The path soon levels off, and you reach a spur trail that extends approximately 200 yards to a rocky promontory with northward views of Lake Angela and Castle Peak, the highest summit in the Donner Pass area. Return to the Mount Judah Trail and after a short distance join an old 4x4 route as you climb gently eastward to a saddle below Donner Peak (8,019 feet). A spur trail takes you to the base of the exfoliating pinnacle, and though reaching the top looks easy, you need basic rock climbing skills to scramble up the easiest summit. Though the views atop Donner Peak are vastly better than those from the rocky promontory we just left, the best views are yet to come.

From the saddle, begin switchbacking up through the thinning mixed conifer forest along the eastern slope of Mount Judah. After approximately 0.7 mile, you reach a saddle between Mount Judah's higher southern summit and its slightly lower northern summit. A short trail leads to the northern summit, but we continue to Mount Judah's true summit just ahead. Follow the exposed ridge, dotted with pink broad-stemmed onion in the early summer, to the barren apex 2.4 miles from the trailhead.

The mountain was named for Theodore Judah, architect of the transcontinental railroad and first chief engineer of the Central Pacific Railroad. Though not a part of Judah's original route, in the mid-1920s a nearly 2-mile-long tunnel was blasted beneath Mount Judah in an effort to ease the grade for locomotives making the trans-Sierra trek. From the summit, if you're lucky, you might be able to watch a train go into the tunnel underneath Mount Judah and emerge on the other side.

From the top of Mount Judah (8,243 feet), the surrounding landscape comes into full view. Donner Lake and the Martis Valley stretch eastward; Anderson Peak and Tinker Knob rise to the south; the now familiar Summit Valley stretches westward; and to the north, imposing Mount Lola and Red Mountain reach toward the sky.

After taking a break and soaking in the view, begin a southwestward, switchbacking descent into a forest of hemlock and, later, fir. At 3.2 miles, reach Mount Judah Loop's southerly junction with the PCT. Veer left (south) for approximately 150 yards to visit Roller Pass, a saddle between Coldstream Valley to the east and Summit Valley to the west, where the Overland Emigrant Trail crossed the Sierra. It is here that emigrants used log rollers to winch wagons up the eastern slope too steep for harnessed oxen to negotiate. Take the short path to the brink to get a better understanding of what the early pioneers faced as they traversed this roadless, rugged range.

Return to the trail junction and continue descending via the PCT. Approximately 0.8 mile past the junction, emerge from the red fir forest onto an open ski run. Cross a 4x4 road and pick up the single-track trail, arriving at the northern junction of the Mount Judah Loop Trail shortly thereafter. From here, retrace your steps back to the trailhead.

9

Rubicon Trail

TYPE: Day hike

SEASON: Late May through September

TOTAL DISTANCE: 5.4 miles one way

RATING: Easy

ELEVATION: 6,333 feet; +765 feet/-511 feet

LOCATION: D. L. Bliss and Emerald Bay State Parks

MAPS: USGS 7.5' Emerald Bay; Trails Illustrated Lake Tahoe Basin No. 803; D.L. Bliss and Emerald Bay State Parks brochure maps

FEES AND PERMITS: A permit is not required for this day hike. D. L. Bliss State Park charges a $10 day-use fee (per vehicle). Parking in the Vikingsholm lot at Emerald Bay State Park costs $10.

CONTACT: D. L. Bliss State Park (530-525-7277; www.parks.ca.gov/?page_id=505); Emerald Bay State Park (530-541-3030; www.parks.ca.gov/?page_id=506).

Though the majority of the 72 miles of shoreline surrounding Lake Tahoe is privately owned, you can find a little slice of heaven within D. L. Bliss and Emerald Bay State Parks, located on the southwestern shore. The Rubicon Trail traverses the adjoining parks and has some of the most splendid views of the lake's cerulean waters and pine-shrouded shoreline. The gentle trail begins near Calawee Cove in D. L. Bliss State Park and culminates at Viking-sholm, a historic Scandinavian mansion, in Emerald Bay State Park.

Since this is a point-to-point hike, you need to arrange for someone to drop you off and pick you up, have two vehicles to shuttle between trailheads, or plan to walk back to where you parked your vehicle. This is one of the easier hikes in the Tahoe Basin, and since its entirety is loaded with tantalizing sights, sounds, and smells, you can walk the trail for as long or as short as you like.

GETTING THERE

From South Lake Tahoe, head north 10.4 miles on CA 89 from its junction with US 50 (the South Lake Tahoe Y) and turn right into D. L. Bliss State Park. Proceed 1 mile, passing the visitor center, to the check-in station where you pay the day-use fee. Continue 0.6 mile along a paved, narrow road, passing alternate trailheads for Lighthouse and Rubicon Trail on your right. At the stop sign, turn right, following the signs to Rubicon Trail. The trailhead parking lot, with restrooms, is 0.6 mile farther.

THE HIKE

Lake Tahoe straddles the border between California and Nevada and bejewels the Sierra crest with its

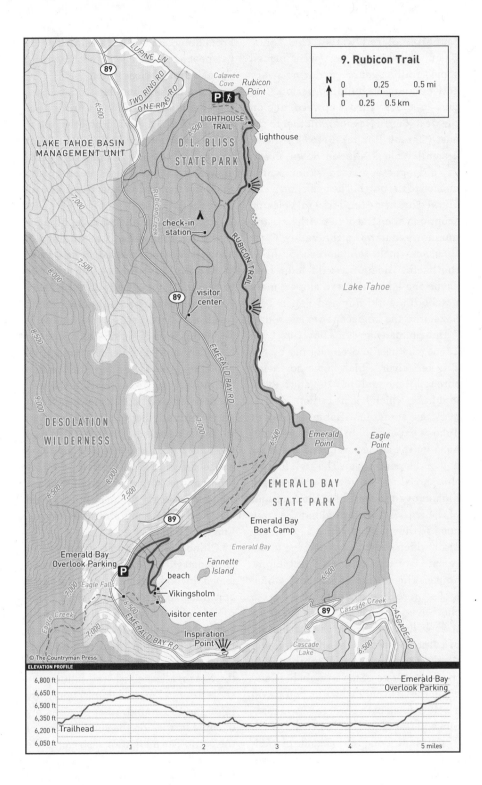

9. Rubicon Trail

N 0   0.25   0.5 mi
   0   0.25   0.5 km

Calawee Cove
Rubicon Point
LIGHTHOUSE TRAIL
lighthouse
LAKE TAHOE BASIN MANAGEMENT UNIT
D.L. BLISS STATE PARK
LUPINE LN
TWO RING RD
ONE RING RD
6,500
7,000
7,500
8,000
8,500
9,000
Rubicon Creek
Rubicon Rd
check-in station
visitor center
RUBICON TRAIL
EMERALD BAY RD
Lake Tahoe
DESOLATION WILDERNESS
7,000
7,500
8,000
8,500
6,500
Emerald Point
Eagle Point
EMERALD BAY STATE PARK
Emerald Bay Boat Camp
Emerald Bay Overlook Parking
Emerald Bay
Fannette Island
beach
Vikingsholm
visitor center
Eagle Falls
Eagle Creek
7,000
6,500
EMERALD BAY RD
Inspiration Point
Cascade Creek
CASCADE RD
Cascade Lake
6,500

© The Countryman Press

ELEVATION PROFILE

6,800 ft
6,650 ft
6,500 ft
6,350 ft
6,200 ft
6,050 ft
Trailhead
1   2   3   4   5 miles
Emerald Bay Overlook Parking

sapphire-colored water. The Tahoe Basin, in which it lies, was formed some 5 million years ago during a very active mountain building period. Two parallel blocks thrust upward, one on the west (Sierra Nevada), another to the east (Carson Range). Between these, a smaller block slipped down, creating a deep, steep-sided valley, which opened to the north. The open north end allowed drainage until several volcanic eruptions filled the outlet with lava and mudflows, damming the valley. Over time, snowmelt, rain, and runoff filled the basin. Glaciers would later help shape the lake's western slopes, most notably Emerald Bay and Fallen Leaf Lake, into the landscape we see today. Although many streams flow into Lake Tahoe, the lake is drained only by the Truckee River, which flows northeast through Reno and into Nevada's Pyramid Lake, which has no outlet.

After some justifiable ogling at Tahoe's expanse of brilliant blue water, head for the signed trailhead at the far end of the parking lot. The trail follows the shoreline; however, you remain high above the water for the first half of the trip. A few steps along the trail, come to the right-branching Lighthouse Trail, which climbs a small ridge to the remains of the Rubicon Point Lighthouse. The neglected beacon, which looks more like an outhouse, was a short-lived endeavor of the early 1900s. It does, however, carry the distinction of being located at the highest elevation (6,300 feet) of any lighthouse in the United States. Stay straight here and enjoy the heavenly views as you travel a well-defined path bordered by manzanita and fragrant tobacco brush.

Continue along the backside of Rubicon Point, where you find several small unofficial trails that descend to its base.

From Rubicon Point, on a calm day, you can peer a remarkable 70 feet down into Tahoe's crystal clear water.

The pine- and boulder-studded path then begins ascending to a precipitous granite bluff, where a protective chain railing has been installed. Watch for osprey foraging in this area. Lucky hikers will spy the predators plunging into the water to nab unsuspecting fish with their sharp talons.

At approximately 0.4 mile, glimpse the old lighthouse perched on the cliff above, and after a short distance arrive at a second junction leading 0.2 mile to the lighthouse itself. Back on Rubicon Trail, continue the gentle ascent, reaching a wood-railed overlook with fantastic views of Mount Tallac and the Nevada shore. At 1 mile, an unsigned lateral takes you to the alternate roadside trailheads you drove past on the way in. Bear left and enter a viewless forest and eventually begin a 1-mile descent to Tahoe's rocky shoreline. Just past the halfway point of the descent, pass another wood-railed viewpoint. In my opinion, this sunny section of trail has some of the best vantages of the rugged western shore as it stretches toward Emerald Point.

Climb again to a tumbling streamlet shrouded with thimbleberry and American dogwood. Past the creek, the climb continues before you descend some rocky stairs and finally arrive at a small sandy beach near the northern end of Emerald Point, an ideal resting spot and a chance to take a chilly swim. From the beach, a less-used trail follows the shore around Emerald Point, eventually rejoining the main trail approximately 0.5 mile farther, on the southern end of the point. The main trail, also called the Bypass Trail, turns inland and enters a forest of incense cedar, Jeffrey pines, white fir, and sugar pines before emerging along the shore once again.

The path is mostly rocky, and several unofficial trails lead down to the water's edge as you meander southwest along the level trail lined with purple lupine and bracken ferns. An obvious swath of denuded hillside at the far end of Emerald Bay marks the site of a 1955 landslide triggered during the construction of CA 89 across a steep, unstable slope.

The path widens as you come into Emerald Bay Boat Camp. At 3.6 miles, veer left on an asphalt road, passing the pier, and picking up the dirt trail on your left a short while later. Follow the trail markers through the campground, crossing several raised walkways before you unfortunately trade the peaceful trail for the bustling area around Vikingsholm.

At a trail fork, go left to reach the beach, where you will find that most visitors lounge on the sand, as the water rarely gets warmer than the mid-60s, even in the hottest weather. Or, stay left and proceed to Vikingsholm, a historic Scandinavian mansion and summer retreat of wealthy heiress Lora J. Knight. Completed in 1929, the house is fashioned after eleventh-century castles found in the fjords of Norway. Hand-hewn timbers were used to construct the home, and granite for the foundation and walls was quarried from behind the house. Intricate carvings and antique furnishings fill rooms that overlook solitary Fannette Island and the azure waters of Emerald Bay. Seasonal guided tours of Vikingsholm are available for a nominal fee (purchase tickets at the visitor center).

You can also explore Eagle Falls, an excellent side trip, once you have reached Emerald Bay. To reach the trailhead, continue south along the paved

LAKE TAHOE SHORELINE

path past Vikingsholm, following signs to Eagle Falls Trail. Join the trail adjacent to the visitor center and proceed 0.2 mile northwest along an easy path to the base of Eagle Falls. The brink of the falls is also visible from the parking area adjacent to CA 89.

When ready, assuming you have arranged a car shuttle, head north on the paved pathway behind Vikingsholm. Hopefully you've saved a little energy. The asphalt trail turns to dirt and climbs 360 vertical feet along a gravel roadbed, via long switchbacks, before depositing you at the parking area along CA 89.

10

Tahoe Meadows

TYPE: Day hike

SEASON: Late June through September

TOTAL DISTANCE: 1.3-mile loop/3.4 miles round trip

RATING: Easy/easy

ELEVATION: 8,711 feet; +74 feet/-74 feet (interpretive loop)/8,726 feet; +286 feet/-247 feet (vista point)

LOCATION: Humboldt-Toiyabe National Forest

MAPS: USGS 7.5' Mount Rose; Trails Illustrated Tahoe Basin No. 803

FEES AND PERMITS: A permit is not required for this day hike.

CONTACT: Humboldt-Toiyabe National Forest, Carson Ranger District (775-882-2766; www.fs.usda.gov/htnf).

Beneath the shadow of Mount Rose, this handicapped-accessible interpretive loop meanders around the edge of lush Tahoe Meadows. In early summer, as the region emerges from its winter coat of snow, the meadow comes alive with birds, butterflies, and elegant wildflowers that add splashes of indigo, fuchsia, and lavender to the carpet of slender grasses. Placards along the trail educate you about the natural and human history of the area. Extend your visit by striking out on the Tahoe Rim Trail to an overlook high above the lake's northeast shore.

GETTING THERE

From US 80 in Truckee, exit at CA 267 (North Shore Boulevard) and drive 12 miles south toward Kings Beach. Turn left onto CA 28 and continue 4.5 miles to Incline Village (you will cross the state line and be in Nevada). At NV 431, turn left and proceed 7.1 miles to Tahoe Meadows. Turn right at the sign and enter the paved parking area, where you will find pit toilets. Parking can be at a premium on summer weekends, so come early or during the week if possible.

THE HIKE

There are two trailheads served by this parking lot, the interpretive loop at the eastern end and the Tahoe Rim Trail (TRT) at the western end. Below you will find an option to extend your visit to this region by hiking to an overlook along the TRT, but first, let's start with the interpretive trail.

Leaving the parking area, you may hear some traffic noise from the nearby highway, but it quickly dissipates, and you are soon serenaded by bird songs and trickling water as you ramble past giant granite boulders and beneath

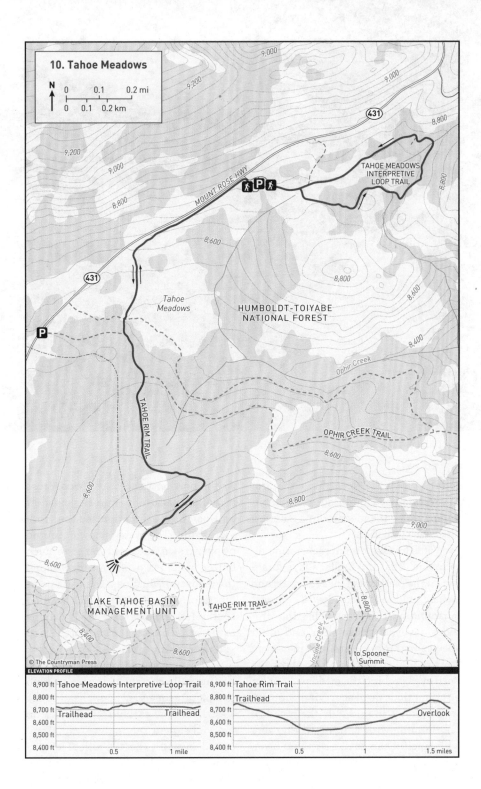

10. Tahoe Meadows

N

| 0 | 0.1 | 0.2 mi |
| 0 | 0.1 | 0.2 km |

9,000

9,000

431

8,800

8,800

TAHOE MEADOWS
INTERPRETIVE
LOOP TRAIL

MOUNT ROSE HWY

9,200

9,000

8,800

8,600

8,800

8,600

431

Tahoe
Meadows

HUMBOLDT-TOIYABE
NATIONAL FOREST

8,400

P

Ophir Creek

OPHIR CREEK TRAIL

8,600

TAHOE RIM TRAIL

8,600

8,800

9,000

8,600

Incline Creek

LAKE TAHOE BASIN
MANAGEMENT UNIT

TAHOE RIM TRAIL

8,800

to Spooner
Summit

8,400

8,600

© The Countryman Press

ELEVATION PROFILE

Tahoe Meadows Interpretive Loop Trail

8,900 ft		
8,800 ft		
8,700 ft	Trailhead	Trailhead
8,600 ft		
8,500 ft		
8,400 ft	0.5	1 mile

Tahoe Rim Trail

8,900 ft		
8,800 ft	Trailhead	
8,700 ft		Overlook
8,600 ft		
8,500 ft		
8,400 ft	0.5	1	1.5 miles

TAHOE MEADOWS INTERPRETIVE LOOP

towering pines. Bear right at the first of several raised footbridges as you circumnavigate the meadow in a counterclockwise direction.

Watch for Clark's nutcrackers, mountain bluebirds, and Steller's jays foraging on the plethora of insects, nuts, and seeds found in the meadow. The forest surrounding the grassy clearing provides cover for these birds and other species that thrive here. You may even spy a red-tailed hawk circling above, its keen eyes probing the meadow floor for a scrumptious meal scurrying about.

Generally, in mid-July the meadow is brimming with delicate wildflowers with fanciful names like elephant head, alpine shooting star, water plantain buttercup, pussy paw, and monkey flower.

At the northern end of the loop, cross a rivulet that drains into the meadow and come to a junction leading to a vista point. The vista is now obscured by overgrown trees, and you have much better vantages of the meadow along the main trail. Just past the vista point junction, turn left onto the TRT heading southwest, and lose your shady canopy as you stroll back to the start of the loop and the parking area.

If the interpretive loop got the blood flowing and you want to do a short climb to a picturesque viewpoint, head to the west end of the parking lot and pick up the well-signed Tahoe Rim Trail. Completed in 2001, the 165-mile TRT circumnavigates the ridge line of the Lake Tahoe Basin. The long-distance loop

Spooner Summit segment of the TRT. Even though we venture only 1.7 of those miles, you get a fine sampling of the many treasures waiting along this National Recreation Trail.

The single-track trail parallels the highway as it descends from the parking area into the lower portion of the meadow. Stay on the trail and avoid trampling the fragile vegetation. The trail bends south, away from the road, into the heart of the meadow and crosses Ophir Creek at 0.7 mile. Just past the burbling year-round stream, the path widens and you enter the mixed conifer forest that forms the distinct meadow perimeter. The intoxicating pine scent, both sweet and pungent at the same time, will no doubt envelop you. Soon you'll come to a T-intersection. Turning right takes you to an alternate roadside trailhead along NV 431. We proceed left, following the blue arrows, which mark the entire TRT.

Through this section, the subalpine forest is relatively open, with majestic firs, stout pines, and nodding hemlocks all coexisting. Stay right at the fork with Ophir Creek Trail, which takes you to Price Lakes and eventually Davis Creek County Park. Begin a gentle climb south and, 1.6 miles from the trailhead, reach a saddle where you get your first views of Lake Tahoe. A short spur trail to your right meanders out to a vista point where you can fully appreciate the scene. From 2,400 feet above the lake, the towering peaks that flank the western shore seem to jut from the serene water like a fortress wall protecting the crown jewel.

From this point, continue south along the TRT for as long as you like, but remember that what goes up must come down. Eventually you'll need to turn around and retrace your steps back to the trailhead.

meanders through wildflower-choked meadows, traverses deep canyons and exposed ridges, passes rushing streams and pristine alpine lakes, and includes some of the most stunning panoramas around.

The TRT passes through two states, six counties, one state park, four National Forests, and three natural wilderness areas. The trail is open to bikers, hikers, and equestrians, but closed to motorized vehicles. Some sections of the trail do not allow biking, or allow it only on even-numbered days.

The TRT Tahoe Meadows Trailhead, at the south end of the parking area opposite the interpretive loop, is the southbound jumping-off point for the 23.3-mile long Tahoe Meadows to

Crag Lake

TYPE: Day hike or overnight

SEASON: Late June through October

TOTAL DISTANCE: 10 miles round trip

RATING: Moderate

ELEVATION: 6,230 feet; +1,290 feet/-27 feet

LOCATION: Eldorado National Forest, Desolation Wilderness

MAPS: USGS 7.5' Meeks Bay, Homewood, Rockbound Valley; Trails Illustrated Lake Tahoe Basin No. 803

FEES AND PERMITS: A free permit is required for this day hike and can be obtained by self-registering at the trailhead kiosk. Overnight trips into the Desolation Wilderness require a permit (fee) from Eldorado National Forest.

CONTACT: Lake Tahoe Basin Management Unit (530-543-2600; www.fs.usda.gov/ltbmu); Eldorado National Forest, Pacific Ranger District (530-644-2349; www.fs.usda.gov/eldorado).

This hike along the beginnings of the Tahoe-Yosemite Trail follows Meeks Creek upstream to a delightful string of lakes. The trail can get busy on summer weekends, but relatively speaking it is much less crowded than other south shore trails leading into Desolation Wilderness and beyond. Though the second lake in the chain is our turnaround point, there are five more to explore before you reach Phipps Pass—any of which makes a fine destination for a longer day trip or overnight jaunt.

GETTING THERE

From Tahoe City, head south 10.6 miles on CA 89 from its junction with CA 28. The trailhead is on the right just past Meeks Bay Resort. Parking can be found along the highway. From South Lake Tahoe, head north 16.5 miles on CA 89 from its junction with US 50 (the South Lake Tahoe Y) and find the trailhead on your left, just past Meeks Bay Campground. Fill out your permit at the information board before starting out.

THE HIKE

The 186-mile Tahoe-Yosemite Trail (TYT) connects Meeks Bay on the western shore of Lake Tahoe to Tuolumne Meadows in Yosemite National Park. Though it's not officially recognized and lacks the notoriety of other long-distance trails, the TYT gives those wanting to test the thru-hiker waters a shorter option than the much lengthier Pacific Crest Trail (PCT). Incidentally, about one-third of the TYT coincides with the PCT.

To begin, go around a locked gate and walk along a wide dirt road. As the level path takes you along the toe of a rocky, forested slope, to your left notice

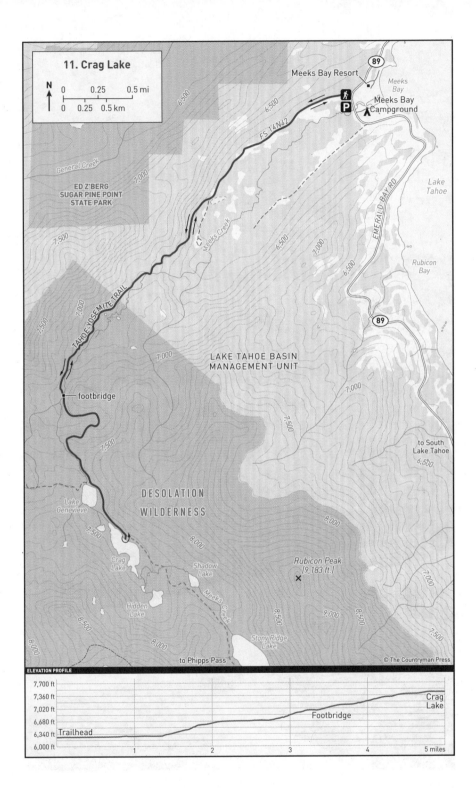

11. Crag Lake

N
| 0 | 0.25 | 0.5 mi |
| 0 | 0.25 | 0.5 km |

Meeks Bay Resort

89

Meeks Bay

Meeks Bay Campground

FS 14N42

6,500

6,500

7,000

General Creek

ED Z'BERG SUGAR PINE POINT STATE PARK

7,500

7,000

Meeks Creek

6,500

7,000

Lake Tahoe

EMERALD BAY RD.

Rubicon Bay

89

TAHOE-YOSEMITE TRAIL

7,500

7,000

LAKE TAHOE BASIN MANAGEMENT UNIT

7,000

footbridge

7,500

7,500

to South Lake Tahoe

6,500

DESOLATION WILDERNESS

Lake Genevieve

7,500

8,000

Crag Lake

Shadow Lake

Rubicon Peak [9,183 ft.]
×

8,000

9,000

8,500

7,000

Hidden Lake

8,500

Meeks Creek

7,500

8,000

8,000

Stony Ridge Lake

8,500

9,000

to Phipps Pass

© The Countryman Press

ELEVATION PROFILE

7,700 ft					
7,360 ft					Crag Lake
7,020 ft					
6,680 ft			Footbridge		
6,340 ft	Trailhead				
6,000 ft					
	1	2	3	4	5 miles

CRAG LAKE

the profusion of saplings and regrowth crowding the meadow after a fire cleared the forest canopy—all vying for water and sunlight. Behind them, on the opposite side of the meadow, is the knobby tip of Rubicon Peak.

Pass a small pond and immediately reach a junction at 1.3 miles. Abandon the road and bear right onto the TYT as the path narrows and begins a steady 0.5-mile climb through a forest thick with lodgepole pines, sugar pines, incense cedar, and white firs. Brewer's lupine, Indian paintbrush, and arnica can be found in the sunnier sections.

Near the crest of the climb, Meeks Creek can be heard splashing to the left. Stroll through the forest, and at 2.3 miles enter Desolation Wilderness. Paralleling the creek, the trail weaves in and out of forested flats and wetter riparian areas filled with greenery. A short 0.3 mile farther along, your stroll becomes a climb as you approach a crossing with the cavorting Meeks Creek. A sturdy wooden footbridge at 3.3 miles takes you across the shallow water, where you promptly angle east away from it. Dodging up a side canyon littered with thimbleberry, vine maple, and currant bushes, the trail makes a circuitous climb, contouring the canyon wall.

Breaking out of the forest, you traverse an open ridge, which grants views of the pine-studded granite landscape and a peek at Lake Tahoe. Rejoining the creek, you once again veer south and follow its pleasant cascades upstream. At 4.5 miles, reach the shore of Lake Genevieve and a junction with the seldom-used General's Creek Trail. Continue along the main trail toward Phipps Pass.

Lake Genevieve is a peaceful gem ringed by pines, its shallow water relatively warm for swimming. Continue south and reach larger and more scenic Crag Lake at 5 miles. A granite slab about midway down the eastern shore is a perfect spot to spread out a picnic and take in the scene. Anglers can test their skills against the resident brook, brown, and rainbow trout. If you are camping here, proceed around the lake to the southern shore for the best and most environmentally friendly sites. Remember to set up camp 100 feet from the water and trail.

Though our hike ends here, it's certainly not the end of the trail. Day hikers looking to extend their trips or backpackers can continue southeast along the TYT and visit Hidden (5.7 miles), Shadow (5.9 miles), Stony Ridge (6.3 miles), Rubicon (8.1 miles), and Grouse (8.6 miles) lakes before the string comes to an end and you have to surmount Phipps Pass.

Cascade Falls and Granite Lake

TYPE: Day hike

SEASON: Late June through October

TOTAL DISTANCE: 1.4 miles round trip/2.2 miles round trip

RATING: Easy/moderate

ELEVATION: 6,920 feet; +111 feet/-211 feet (Cascade Falls)/6,920 feet; +776 feet/-33 feet (Granite Lake)

LOCATION: Eldorado National Forest, Desolation Wilderness

MAPS: USGS 7.5' Emerald Bay; Trails Illustrated Lake Tahoe Basin No. 803

FEES AND PERMITS: If Cascade Falls is your only destination, you do not need to fill out a permit, since the Cascade Falls Trail does not cross into Desolation Wilderness. Those making the trek to Granite Lake and beyond must obtain a free permit at the trailhead kiosk.

CONTACT: Lake Tahoe Basin Management Unit (530-543-2600; www.fs.usda.gov/ltbmu); Eldorado National Forest, Pacific Ranger District (530-644-2349; www.fs.usda.gov/eldorado).

The Bayview trailhead is a popular starting point for day hikers and backpackers alike. Two trails leave from here—Cascade Falls Trail and Bayview Trail—both with something unique to offer. The former visits Cascade Falls, a tumbling cataract that spills 150 feet into Cascade Lake. The path is easy to follow and offers impressive vistas of the Tahoe Basin along the way. Come in the spring, as by late summer the falls are but a wee trickle. Unlike the mild gradient of the Cascade Falls Trail, Bayview Trail is a steady uphill trudge. Part of the way up, enjoy a spectacular bird's-eye view of Emerald Bay and the expansive Lake Tahoe. In the end, energize yourself with a refreshing swim in peaceful Granite Lake.

GETTING THERE

From South Lake Tahoe, head north 7.3 miles on CA 89 from its junction with US 50 (the South Lake Tahoe Y) and turn left into Bayview Campground (just opposite Inspiration Point). Proceed 0.1 mile through the campground to the trailhead parking area.

THE HIKE

From the information board, proceed 25 feet up the trail to a signed fork (right for Granite Lake, left for Cascade Falls). Veer left and make the short excursion to Cascade Falls first. The wide path heads east through a forest of Jeffrey pine and white fir. Not far from the trailhead, a path from the campground joins in on the left and the route bends southward along a sandy flat.

Abandon the shady conifers, and at 0.25 mile begin a short, rocky ascent. Manzanita, chinquapin, and huckleberry oak now line the path. Cresting

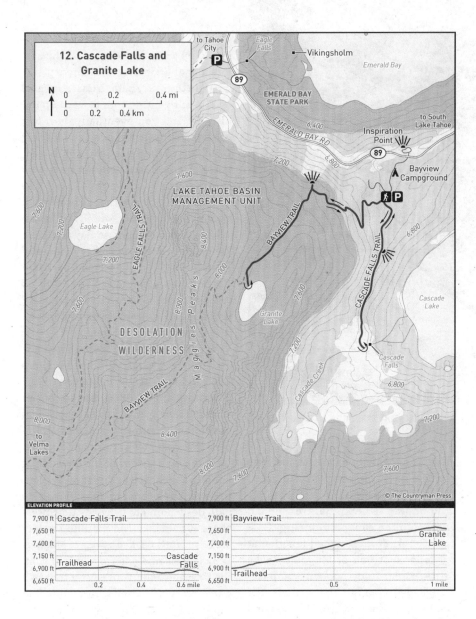

12. Cascade Falls and Granite Lake

ELEVATION PROFILE

Cascade Falls Trail — Trailhead ... Cascade Falls
(7,900 ft / 7,650 ft / 7,400 ft / 7,150 ft / 6,900 ft / 6,650 ft; 0.2 / 0.4 / 0.6 mile)

Bayview Trail — Trailhead ... Granite Lake
(7,900 ft / 7,650 ft / 7,400 ft / 7,150 ft / 6,900 ft / 6,650 ft; 0.5 / 1 mile)

a knoll, gain your first view of the surrounding environs—spread out at your feet some 400 feet below is oblong, forest-ringed Cascade Lake, another moraine-dammed loch so typical of Tahoe's south shore. In the distance, the placid deep blue waters of Lake Tahoe give way to the towering Carson Range that borders its eastern shore.

Descend the brushy hillside, picking your way among the boulders that clutter the path. The trail then begins a mild ascent over some exposed granite slabs made slippery by a thin layer of sand. This section is short, but might result in a bit of anxiety for acrophobes and parents with young children. As you approach, the rumble of the falls grows louder, and you spot the frothy water spilling over a granite ledge. It's not the

STONE STAIRCASE TO CASCADE FALLS

most photogenic of cataracts, and this profile view is the best you will get of the overall cascade.

Rounding a bend, gain expanded views into the canyon funneling Cascade Creek. From a signed junction at 0.6 mile, spot one of Maggies Peaks to the right, and, opposite, a pyramid-shaped mountain that occludes the craggy tip of Mount Tallac. Turn left and make your way down the boulder-lined path. The trail peters out near the brink of the falls, where you can scout out the perfect picnic spot from which to enjoy the sights and sounds.

When ready, return to the first trail junction near the information board. With your warm-up complete, you can now tackle the steep route to Granite Lake. From the trail junction, head west

into a dense mixed conifer forest dominated by white firs. You'll find the soft forest floor underfoot much more pleasing than the rocky path to Cascade Falls.

The unrelenting trail zigzags up the hillside, and you eventually gain forest-framed views of Lake Tahoe. Enter Desolation Wilderness at 0.4 mile and, not long after, cross the outlet stream for Granite Lake.

At 0.6 mile, leave the trail and walk 25 feet to an overlook, where you have a sublime vista of Emerald Bay and Lake Tahoe. Peer down on solitary Fannette Island and the delta formed by Eagle Creek as it spills into the bay. With its velocity reduced, it can no longer carry its load of alluvium and rapidly deposits it at the mouth of the river.

Leaving this lovely scene, dive back into the forest and continue climbing. The gradient eases a bit as you follow Granite Lake's alder-choked outlet stream. In the spring, find an assortment of wildflowers crowding the fern, thimbleberry, and currant understory that lines the outer edges of the creek. Spot Granite Lake through the trees, but continue along the trail to an obvious side path descending to its shady northwest shore at 1.1 miles. The sparkling waters are beautifully backed by one of Maggies Peaks (the same one we admired from the Cascade Falls Trail). After that stiff climb, reward yourself with a refreshing dip in the lake's relatively warm water before returning to the trailhead.

Backpackers or ambitious day hikers can continue along the Bayview Trail, which intersects the Eagle Falls Trail 1.5 miles past Granite Lake and, eventually, the Pacific Crest Trail. Strong day hikers might consider a challenging semi-loop that visits Upper Velma, Fontanillis, and Dicks Lakes before returning along the Bayview Trail (11 miles round trip).

GRANITE LAKE

Mount Tallac

TYPE: Day hike

SEASON: Late June through September

TOTAL DISTANCE: 9.2 miles round trip

RATING: Strenuous

ELEVATION: 6,440 feet; +3,295 feet/-0 feet

LOCATION: Eldorado National Forest, Desolation Wilderness

MAPS: USGS 7.5' Emerald Bay; Trails Illustrated Tahoe Basin No. 803

FEES AND PERMITS: A free permit is required for this day hike and can be obtained by self-registering at the trailhead kiosk.

CONTACT: Lake Tahoe Basin Management Unit (530-543-2600; www.fs.usda.gov/ltbmu); Eldorado National Forest, Pacific Ranger District (530-644-2349; www.fs.usda.gov/eldorado).

The steep, rocky, high-altitude trek to the summit of Mount Tallac is undeniably grueling. At 9,735 feet, Mount Tallac is the dominant feature of the southwestern shore of Lake Tahoe. Tackling this imposing peak is a formidable challenge, but one definitely worth taking on. The trail is jam-packed with stellar views, not to mention the sublime panorama of Lake Tahoe, Fallen Leaf Lake, and Desolation Wilderness waiting for you at the top. Mount Tallac's accessibility makes it one of the most popular day hikes in the basin, so don't expect to be huffing and puffing alone.

GETTING THERE

From South Lake Tahoe, head north 3.9 miles on CA 89 from its junction with US 50 (the South Lake Tahoe Y) and turn left onto Mt. Tallac Road (just opposite the Baldwin Beach turnoff). Proceed 1 mile along the paved though rough and narrow road to the trailhead parking area. There are no facilities at the trailhead.

THE HIKE

Fill out your free permit at the information board and set out on an old gravel roadbed lined with sage and Jeffrey pines. Just past the 0.5-mile mark, the trail follows the uphill contour of a fire-scarred ridge blanketed with manzanita, where you gain your first magnificent view of the trek—a precursor of what is yet to come. To the west, Mount Tallac rises on the ridgeline, beckoning you farther. To the east, Fallen Leaf Lake spreads out before you, its watery margins bordered with a dense mass of conifers.

Glaciers once dominated this terrain. As they crept across the landscape they

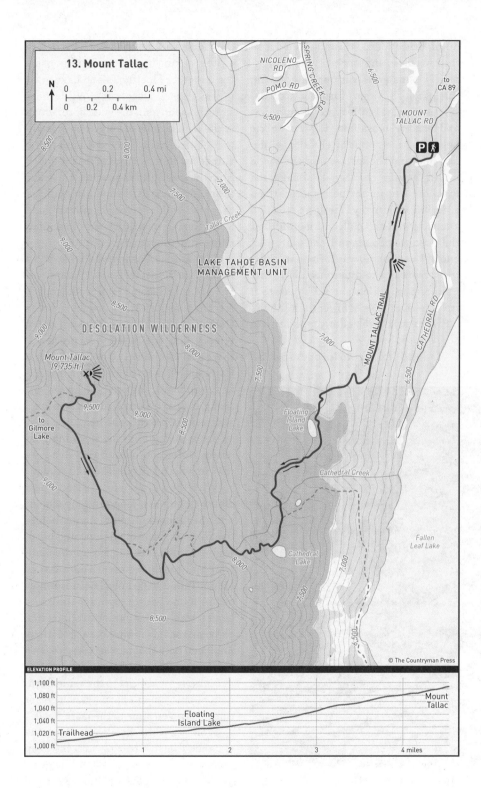

13. Mount Tallac

N
0   0.2   0.4 mi
0   0.2   0.4 km

NICOLENO RD

POMO RD

SPRING CREEK RD

to CA 89

MOUNT TALLAC RD

6,500

6,500

Tallac Creek

7,000

7,500

8,000

8,500

9,000

LAKE TAHOE BASIN
MANAGEMENT UNIT

DESOLATION WILDERNESS

8,500

8,000

7,500

7,000

MOUNT TALLAC TRAIL

CATHEDRAL RD

6,500

Mount Tallac
(9,735 ft.)

9,500

9,000

8,500

to Gilmore Lake

9,000

Floating
Island
Lake

Cathedral Creek

Fallen
Leaf Lake

Cathedral
Lake

8,000

7,500

7,000

6,500

8,500

© The Countryman Press

ELEVATION PROFILE

1,100 ft				Mount Tallac
1,080 ft				
1,060 ft		Floating		
1,040 ft		Island Lake		
1,020 ft	Trailhead			
1,000 ft				
	1	2	3	4 miles

dug debris underneath and carried it on their surfaces and frozen in their interiors. This material was deposited along the glacier's sides, forming parallel ridges of debris called lateral moraines and terminal moraines, ridges of debris heaped at the snout or end of the glacier marking the farthest extent of the ice. In the case of Fallen Leaf Lake, the moraine along its northern shore formed a low hill, effectively creating a dam and allowing water to collect. Emerald Bay, the curious appendage at the southwest end of Lake Tahoe, was formed in much the same way, the difference being that its moraine, which should separate it from the main lake, is lower than Tahoe's current water level, allowing the two to connect.

The well-worn footpath ducks behind

HIKER ASCENDING MOUNT TALLAC

the ridge and descends briefly before switchbacking up and coming alongside the outlet for Floating Island Lake at 1.3 miles. Pass a Desolation Wilderness sign and soon gain the lakeshore, which is rife with hordes of voracious mosquitoes. Quickly skirt the lake, apparently named for clumps of grass that break off from the shore and float about, and trade the shady forest for an open, dry hillside carpeted with sagebrush, currant, and a smattering of wildflowers, including spreading phlox and groundsel.

Step across Cathedral Creek; at 2.1 miles ignore a steep trail bound for Fallen Leaf Lake and veer right (south). A scant 0.2 mile farther, you reach petite Cathedral Lake, whose peaceful shore tempts you to linger—but press on, there's much climbing to do. Beyond Cathedral Lake, the gradient intensifies significantly as you plod up a steep, rocky, exposed slope. The climb is long, and poor footing doesn't help the cause, so pause and admire the stunning panorama unfolding behind you—it's sure to take your mind off the uphill trudge.

With the aid of cairns, ascend past chunky boulders, along brushy slopes, and through small pine stands before reaching the base of an imposing headwall of loose talus. Zigzag up the main trail and reach the crest southeast of Mount Tallac at 3.3 miles. Because snow can be found here, clinging to the rocky slopes well into summer, trailblazing, early-season hikers have cut a precarious unofficial path that tackles the scree in a more direct fashion—heading straight up it. Both eventually get to the same destination, but you will have a much easier time of it if you stick to the main trail.

From atop the headwall, enjoy the expanded westward view into the deep recesses of Desolation Wilderness. With the hard part behind you, head

PEERING INTO DESOLATION WILDERNESS FROM MOUNT TALLAC SUMMIT

northwest up the more gently sloping backside of Mount Tallac. The rocky path is festooned with tufts of hardy grass, scrubby whitebark pine, and colorful wildflowers. Watch for furry marmots scurrying about or sunning themselves.

The steady ascent eventually leads to a signed junction at 4.3 miles with a trail that heads to Gilmore Lake. Turn right and begin the final 0.3-mile push to the summit. Regain the view of Lake Tahoe on an exposed ridge just shy of the metamorphic peak. From here, the trail grows vague, but the goal is obvious. Scramble to the top of the windswept peak and savor the vista.

Lake Tahoe dominates the scene, its deep blue water hemmed by a perfect ring of mountains. To the south, mile upon mile of rugged, majestic terrain stretches toward Carson Pass and beyond. Desolation Wilderness's stark granite landscape fills the scene over your shoulder. Spot shimmering Gilmore Lake to the southwest, followed by Susie Lake, and beyond it Lake Aloha tucked beneath the snow-capped pinnacles of Pyramid and Ralston Peaks.

When you've had your fill, begin the knee-pounding descent to the trailhead back along the same path.

Echo Lake to Lake Aloha

Venture into the heart of Desolation Wilderness on this busy path to sparkling, island-studded Lake Aloha. The trail's accessibility, high-elevation starting point, and convenient water taxi shortcut make it an easy way to experience the riches of the region with relatively little effort (read: expect lots of company). Nonetheless, with a boon of scenic lakes dotting the rugged landscape there is plenty of space for everyone to spread out.

GETTING THERE

From South Lake Tahoe, head south 10 miles on US 50 from its junction with CA 89 (the South Lake Tahoe Y) and turn right onto Johnson Pass Road (about 1.25 miles west of Echo Summit). Proceed 0.5 mile and turn left onto Echo Lakes Road. Another 0.9 mile takes you to the upper parking area. From here, walk down to Echo Chalet boat dock (0.2 mile), where you can arrange for the water taxi. If you plan on walking, the trail begins across the spillway. Either way, be sure to fill out a permit at the trailhead information board.

THE HIKE

The section of Pacific Crest Trail (PCT) that follows the northern shoreline of Lower and Upper Echo Lake offers fine views, but is quite honestly a rather uneventful 2.5 miles. You stay well above the waterline and traipse behind cottages and cabins that line the shore. I recommend you save time and energy by boarding the water taxi that departs from the Echo Chalet boat dock and deposits you at the public landing at the far western end of Upper Echo Lake. The taxi runs "on demand" during operating

TYPE: Day hike or overnight

SEASON: Mid-July to October

TOTAL DISTANCE: 6.8 miles round trip with water taxi (11.8 miles without water taxi)

RATING: Moderate

ELEVATION: 7,433 feet; +914 feet/-174 feet

LOCATION: Eldorado National Forest, Desolation Wilderness

MAPS: USGS 7.5' Echo Lake, Pyramid Peak; Trails Illustrated Lake Tahoe Basin No. 803

FEES AND PERMITS: A free permit is required for this day hike and can be obtained by self-registering at the trailhead kiosk. Overnight trips into the Desolation Wilderness require a permit (fee) from Eldorado National Forest. The water taxi charges $14 one way, with a three-person (or $42) minimum.

CONTACT: Lake Tahoe Basin Management Unit (530-543-2600; www.fs.usda.gov/ltbmu); Eldorado National Forest, Pacific Ranger District (530-644-2349; www.fs.usda.gov/eldorado); Echo Lakes Chalet Taxi Service (530-659-7207; www.echochalet.com/taxi.htm).

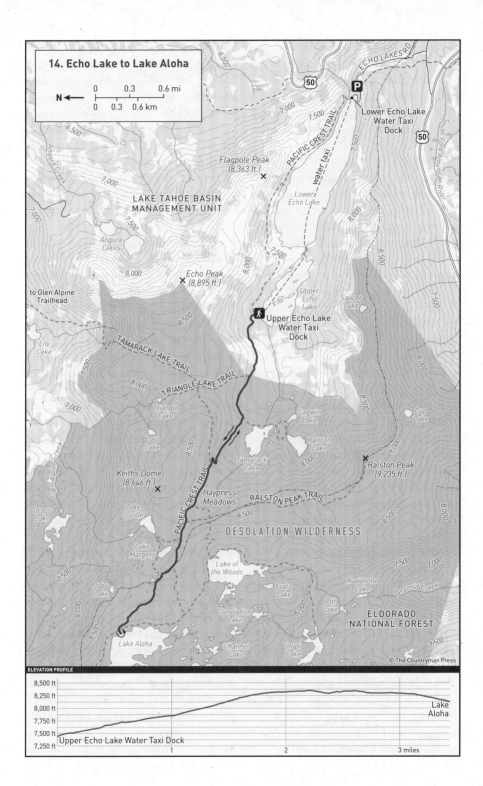

14. Echo Lake to Lake Aloha

0   0.3   0.6 mi
0   0.3   0.6 km
N ←

ECHO LAKES RD

50

Lower Echo Lake
Water Taxi
Dock

50

South Fork American River

PACIFIC CREST TRAIL

water taxi

Flagpole Peak
(8,363 ft.) ✕

LAKE TAHOE BASIN
MANAGEMENT UNIT

Lower
Echo Lake

Angora Creek

Angora
Lakes

Echo Peak
(8,895 ft.) ✕

Upper
Echo
Lake

Saucer
Lake

🚶 Upper Echo Lake
Water Taxi
Dock

to Glen Alpine
Trailhead

TAMARACK LAKE TRAIL

Lily
Lake

TRIANGLE LAKE TRAIL

Triangle
Lake

Cagwin
Lake

Cup
Lake

Ralston
Lake

Lost
Lake

Tamarack
Lake

Ralston Peak
(9,235 ft.) ✕

Keiths Dome
(8,646 ft.) ✕

PACIFIC CREST TRAIL

Haypress
Meadows

RALSTON PEAK TRAIL

Glen Alpine Creek

Grass
Lake

Lake
Lucille

DESOLATION WILDERNESS

Lake
Margery

Lake of
the Woods

Avalanche
Lake

Pyramid Creek

Jabu
Lake

Frata
Lake

Pitt
Lake

ELDORADO
NATIONAL FOREST

Desolation
Lake

Lake Aloha

Channel
Lake

Ropi
Lake

© The Countryman Press

ELEVATION PROFILE

8,500 ft
8,250 ft
8,000 ft
7,750 ft
7,500 ft
7,250 ft

Lake
Aloha

Upper Echo Lake Water Taxi Dock

1   2   3 miles

hours and when the narrow channel connecting the lakes is passable by boat (typically July 4 to Labor Day weekend). A phone near the Upper Echo Lake dock provides direct access to the resort when you're ready to be picked up after your hike.

From the boat landing on Upper Echo Lake, with a fresh set of legs, head uphill 0.1 mile to your main path, the PCT, and turn left (a sign posted on a tree ensures you won't miss this junction on the way back). The rocky trail climbs gently to a wilderness boundary sign at 0.7 mile, followed immediately by a junction with the northbound Triangle Lake Trail. This is the first of two pathways leading to Triangle Lake, this one being the shorter, steeper route. It is also the first of many trails shooting off the PCT that you should bypass if Lake Aloha is your primary destination.

Forsaking the shady woodland, enjoy over-the-shoulder views of the forested valley cradling the Echo Lakes as you climb. Intersect a spur trail heading left to a trio of picturesque gems—Tamarack, Ralston, and Cagwin—all gloriously backdropped by Ralston Peak, the highest bump on the ridgeline.

Keep to the main trail and begin a moderate climb through the granite landscape, stippled with contorted pines, as Tamarack Lake comes into view to your left. Ascend a pair of long switchbacks to a forested bench and an eastbound lateral, at 1.8 miles, heading toward Triangle Lake and ultimately Lily Lake. This trail originates at the Glen Alpine Trailhead south of Fallen Leaf Lake, another gateway into this stunning natural wonderland.

Stay on the PCT and continue on your northwestward course. The trail gradient eases, and a short 0.3 mile farther you skirt grassy Haypress Meadows and reach the first of two trails descending to Lake of the Woods, a popular overnight destination, evidenced by its heavily used shoreline. The 0.6-mile trail runs into the northeastern shore of this pine-ringed lake. By tracing the bank 1.5 miles south and then west, you can also visit Ropi Lake, where the trail peters out, although there are several other lakes in the area. With a good topographic map and sharp navigation skills, they are fantastically solitudinous.

Back on the PCT, reach the high point of the journey and ignore the Ralston Peak Trail (left) and, later, the southward intersection with a potentially waterlogged, looping trail that visits Lake Margery and Lake Lucille (right) at 2.5 miles. Farther still, pass a junction to the west (left) bound for Lake Aloha's southeast shore (take note of this junction, as it is a possible return route) and instead continue along the PCT, immediately passing the north end of the Lake Margery/Lake Lucille loop (right). From here, the trail gently descends, breaks out of the forest cover, and collides with the eastern shore of shallow Lake Aloha at 3.4 miles.

The sprawling lake occupies an enormous granite valley that was dammed to create a high-mountain reservoir. Dead tree trunks and a plethora of granite blobs dot the crystalline waters, which are backed by the imposing Crystal Range—Pyramid Peak and Mount Price dominating the ridgeline. While there is water as deep as 20 feet in places, there are many spots where you can wade across the lake. Add to this the annual drawdown, and by late summer the lake isn't nearly as spectacular. Because of this significant fluctuation in water level, visiting in late July or

ROCKY TRAIL TO LAKE ALOHA AND BEYOND

early August offers the best scenery and opportunity for swimming.

Backpackers should turn left, where they can find the best campsites along the southeast shore. Day hikers can return via the same trail or venture 0.6 mile south alongside the east shore to a junction with the first Lake Aloha Trail, which veers northeast and rejoins the PCT after 0.5 mile. From here, turn right and make your way back to the boat landing.

III.

TRANS-SIERRA PASSES

15

Round Top Lake Loop

TYPE: Day hike

SEASON: June to October

TOTAL DISTANCE: 5-mile loop

RATING: Moderate

ELEVATION: 8,198 feet; +1,214 feet/-1,214 feet

LOCATION: Eldorado National Forest, Mokelumne Wilderness

MAPS: USGS 7.5' Caples Lake, Carson Pass; USFS Mokelumne Wilderness

FEES AND PERMITS: A permit is not required for this day hike. There is a $5 day-use fee (per vehicle).

CONTACT: Eldorado National Forest, Amador Ranger District (209-295-4251; www.fs.usda.gov/eldorado).

This fantastic loop hike breaches the northern boundary of uncrowded Mokelumne Wilderness. Wander past hillsides exploding with seasonal wildflowers, in the shadow of brooding sawtooth ridges of volcanic rock, and take respite along the shores of two picturesque lakes. You even have the option of adding a notch to your peak-bagger's belt—if you're into that sort of thing—by climbing to the summit of Round Top (10,381 feet), the tallest peak within the Mokelumne Wilderness.

GETTING THERE

From the intersection of CA 88 and CA 89 (also known as Picketts Junction in Hope Valley), drive 10.5 miles west on CA 88 (Carson Pass) to the turnoff for Woods Lake. Follow the narrow road 1 mile to the small trailhead parking area equipped with pit toilets. Pay the day-use fee at the kiosk adjacent to the parking area, then walk south along the access road, crossing a bridge over Woods Creek, and find the trailhead on your right.

THE HIKE

The 105,165-acre Mokelumne Wilderness sprawls across portions of the Eldorado, Stanislaus, and Humboldt-Toiyabe National Forests. Its rugged terrain is characterized by dark, colorful peaks, reminders of the Sierra Nevada's volcanic past. Here you will find a pleasant mix of characteristically stark granite terrain intermingled with rich volcanic rock, creating a dramatic scene.

The well-defined trail begins by paralleling the campground access road. Quickly come to a trail fork and veer left toward Winnemucca Lake. You will be completing the loop in a clockwise

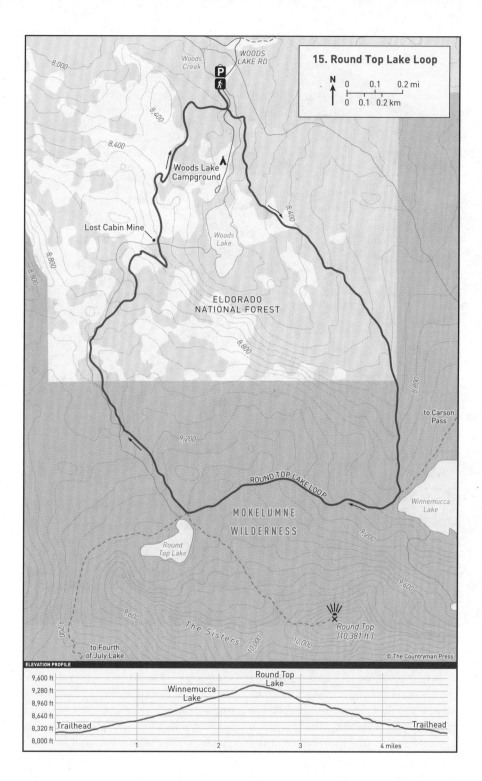

15. Round Top Lake Loop

N

| 0 | 0.1 | 0.2 mi |

| 0 | 0.1 | 0.2 km |

WOODS LAKE RD

Woods Creek

P

Woods Lake Campground

Lost Cabin Mine

Woods Lake

ELDORADO NATIONAL FOREST

to Carson Pass

ROUND TOP LAKE LOOP

Winnemucca Lake

MOKELUMNE WILDERNESS

Round Top Lake

The Sisters

to Fourth of July Lake

Round Top (10,381 ft.)

© The Countryman Press

ELEVATION PROFILE

		Round Top Lake		
9,600 ft				
9,280 ft		Winnemucca Lake		
8,960 ft				
8,640 ft				
8,320 ft	Trailhead			Trailhead
8,000 ft		1	2	3	4 miles

ROUND TOP

direction, and the right fork represents the return leg of the journey. Cross the access road and pick up the trail on the opposite side. From here, cross a wooden footbridge spanning willow-lined Woods Creek and proceed upstream along its eastern bank. With the creek burbling on the right, make your way through a mixed forest of lodgepole and western white pines and graceful mountain hemlocks before coming to a junction at 0.4 mile. Veer left and watch for mountain pennyroyal, spirea, and triteleia sprinkled along the trail.

Begin a mild but steady uphill climb, passing an arrastra, a crushing device early Mexicans used for pulverizing ore, at 1 mile. As you continue, the thinning forest allows slivers of views of the surrounding mountainside before eventually emerging at the base of a low ridge. While the outlet creek for Winnemucca Lake serenades you from below, the trail continues south along an open hillside exploding with an assortment of wildflowers. Woolly mule's ear, lupine, paintbrush, aster, and cinquefoil carpet the slope in a magnificent display while Round Top's hulking presences fills the skyline.

Pass the boundary sign announcing entry into the Mokelumne Wilderness and enjoy the lovely cascades taking shape between the willow- and heather-lined creek sides. Several small unofficial paths lead down to the water. At 1.8 miles, reach a signed junction and Winnemucca Lake. To the east lies the rounded hump of Elephants Back and, due north of that, Red Lake Peak and Carson Pass. The pass was named after Christopher "Kit" Carson, a man indelibly linked with early Western exploration and expansion. He was a trapper, Indian agent, and soldier best known for his work as a guide to the expeditions of John C. Frémont.

From the junction, head west toward Round Top Lake. Carefully cross Winnemucca's outlet stream, and head uphill once again. Colorful columbine and heather blossoms add to the trailside bouquet. Gain over-the-shoulder views of Winnemucca Lake as you journey higher and cross several seasonal drainages. Crest a saddle between Round Top and Winnemucca Lakes, noticing the wind-battered whitebark pines that dot the landscape. The now single-track trail cuts across the grassy saddle and drops down toward Round Top Lake, beautifully backdropped by The Sisters, a pair of dark, craggy peaks.

As you approach Round Lake, a spur trail heads left (southeast) to the summit of Round Top, an old volcanic vent. This out-and-back side trip is no easy task and should be attempted only by experienced hikers. The scree-covered terrain makes travel difficult and frustrating; however, the 360-degree view from the knobby peak is a well-deserved reward. By climbing to the summit, you add almost 2 miles and a little over 1,000 vertical feet to your hike, putting it in the strenuous classification.

Back on the main trail, from the signed junction near Round Lake, at 2.7 miles, head northwest toward Woods Lake. Views expand both north and west as you descend the rocky trail beside Round Lake's willow-congested outlet stream. Exit Mokelumne Wilderness and descend a series of short, steep switchbacks. The forest thickens and views disappear. At 3.8 miles, reach Lost Cabin Mine, marked by dilapidated buildings and rusted car frames. Though mining operations ceased many years ago, the claim is still active and there are signs posted everywhere letting you know that this is private property.

The trail's moderate descent continues down a boulder-strewn hillside dotted with mountain hemlock. Catch glimpses of Woods Lake through the trees. Boulder-hop across Round Lake's outlet creek, and at 4.2 miles reach a junction with an old road. Bear right and follow the trail, wider now, downhill. Just before a metal gate, turn left on a narrow path heading to the trailhead parking area. Close the loop 0.4 mile later and veer left to reach the trailhead.

16

Meiss Meadow to Round Lake

Taking advantage of the Pacific Crest Trail and Tahoe Rim Trail, this pleasant hike wanders through a broad meadow brimming with wildflowers to Round Lake, the largest body of water in the Upper Truckee River Basin. Though you can access Round Lake via trailheads at either Meiss Meadow or Big Meadow, the former, albeit a longer path, is less frequently used, which equals more solitude for you.

GETTING THERE

From the intersection of CA 88 and CA 89 (also known as Picketts Junction in Hope Valley), drive 8.9 miles west on CA 88 (Carson Pass) to the Meiss Meadow trailhead parking area on the north side of the road. Pay the day-use fee at the kiosk near the trailhead.

THE HIKE

The Pacific Crest Trail is a 2,650-mile National Scenic Trail that runs from Mexico to Canada through California, Oregon, and Washington. Though the hike to Round Lake rambles along only a small slice of this fantastic trail, each year hundreds of people attempt to thru-hike the trail's entire length in one season—an incredible physical and logistical feat, to say the least.

Departing from the northwest end of the parking area, enter an open forest of lodgepole pines, western junipers, and quaking aspens. The trail parallels the highway for a spell, making vehicle noise an unfortunate reality for the first 0.7 mile. Southward, a marvelous panorama encompassing Elephants Back and Round Top is on full display. Indian paintbrush, mountain pennyroyal, nude buckwheat, and lupine color the boulder- and sage-strewn hillside you

---

TYPE: Day hike

SEASON: June to October

TOTAL DISTANCE: 10 miles round trip

RATING: Moderate

ELEVATION: 8,584 feet; +464 feet/-1,012 feet

LOCATION: Eldorado National Forest, Lake Tahoe Basin Management Unit

MAPS: USGS 7.5' Carson Pass, Caples Lake, Echo Lake; Trails Illustrated Lake Tahoe Basin No. 803

FEES AND PERMITS: A permit is not required for this day hike. There is a $5 day-use fee (per vehicle).

CONTACT: Eldorado National Forest, Amador Ranger District (209-295-4251; www.fs.usda.gov/eldorado); Lake Tahoe Basin Management Unit (530-543-2600; www.fs.usda.gov/ltbmu).

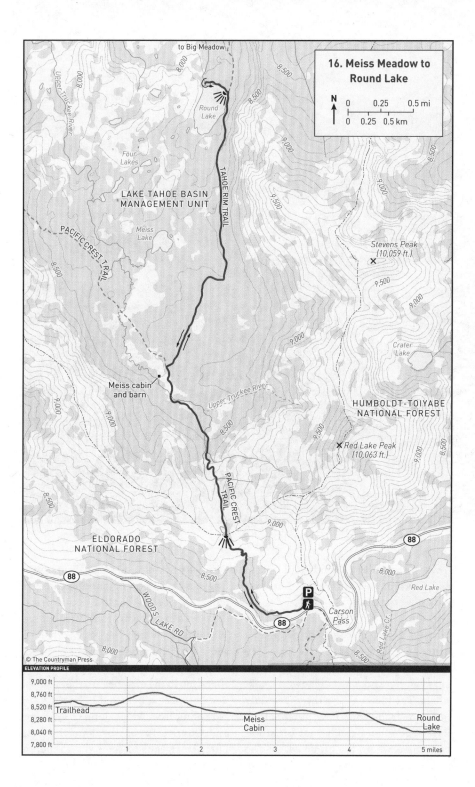

to Big Meadow

16. Meiss Meadow to Round Lake

N

| 0 | 0.25 | 0.5 mi |
| 0 | 0.25 | 0.5 km |

Round Lake

Upper Truckee River

Four Lakes

TAHOE RIM TRAIL

LAKE TAHOE BASIN MANAGEMENT UNIT

Méiss Lake

PACIFIC CREST TRAIL

Stevens Peak (10,059 ft.)

Crater Lake

Meiss cabin and barn

Upper Truckee River

HUMBOLDT-TOIYABE NATIONAL FOREST

Red Lake Peak (10,063 ft.)

PACIFIC CREST TRAIL

88

ELDORADO NATIONAL FOREST

88

WOODS LAKE RD

88

P

Carson Pass

Red Lake

Red Lake Dr.

© The Countryman Press

ELEVATION PROFILE

9,000 ft					
8,760 ft					
8,520 ft Trailhead					
8,280 ft		Meiss Cabin		Round Lake	
8,040 ft					
7,800 ft	1	2	3	4	5 miles

BLUE FLAG IRIS FLANKING THE PACIFIC CREST TRAIL

traverse. Rounding a bend, Caples Lake and Covered Wagon Peak come into view over the treetops.

Soon the trail bends north and crosses a pair of seasonal drainages near the 1-mile mark. Zigzag up a dry hillside blanketed with woolly mule's ears, sage, and sulphurflower buckwheat. The views across the valley only improve from your new perspective. Pass a pond and catch your breath at 1.25 miles, where the grade eases. The single-track trail slices through a grassy saddle that is spectacularly adorned with western blue flag iris. The views from this high point along the trail are amazing. Rising behind you are the dark, volcanic peaks of the Mokelumne Wilderness, which harbor patches of snow well into summer, and up ahead, on a clear day, Lake Tahoe can be seen sparkling in the distance. To the east lies Red Lake Peak, believed to be the vantage point from which John C. Frémont and Charles Preuss became the first Euro-Americans to see Lake Tahoe, in February 1844.

The trail becomes rocky again and

you begin a mild descent, crossing several seasonal drainages. Depending on the time of year, they can be either bone dry or filled with enough water to give you a chance to hone your boulder-hopping skills. All these small, snowmelt-fed creeklets are dashing toward the deep ravine directly to the west, in which flows the fledgling Truckee River.

As you descend, keep an eye out for prairie smoke. This curious flower has fuzzy tendrils creating a twisted mass that resembles a troll doll's hair when poofed up—Mother Nature does have a sense of humor.

Easily rock-hop across the peaceful river, beyond which the trail levels as you enter the southern fringe of pastoral Meiss Meadow, with Sierra penstemon, bistort, aster, California corn lily, and groundsel scattered about. Cross the Truckee River once again, and at 2.6 miles come to a small unofficial path leading left toward the Meiss cabin and barn, built in the late 1880s by a pioneering family who drove cattle here each summer for grazing. Fortunately, the Forest Service banned cattle in the area several years ago, in an effort to restore the declining meadows and fisheries.

Shortly thereafter, reach a trail fork and bear right on the Tahoe Rim Trail as it continues north toward Round Lake. The mild gradient makes for easy walking as the trail undulates through lodgepole forest and pocket-size meadows. Easily cross a rocky creek and later Round Lake's inlet. At 4 miles, begin a moderate descent to Round Lake's shore. Follow the trail along the eastern shoreline to an unofficial path (left) that departs the main trail and skirts the north side of the lake. From this junction, you have a wonderful view of Round Lake and the towering buttress of volcanic cliffs that border its east side.

Follow the unofficial path to the lake's outlet, where you can unpack a picnic and take a break before heading back the same way you came.

If you can arrange a car shuttle, another option is to walk point-to-point from Meiss Meadow to Big Meadows. Both trailheads are easily accessible from the highway, and the driving distance between the two is only about 15 miles. A car shuttle or key swap means that you don't have to backtrack, shortening the trek to a mere 7.5 miles round trip.

MEISS MEADOW CABIN

Granite Lake

TYPE: Day hike or overnight

SEASON: June to October

TOTAL DISTANCE: 4 miles round trip

RATING: Easy

ELEVATION: 8,171 feet; +597 feet/-44 feet

LOCATION: Eldorado National Forest, Mokelumne Wilderness

MAPS: USGS 7.5' Carson Pass, Pacific Valley; USFS Mokelumne Wilderness

FEES AND PERMITS: A permit is not required for this day hike. Overnight trips into the Mokelumne Wilderness require a free permit from Eldorado National Forest.

CONTACT: Eldorado National Forest, Amador Ranger District (209-295-4251; www.fs.usda.gov/eldorado).

Sufficiently hidden off the main highway to deter windshield naturalists zipping by, the Blue Lakes area and its easily accessible backcountry offer a collection of lakes set amid an often-overlooked nook of Mokelumne Wilderness. This easy jaunt to Granite Lake rambles through quiet forests and wildflower-filled meadows on the way to a rock-encircled gem perfect for swimming, picnicking, or simply lounging about.

GETTING THERE

From the intersection of CA 88 and CA 89 (also known as Picketts Junction in Hope Valley), drive 2.4 miles west on CA 88 (Carson Pass) and turn left onto paved Blue Lakes Road. Drive 11.5 miles to a T-intersection near Lower Blue Lake. Turn right and proceed 1.5 miles to Middle Creek Campground on the narrow, mostly unpaved road. Find the trailhead (signed for Grouse Lake) on your left just past the campground.

THE HIKE

Washoe and Sierra Miwok peoples originally inhabited this region of the Sierras. They hunted seasonally for local game and gathered plants for food and medicine. It is also believed that they used a portion of the Mokelumne Wilderness as a major thoroughfare for social interaction and trade.

In 1848, a Mormon Battalion, recently discharged from their post fighting in the Mexican-American war, sought a route across the Sierra Nevada that avoided the infamous Truckee River Route, scene of the Donner Party tragedy a mere two years before. Traveling from Sutter's Fort to Salt Lake City, they pioneered a trail, most likely following

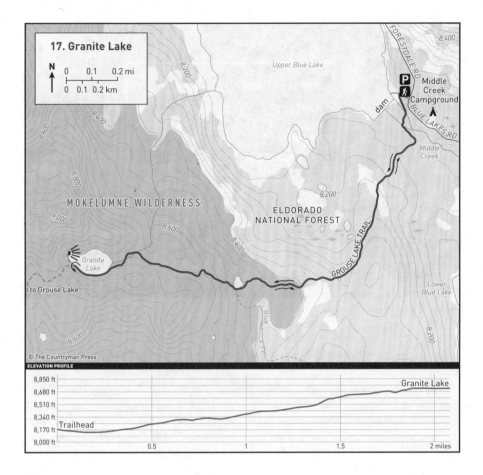

17. Granite Lake

ELEVATION PROFILE

a Native American route, just south of present day Carson Pass. Coined the Carson River Route, this trail subsequently carried thousands of emigrants to California's fabled fields of gold.

In the 1860s, the area had its own short-lived run at gold and silver mining southwest of Blue Lakes, but by the turn of the twentieth century the region saw more stockmen and shepherds grazing cattle and sheep than anything else. The passage of the Wilderness Act in 1964 secured the future of this fantastic landscape, preserving it for generations to come.

From the parking lot, head toward Upper Blue Lake and cross its wide

spillway on a steel bridge. A sign directs you left onto Grouse Lake Trail, which begins by paralleling the spillway in its downhill course toward Middle Creek and eventually Lower Blue Lake. Beneath the shade of lodgepole pines and mountain hemlocks, the trail soon crosses peaceful Middle Creek via a fallen tree.

The trail then bends southwest and begins a mild ascent away from the creek. Red firs and western white pines eventually join the forest mix, while California corn lily and golden yarrow add splashes of color. At 0.7 mile, reach a crest and enjoy level walking and glimpses of the surrounding peaks

TRAILHEAD SIGN POINTING THE WAY

through the trees before resuming the climb.

The trail weaves in and out of forested sections and open rocky hillsides, crossing the boundary for Mokelumne Wilderness near the 1-mile mark. Quickly come to a lovely little unnamed pond ringed by pines and clumps of granite. The trail is a little vague here, but, when in doubt, stick close to the southern shore and you will spot the trail as it climbs northwest away from the water.

The grade steepens for a while and the views improve slightly as you venture higher. The steady climb eases and you come to a verdant area decorated with aster, Sierra penstemon and Brewer's lupine. Leaving the wildflowers and snaking through the forest, the trail dries out again before cutting through a notch in a rocky knoll and dropping down to the willow-lined outlet for Granite Lake at 1.8 miles. Walk along the outlet's southern bank before cresting the

southeastern rim of the bowl confining Granite Lake's clear water.

As you would expect, the lake is encircled by a granitic barrier that is dotted with willows, heather, and scattered conifers. Campers and picnickers will find nice resting spots among the pines on the southwest shore. By continuing a short way along the trail to the western lip of the bowl, you can have sweeping views of the surrounding terrain. When ready, retrace your steps to the trailhead.

Backpackers can delve deeper into Mokelumne Wilderness by continuing on to Grouse Lake (12 miles round trip). The lake is crystal clear and surrounded by forested shores and rocky outcrops. There are plenty of places to set up camp around the lake. While there, take a refreshing swim, venture to the summit of Deadwood Peak, and revel in the oodles of stars winking at you from your secluded backcountry bivouac.

GRANITE LAKE

Bull Run Lake

TYPE: Day hike or overnight

SEASON: Late June through mid-October

TOTAL DISTANCE: 7.4 miles round trip

RATING: Moderate

ELEVATION: 7,895 feet; +1,023 feet/-521 feet

LOCATION: Stanislaus National Forest, Carson-Iceberg Wilderness

MAPS: USGS 7.5' Pacific Valley, Spicer Meadow Reservoir; USFS Carson-Iceberg Wilderness

FEES AND PERMITS: A permit is not required for this day hike. Overnight trips into the Carson-Iceberg Wilderness require a free permit from Stanislaus National Forest.

CONTACT: Stanislaus National Forest, Calaveras Ranger District (209-795-1381; www.fs.usda.gov/stanislaus).

Open meadows, old-growth forests, and a clear mountain lake are waiting for you on this trek into the rugged Carson-Iceberg Wilderness. Though you've got some climbing to do, the trail has a nice balance of ups and downs, and level spots too. Whether you're out for the day or camping overnight, Bull Run Lake is sure to please even the most discriminating hiker. Early season visitors should be prepared for several fords across snowmelt-swollen creeks.

GETTING THERE

From its intersection with CA 89 near Markleeville, drive 22.4 miles west on CA 4 (Ebbetts Pass) to Stanislaus Meadow, located on the south side of the road. There are no facilities here. Park in the dirt lot adjacent the highway, or, if you have a high-clearance vehicle with four-wheel drive, proceed down the narrow, rutted fire road (Forest Road 8N13) 0.5 mile to a small parking area near the true trailhead.

THE HIKE

Ebbetts Pass is named after "Major" John Ebbetts, a California pioneer credited with the first recorded crossing in 1851. The route was infrequently used until silver was discovered east of the Sierra in the late 1850s. This prompted merchants from the Gold Rush town of Murphy to finance the present route through Ebbetts Pass to transport supplies to the miners more easily. The route eventually became part of the state highway system in the 1920s (CA 4).

This is arguably the most obscure and least traveled of all the trans-Sierra routes because of its steep grade and overabundance of hairpin turns. A large

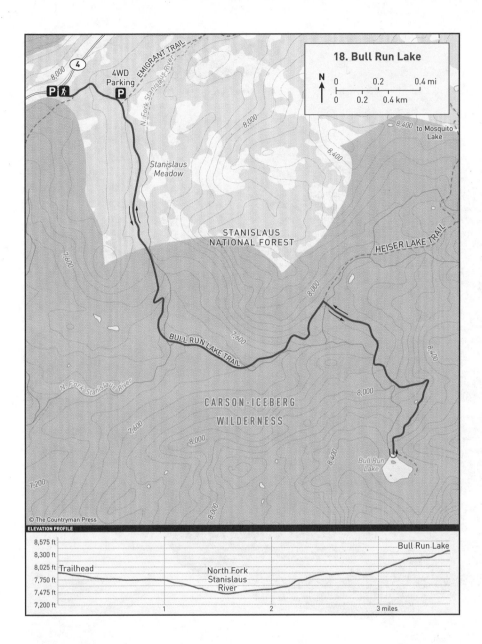

ELEVATION PROFILE

8,575 ft			Bull Run Lake
8,300 ft			
8,025 ft	Trailhead		
7,750 ft		North Fork	
7,475 ft		Stanislaus	
7,200 ft		River	

1　　　　2　　　3 miles

section of the highway traversing the pass is narrower than two lanes—with no dividing line—but don't let this deter you. It travels through some of the most scenic countryside around, so scenic in fact that it was designated a National Scenic Byway (incidentally, Tioga Pass also makes the list).

Start by walking downhill on a fire road that heads south from the parking area adjacent CA 4. It's not long before your path intersects the Emigrant Trail. Continue along the road, soon coming to Stanislaus Meadow, an expansive clearing that is incised by the fledgling North Fork Stanislaus River. The road follows

BULL RUN LAKE

the western fringe of the meadow before coming to the official trailhead at 0.5 mile. Those who drove along the fire road must park here.

The trail narrows past the information board as you walk amid mountain hemlocks, red firs, and lodgepole pines. The barbed wire fence to your left and the thick forest to your right are sure to keep you on track. Level walking takes you to a boundary sign for Carson-Iceberg Wilderness, beyond which you lose the barbed wire and begin a mild descent.

You are no doubt wondering about the wilderness's odd hyphenated moniker. (No, there aren't any large floating masses of ice here!) The name comes from two prominent geographic features: the Carson River, named after famed explorer Kit Carson, and a granite formation called "The Iceberg" on the southern boundary of the wilderness.

The trail loosely follows the North Fork Stanislaus River to the low point of the jaunt at 1.5 miles, where you cross several branches of the river and the outlet for Bull Run Lake. Early season hikers can expect to get their feet wet; however, late summer typically finds the river bone dry. Enjoy the lupine, California corn lily, and groundsel that fill the spaces in between the crossings. Beyond the river a mild ascent ensues, followed by level walking, which takes you to yet another ford of Bull Run's outlet at 2 miles.

The gradient steepens as you ascend an open, rocky hillside and gain views of the pine-scattered granite landscape.

While the trail is not endowed with a profusion of wildflowers, they do add splashes of color here and there. Their absences make those flowers we do encounter all the more treasured.

The steady climb eases after 0.5 mile, and you reach a junction with the Heiser Lake Trail. Turn right and immediately boulder-hop across Heiser Lake's outlet stream.

The trail meanders through the forest, crossing a series of seasonal streams before beginning the second major climb of the hike. Follow the route as it traverses the rocky landscape and ascends along smooth granite slabs. The clearly defined path falters at times, but cairns help guide you until a more obvious trail reappears. A handful of steep switchbacks carry you up a narrow ravine. Leveling off once again, you wander past a murky pond before making the final push to the lakeshore.

Crest the top of a ridge and arrive at Bull Run Lake at 3.7 miles. The trail continues around the eastern shore but soon peters out. The crystalline lake is ringed by pines and is almost completely encircled by an imposing fortress of rock. A breach in the northern wall grants access to this most picturesque scene. In the center of the lake, a dollop of granite forms an island that is quite possibly the most perfect sunbathing spot in the entire Sierra Nevada.

Set up camp or spread out a picnic at one of the many ideal locations around the lake. When ready, return via the same path.

Calaveras Big Trees State Park—South Grove

TYPE: Day hike
SEASON: Mid-May through October
TOTAL DISTANCE: 5.4-mile semi-loop
RATING: Easy
ELEVATION: 4,431 feet; +800 feet/-800 feet
LOCATION: Calaveras Big Trees State Park
MAPS: USGS 7.5' Stanislaus, Crandall Peak; Calaveras Big Trees State Park brochure map
FEES AND PERMITS: A permit is not required for this day hike. There is a $10 day-use fee (per vehicle).
CONTACT: Calaveras Big Trees State Park (209-795-2334; www.parks.ca .gov/?page_id=551).

Explore the remote Calaveras South Grove on this easy, well-marked trail through a pristine grove of giant sequoias, earth's largest living objects. Protected as a natural preserve, this area offers a rare opportunity to wander through an ancient undisturbed forest ecosystem in its primeval conditions. This pleasant forest walk passes several notable specimens including the Agassiz Tree—the largest tree in the park.

GETTING THERE

From Angel's Camp, drive 22.1 miles east on CA 4 (Ebbetts Pass) to the turnoff for Calaveras Big Trees State Park. Proceed to the entrance station and pay the day-use fee. From the entrance, drive 8 miles along paved Walter W. Smith Memorial Parkway to the South Grove parking lot.

THE HIKE

In 1852, while Augustus T. Dowd was tracking a wounded grizzly bear, he happened upon a forest of enormous trees—what we now refer to as the Calaveras North Grove. When he told others of what he had found, no one believed him. After Dowd led a group of men to his find, word of the extraordinary giants spread rapidly, bringing a flurry of curious visitors and the exploits of enterprising individuals looking to make a buck. Coming under the purview of the State of California in 1931, Calaveras Big Trees State Park is considered the state's longest continuously operated tourist facility.

After a stop at the visitor center, make your way to the South Grove trailhead. The South Grove contains approximately 1,000 large sequoias, about 10 times as many as the smaller North

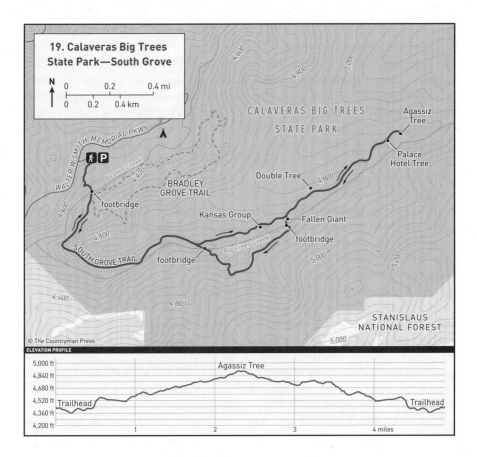

19. Calaveras Big Trees State Park—South Grove

N

| 0 | 0.2 | 0.4 mi |
| 0 | 0.2 | 0.4 km |

CALAVERAS BIG TREES STATE PARK

Agassiz Tree

Palace Hotel Tree

WALTER W SMITH MEMORIAL PKWY

Beaver Creek

Double Tree

BRADLEY GROVE TRAIL

Kansas Group

Fallen Giant

footbridge

footbridge

SOUTH GROVE TRAIL

Big Trees Creek

footbridge

STANISLAUS NATIONAL FOREST

© The Countryman Press

ELEVATION PROFILE

Agassiz Tree

Trailhead

Trailhead

5,000 ft / 4,840 ft / 4,680 ft / 4,520 ft / 4,360 ft / 4,200 ft

1   2   3   4 miles

Grove in the main area of the park. Find the path across from the restrooms and head south, soon crossing Beaver Creek, a popular summer swimming hole, via footbridge.

Although the Sierra Nevada foundation is granite, you won't see much of the salt-and-pepper flecked rock in the park, as it is almost completely covered by soil and alluvium. One exception is the channel carrying Beaver Creek. Here the soil has been eroded, revealing the underlying bedrock.

Climb away from the creek, and at 0.3 mile, reach a junction with the Bradley Grove Trail. This 2.5-mile loop wanders through a grove of young sequoias planted in the 1950s by South Grove

caretaker Owen Bradley. A logging operation left its mark on the area, but despite man's effort to destroy it, nature has restored itself in fine fashion. In the eloquent words of John Muir: "Nature is always lovely, invincible, glad, whatever is done and suffered by her creatures. All scars she heals, whether in rocks or water or sky or hearts."

With Beaver Creek splashing in the ravine to your right, gently ascend a hillside thick with a mix of conifers and mountain dogwood. In the spring, dogwood blossoms bedeck the understory in a showy display that enlivens the forest. Contrary to what you might think, the small, buttonlike center of the blossom is the actual flower. Surrounding this are large, egg-shaped white bracts, which are actually modified leaves. The leaves typically turn crimson in the autumn, painting a whole new scene.

Rounding a bend, you trade the tumbling of Beaver Creek for Big Trees Creek and you follow it upstream to the western boundary of the preserve. At 1.1 miles, cross a dirt road and officially enter the South Grove. Soon you'll reach a junction and bear left. This is the beginning of the loop part of the journey.

As you travel northeast through the tranquil grove, begin to notice scattered rust-colored trunks rising about. Unlike their closely related cousin, the coast redwood, sequoia trees (also called Sierra redwoods) do not grow in pure stands. Instead they thrive in mixed coniferous forests of white fir, sugar pine, and incense cedar. In California, these stately giants are found within a narrow belt along the western slope of the Sierra, where the optimal altitude, temperature, rainfall, and soil type converge, encouraging their growth.

To your right, pass the Kansas Group, a cluster of three large sequoias, before coming to another junction at 1.75 miles. Stay straight and pass Double Tree, a pair of sequoias growing so close together they appear as one. Continue along the somewhat overgrown trail as it winds toward Palace Hotel Tree, named in the 1870s after its apparent resemblance to the courtyard carriage entrance of San Francisco's newly opened Palace Hotel (it's a stretch). At 2.5 miles, reach the end of the official trail and the Agassiz Tree, named after Louis Agassiz, the Swiss-born zoologist who became one of America's leading naturalists. This specimen is the largest sequoia in the park, at 25 feet in diameter and 250 feet tall.

Although a sign here marks the end of the trail, a faint footpath continues into the upper portion of the grove. If you are up for a little freelancing and are comfortable navigating through an unfamiliar forest, venture farther and explore The Moody Group, named for

BRIDGE OVER BEAVER CREEK

TRAIL THROUGH THE SOUTH GROVE

nineteenth-century evangelist Dwight Moody; Smith Cabin Tree, named for Alexander Jackson "Trapper" Smith, who lived in the hollowed-out behemoth in the late 1850s; and Old Goliath, which, as the story goes, came crashing down during a violent windstorm.

Return to the last junction and bear left onto the loop trail. Immediately pass through a tunnel in a fallen giant, beyond which you cross Big Trees Creek on a wooden footbridge. From here the trail meanders through the quiet forest, passing several other sequoias en route to a second footbridge over Big Trees

Creek and the close of the loop trail at 4.1 miles. Turn left at the junction and retrace your steps to the trailhead.

If you're looking for a shorter option, the much more frequented North Grove has an accessible, 1.5-mile interpretive loop near the visitor center. The stump of the tree that originally caught Dowd's eye—the Discovery Tree—is located along the trail. Not long after Dowd found it, it was felled at the hands of five men over 22 days to be put on display. Other notable North Grove trees include Three Graces, Abraham Lincoln, and Old Bachelor.

Sonora Pass

TYPE: Day hike

SEASON: Late July to October

TOTAL DISTANCE: 8.6 miles round trip

RATING: Moderate to strenuous

ELEVATION: 9,626 feet; +1,640 feet/-502 feet

LOCATION: Stanislaus National Forest, Humboldt-Toiyabe National Forest, Emigrant Wilderness

MAPS: USGS 7.5' Sonora Pass; USFS Emigrant Wilderness

FEES AND PERMITS: A permit is not required for this day hike.

CONTACT: Stanislaus National Forest, Summit Ranger District (209-965-3434; www.fs.usda.gov/stanislaus).

Striking south along the Pacific Crest Trail from Sonora Pass, this challenging hike climbs through moonlike terrain to a windswept saddle just east of Leavitt Peak. From this airy perch, you have mile upon mile of High Sierra resplendence spread out before you in spectacular display. Be sure to call ahead for trail conditions, as snow may linger well into summer, making sections of this steep trek potentially dangerous. Pack plenty of water, a windbreaker, and sun protection, as you will be well above treeline for most of the hike. Be cognizant of sudden weather changes and the reduced level of oxygen at this altitude.

GETTING THERE

From US 395, 17 miles north of Bridgeport, turn onto CA 108 (Sonora Pass) and drive 14.6 miles west. Notice the trailhead marker on the south side of the highway as you crest Sonora Pass. There is limited parking here along the road, or you can proceed 100 yards farther and turn right into the parking/picnic area. From a dirt path on the south end of the parking area, walk south 0.2 mile back to the pass itself, where you cross the highway and arrive at the signed trailhead.

THE HIKE

At 9,626 feet, Sonora Pass is the second highest road crossing of the Sierra Nevada, with Tioga Pass, at 9,945 feet, taking the top spot. With mules, horses, and oxen, the brave Bartleson-Bidwell Party, the first organized group of emigrants to traverse the Sierra Nevada, crossed the pass in October 1841. The route was not attempted by wagon until 1852. Two years later, John "Grizzly" Adams crossed the pass and reported:

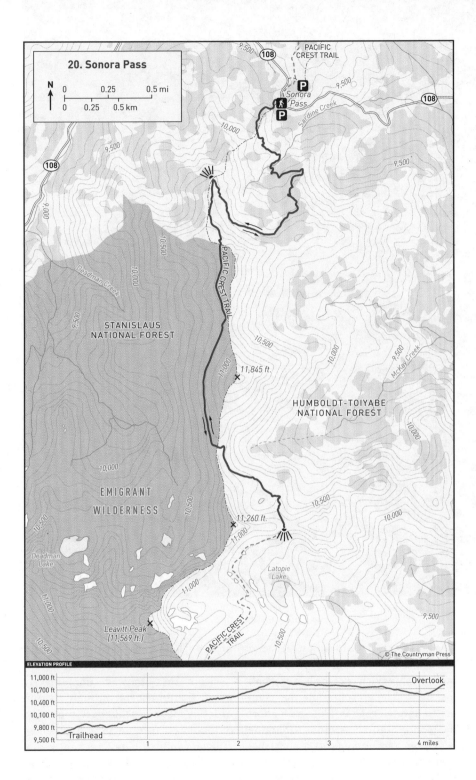

20. Sonora Pass

N

0   0.25   0.5 mi
0   0.25   0.5 km

PACIFIC CREST TRAIL

108

Sonora Pass

108

Sardine Creek

9,500

9,500

9,500

10,000

10,000

108

9,500

9,000

10,500

Deadman Creek

10,000

9,500

STANISLAUS NATIONAL FOREST

PACIFIC CREST TRAIL

10,500

10,000

McKay Creek

9,500

11,000

11,845 ft.

HUMBOLDT-TOIYABE NATIONAL FOREST

10,000

10,500

10,000

10,500

10,000

EMIGRANT WILDERNESS

10,000

10,500

11,260 ft.

11,000

Latopie Lake

10,500

Deadman Lake

11,000

11,000

10,500

Leavitt Peak (11,569 ft.)

10,500

PACIFIC CREST TRAIL

9,500

© The Countryman Press

ELEVATION PROFILE

11,000 ft				Overlook
10,700 ft				
10,400 ft				
10,100 ft				
9,800 ft				
9,500 ft	Trailhead			
	1	2	3	4 miles

SONORA PASS

"On all sides lay old axle-trees and wheels, some broken, some perfect, melancholy evidence of the last season's disasters." The present route was completed as a toll road in 1865 in an effort by Mono, Stanislaus, and Tuolumne counties to recoup some of the construction costs. The round trip from Sonora to Bridgeport, what we now drive in a matter of hours, was said to have taken a six-horse team three weeks to complete.

From the highway, immediately begin a mild ascent through a stand of lodgepole and whitebark pine. The duff-colored ground is enlivened by lavender lupine, blue flax, and woolly sunflower. The trail then dips to cross several gullies, the most notable being

Sardine Creek at 0.6 mile. Watch for alpine buckwheat, woolly mule's ear, and mountain helenium as you approach the willow-lined channel.

Resume climbing and spot ruddy-colored Sonora Peak and its attendant ridgeline north across the valley. Catch your breath at a bend in the trail and admire the expanded view of hill and dale as they roll into the eastern horizon. The gradient steepens and you duck behind a hill, losing the panorama for the moment. The rocky, exposed terrain negates any chance of getting off course and makes it easy to see the trail gently rising on the canyon wall ahead.

From a distance, this barren landscape appears devoid of life, but here walking through it, you can see it is rife with a hardy community of alpine plants, all well adapted to this harsh, unforgiving environment. Some plants have evolved interesting adaptations, including growing low and small to withstand high winds and stay warm. To cope with near drought conditions during the short summer growing season, many have developed specialized means to conserve and capture moisture; because manufacturing scent uses up valuable water, many plants produce relatively large flowers instead to attract pollinators.

Continue your uphill march beneath a colorful unnamed rampart of chunky volcanic rock as you circle the headwall in a clockwise direction. Spy the highway coursing below as you pass through clumps of stunted whitebark pine clinging to the hillside.

The trail doubles back on itself at 2.1 miles and heads south toward a saddle that's just west of our unnamed peak along the Sierra Crest. Near the bend, scramble to the ridgetop and enjoy expanded westward views of Night Cap Peak, Chipmunk Flat, and Red Peak. Back on the main trail, gain the saddle at 2.4 miles, where views improve once again to include Leavitt Peak, the tallest in a wall of 11,000-foot pinnacles forming an imposing bulwark that flanks Blue Canyon below.

The crest you now traverse is the topographical dividing line where the waters of the region part. Creeks flowing east tumble into the Great Basin, while westward flows hit the Stanislaus River and eventually spill into the Pacific Ocean.

With the major climbing behind you, the trail levels off and begins a general descent south along a steep wall and briefly penetrates the northeastern tip of Emigrant Wilderness. Watch for lingering snow along this section, which can be very treacherous. If you are early in the season, carry an ice axe just in case. At 3.6 miles, reach another saddle, where you can look down upon grimly named Deadman Lake to the south and Sardine Meadow to the north.

Past the saddle, the trail descends to more level walking and then culminates with a final steep climb to your goal—a lofty 10,800-foot notch overlooking the dusky volcanic landscape magnificently studded with a bevy of striking alpine lakes. Nearest you is Latopie Lake, followed by Koenig and Leavitt Lakes. On a clear day you can even see Mount Conness, Mount Lyell, and a host of other lesser peaks that form Yosemite's granite skyline.

If you aren't satisfied with the view (although that's highly unlikely) and can muster the energy, scramble to the summit of Leavitt Peak (11,569 feet). The easiest way is to continue south on the PCT and ascend along the southeast ridge.

Leavitt Meadow to Lane Lake

TYPE: Day hike or overnight

SEASON: Mid-May through October

TOTAL DISTANCE: 6.6 miles round trip

RATING: Moderate

ELEVATION: 7,120 feet; +686 feet/-505 feet

LOCATION: Humboldt-Toiyabe National Forest

MAPS: USGS 7.5' Pickel Meadow; USFS Toiyabe National Forest – Bridgeport Ranger District

FEES AND PERMITS: A permit is not required for this day hike. Overnight trips into the Hoover Wilderness require a permit (fee) from Humboldt-Toiyabe National Forest.

CONTACT: Humboldt-Toiyabe National Forest, Bridgeport Ranger District (760-932-7070; www.fs.usda.gov/htnf).

Tranquil Leavitt Meadow rests at the base of the eastern slope of Sonora Pass and is bisected by the West Walker River. Because the roughly 2-mile-long meadow is only at 7,000 feet elevation and is situated on the drier eastern side, it is often free of snow in May. There are several lakes in the area that make great destinations for day hikes or overnights. The relatively mild gradient and multitude of options makes Leavitt Meadow a popular jumping off spot for early season rambles into the backcountry.

GETTING THERE

From US 395, 17 miles north of Bridgeport, turn onto CA 108 (Sonora Pass) and drive 7 miles west. The trailhead parking area is on the south side of CA 108, just west of Leavitt Meadow Campground.

THE HIKE

From the north end of the Leavitt Meadows Trailhead parking lot (near the trailhead sign) follow a short footpath toward Leavitt Meadows Campground, crossing Brownie Creek via a log footbridge. Join the Leavitt Meadows Campground access road and continue 1,000 feet north to the new West Walker River Bridge, where the trail begins. There are restrooms at the trailhead parking lot and campground.

After crossing the West Walker River footbridge, follow the trail up and to the right. When you crossed the lively river, you no doubt noticed the old bridge just upstream. Keep straight when the path to the old bridge appears to your right. At 0.2 mile come to a signed junction that heads to Secret Lake. There is an option here to turn this hike into a partial loop by venturing to Secret Lake either going or coming. We continue along the West

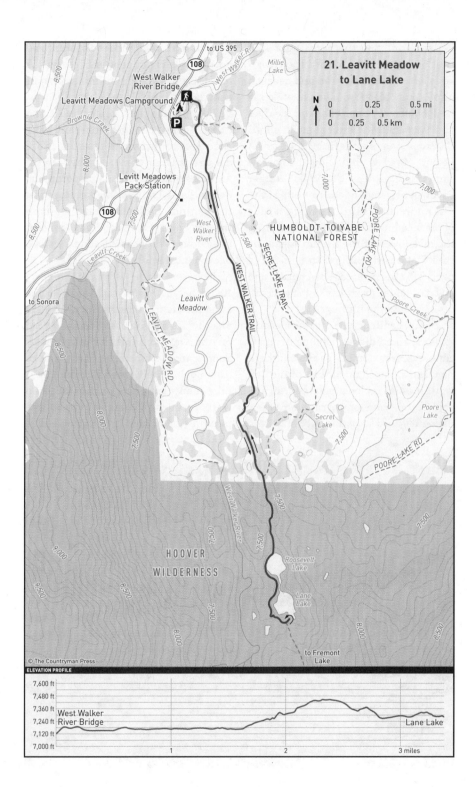

ELEVATION PROFILE

West Walker
River Bridge

Lane Lake

Walker Trail. Shortly thereafter a spur trail branches right toward the river—keep left on the main trail and descend into Leavitt Meadow. If you mistakenly wander off course and end up at the river you can backtrack without much effort.

Cross the northern perimeter of Leavitt Meadow and follow the narrow sage-lined trail as the West Walker River gently meanders to your right. The rolling trail skirts the eastern edge of the meadow and is fairly level. Across the meadow spot the Leavitt Meadows Pack Station, which offers trail rides and pack trips in the area. Use caution and always yield right of way if you encounter horses on the trail.

As you continue, views of the meadow expand, and a distant skyline of snow-capped spires dominates the southern panorama. Pause under one of the Jeffrey pines sprinkled along the trail and soak in the symphony of rustling aspen, melodious bird song, and babbling river.

Several spur trails and stock paths head down to the river along this section. A tempting detour if angling is on your agenda.

At 1.75 miles, the trail starts climbing in earnest and changes from sandy and shadeless to rocky and forested. Wander past a series of murky ponds and at 2.5 miles—the elevation high point—the Secret Lake Trail option we passed at the beginning of the hike joins in on the left. Shortly thereafter you arrive at the Hoover Wilderness boundary and a backcountry information board.

It was near this spot in the early 1850s that brave emigrant wagon trains attempted to traverse the Sierra Nevada via the "West Walker-Sonora Road" on the way to southern mines near Sonora and Columbia, the most famous group being the Clark-Skidmore Party. Like many emigrant parties heading west during this time, progress was painfully slow and treacherous. The

LEAVITT MEADOW AND THE PLACID WEST WALKER RIVER

HIKER TAKING A BREAK ALONG THE SHORE OF LANE LAKE

Clark-Skidmore Party ran out of food, had to engineer means of moving their wagons over steep, rocky terrain, and was plagued by desertion. While the remnants of the Clark-Skidmore Party did eventually arrive in Columbia, their journey up and over the Sierra Nevada that was supposed to take 10 days ended up lasting over a month.

In 1853, Major John Ebbetts led an expedition for the Atlantic & Pacific Company to find a possible railroad crossing over the Sierra Nevada. Upon witnessing the number of abandoned wagons and dead livestock strewn along the West Walker-Sonora route he quickly eliminated it from consideration and advised no emigrant take it. However, the route continued to be utilized and, in 1863, Hiram Leavitt, an early settler, innkeeper, and judge built a hostelry at the east end of Sonora Pass to serve the growing numbers of travelers between Sonora and Aurora, primarily miners headed to nearby Bodie.

From the signboard, the trail descends 0.5 mile to the northern shore of Roosevelt Lake. Enjoy the view before following the sandy trail along the western shoreline and pass an appealing campsite on a knoll overlooking the southern shore. A short distance further and you arrive at Lane Lake. The lakes are connected by a narrow log-strewn saddle. From a clearly used campsite situated on the northern shore, enjoy views of the crystalline water and surrounding peaks poking above the pines. Continue around to the southern shore where a small peninsula that juts into the lake makes for another fine campsite or spot to jump in and refresh yourself before returning the way you came.

If you are planning an overnight, campsites are limited at both lakes, and the relatively easy access means the lakes can get quite busy in the summer.

As mentioned previously there are several options for additional exploring in this area. You can turn this hike into a partial loop by combining the West Walker Trail and Secret Lake Trail or continue past Lane Lake and on to Fremont Lake and beyond if you are up for a multi-day excursion.

22

Bennettville Trail

TYPE: Day hike

SEASON: June through October

TOTAL DISTANCE: 3.9 miles round trip

RATING: Easy

ELEVATION: 9,544 feet; +359 feet/-0 feet

LOCATION: Inyo National Forest

MAPS: USGS 7.5' Tioga Pass; Trails Illustrated Yosemite NE—Tuolumne Meadows & Hoover Wilderness No. 308 (trail partially shown)

FEES AND PERMITS: A permit is not required for this day hike.

CONTACT: Inyo National Forest, Mono Lake Ranger District (760-647-3044; www.fs.usda.gov/inyo).

Steeped in Sierra mining history and fantastic subalpine landscapes, this easy day hike is perfect for a summer afternoon. Just outside Yosemite National Park, explore the remains of short-lived Bennettville, a town of great expectation in 1882, and skirt a peaceful chain of lakes connected by the sinuous flow of aptly named Mine Creek.

GETTING THERE

From US 395, 1 mile south of Lee Vining, turn onto CA 120 (Tioga Pass) toward Yosemite National Park. Drive 9.8 miles west and turn right onto Saddlebag Lake Road. Proceed 0.1 mile farther to the small parking area on the left, prior to reaching Junction Campground. Walk toward the campground and across the bridge spanning Lee Vining Creek and immediately find the trailhead on the right.

THE HIKE

The trail sets out briefly along the grassy west bank of Lee Vining Creek, but quickly bends away and climbs a short hill blanketed with a sparse forest of lodgepole pines. Skirting Junction Campground from above, angle toward Mine Creek and eventually meet up with it, splashing below in a chasm of dark metamorphic rock. Now, following the creek upstream, look for nude buckwheat and Sierran raillardella sprouting from the rocky terrain. Come to a grassy meadow and step across a small streamlet. Continue your ramble under the shady pines, enjoying the sounds of the creek and the lovely pools and cascades it creates in its rush to rendezvous with Lee Vining Creek. At 0.9 mile, arrive at an interpretive plaque below Bennettville, a short-lived Sierra mining town.

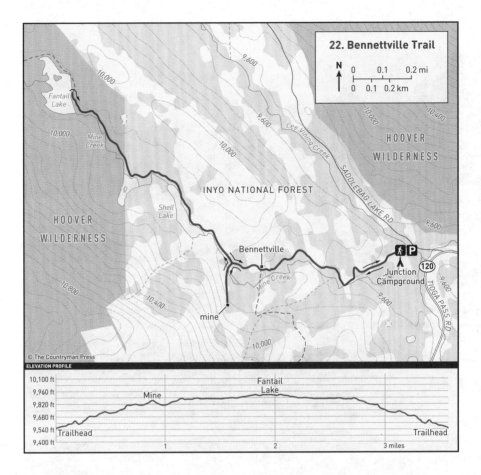

ELEVATION PROFILE

In 1874, William Brusky, a young sheep herder, stumbled across a rusty pick, shovel, and a flattened tin can wedged in the rocks of Tioga Hill. Left by George W. Chase some 15 years prior, the tin can was etched with a location notice marking what was believed to be a rich silver vein—the "thundering big silver ledge." This fateful discovery sparked a small silver rush and gave rise to the town of Bennettville, named after Thomas Bennett, president of the Great Sierra Consolidated Silver Mining Company.

With great expectations, the directors of the Tioga Mine ordered the latest mining technology—16,000 pounds worth to be exact. The equipment was to be transported from Lundy Canyon, some 9 miles away, up and over the rugged Sierra to the mine. Over a two-month period in late winter, a team of 12 men and a pair of mules hoisted, pulled, and dragged the equipment on sleds through blinding snowstorms and near-zero temperatures. Subsequently, the Great Sierra Wagon Road was constructed, linking Bennettville to Sonora to the west, reducing the burden of transporting equipment and supplies into the remote mine and standing ready to carry a bonanza of silver out, hopefully.

After two years with the new

MINE CREEK AND MOUNT DANA IN THE DISTANCE

machinery and upwards of 1,700 feet of tunnel dug, the propitious ledge of silver was nowhere to be found. Investors, now skeptical of the mine's profitability, backed out, effectively ceasing operations. No ore was ever mined or hauled out of Tioga Mine, and the town of Bennettville slipped slowly into obscurity as people realized the once envisioned town of 50,000 people was never going to become reality. The one positive nugget of this woeful tale is the creation of the Great Sierra Wagon Road, which eventually served as the foundation for Tioga Pass. In 1910, the eastern segment from Lee Vining to Tioga Pass was opened, linking east to west and forming the highest and arguably one of the most scenic mountain roads in all of California.

Climb a small knoll and explore the two restored wooden buildings, which stare vacantly across the canyon to a cascade of copper-colored scree, the tailings of a fruitless mine.

Shortly beyond Bennettville, you come to an unsigned trail fork. Veer left and descend to a slippery log crossing over Mine Creek, then up the opposite canyon wall for 0.15 mile to the actual mine. Explore the rusty equipment scattered about and peer into the rocky orifice (now barricaded) before returning the way you came.

Back at the fork, rejoin the main trail by turning left. Round a bend where views expand northwest into the canyon to include a verdant basin and its peacefully meandering creek. Mount Conness (12,590 feet), a formidable challenge on Yosemite's northeastern boundary, dominates the granite skyline.

Approaching the shore of Shell Lake at 1.4 miles, gain stunning over-the-shoulder views of Mount Dana (13,057 feet), Yosemite's second highest peak. Come to a Y-junction and veer left to walk along the shore, or right to stay above it (less buggy). The two eventually reconvene at the far end of the lake. Progressing along the single-track trail, pass another unnamed lake to the left and eventually come to a boundary sign for 3,883-acre Harvey Monroe Hall Research Natural Area (RNA). This was one of the first established in California (1933) as part of a nationwide program developed to protect a network of federally administered public lands for the purpose of maintaining biological diversity, providing baseline ecological data, and encouraging research and education. Specifically, the Harvey Monroe Hall RNA has been used to study the social organization of Belding ground squirrels, the dynamics of windblown detritus in snow banks, and the community structuring of subalpine forest birds.

Forging deeper into the canyon, arrive at shallow Fantail Lake at 2.1 miles. Watch for cassiope blooming along the trail, its nodding bell-shaped flowers said to be a favorite of John Muir, who wrote: "Her blossoms . . . so beautiful as to thrill every fibre of one's being . . . No evangel among the mountain plants speaks Nature's love more plainly than cassiope. Where she dwells, the redemption of the coldest solitude is complete. The very rocks and glaciers seem to feel her presence and become imbued with her own fountain sweetness."

The trail continues around the lake; however, we retreat from this subalpine paradise and return to the trailhead.

Twenty Lakes Basin

TYPE: Day hike or overnight

SEASON: Late June through October

TOTAL DISTANCE: 4.5-mile loop

RATING: Easy to moderate

ELEVATION: 10,071 feet; +600 feet/-600 feet

LOCATION: Inyo National Forest, Hoover Wilderness

MAPS: USGS 7.5' Tioga Pass, Dunderberg Peak; Trails Illustrated Yosemite NE—Tuolumne Meadows & Hoover Wilderness No. 308 (northern part of loop is not shown)

FEES AND PERMITS: A permit is not required for this day hike. Overnight trips into the Hoover Wilderness require a permit (fee) from Inyo National Forest. The water taxi charges $13 per person, round trip.

CONTACT: Inyo National Forest, Mono Lake Ranger District (760-647-3044; www.fs.usda.gov/inyo); Saddlebag Lake boat taxi (www.saddlebaglakeresort.com/boats.html).

It's hard to imagine another hike with as much austere alpine scenery as this short loop that penetrates the southern corner of Hoover Wilderness. Wander past a chain of stunning lakes, made all the more remarkable by the serrated, snow-speckled skyline that forms the backdrop of this rugged landscape. Spread out a picnic, cast a line, or just linger at any of these tranquil gems.

While such beauty has not gone unnoticed, Twenty Lakes Basin is relatively uncrowded, particularly by the standards of Yosemite, which is just a stone's throw away. By utilizing the water taxi that departs Saddlebag Lake's south shore, you can forgo the relatively uneventful trail that skirts the shoreline and save your energy for the "good stuff." If you opt to walk it, add 3 miles to your jaunt. Oh, and don't forget the bug juice.

GETTING THERE

From US 395, 1 mile south of Lee Vining, turn onto CA 120 (Tioga Pass) toward Yosemite National Park. Drive 9.8 miles west, and turn right onto Saddlebag Lake Road. Immediately come to a fork and veer right. Proceed 2 miles on this unpaved road to a large trailhead parking area.

THE HIKE

From the water taxi dock, peer northwest to the far shore of Saddlebag Lake and get a glimpse of the tantalizing scenery awaiting your lug soles. After a 10-minute boat ride, arrive at the boat landing on the north shore. Follow a faint path up the rise to the main trail. If you walked from the marina, this junction is where you will join the loop trail described in this hike. You will be going

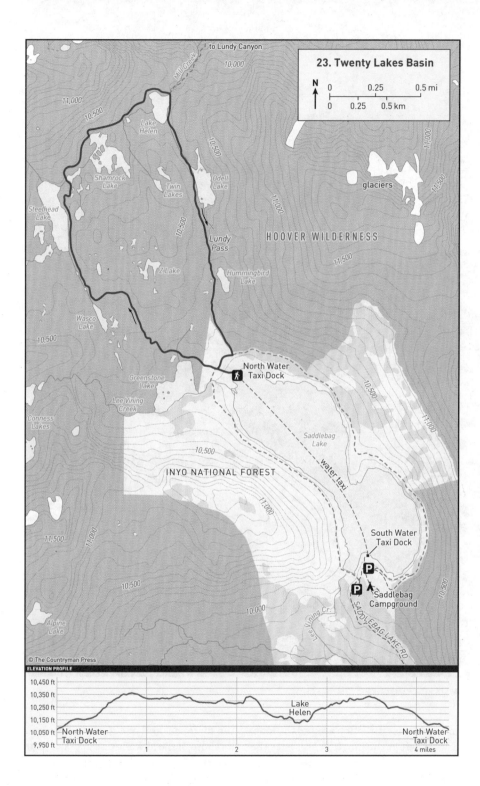

23. Twenty Lakes Basin

to Lundy Canyon

Mill Creek

10,000

11,000

10,500

Lake Helen

Shamrock Lake

Twin Lakes

Odell Lake

10,500

Steelhead Lake

10,500

Lundy Pass

11,000

HOOVER WILDERNESS

glaciers

11,000

11,500

11,500

Z Lake

Hummingbird Lake

Wasco Lake

10,500

Greenstone Lake

North Water Taxi Dock

10,500

11,000

Lee Vining Creek

Conness Lakes

10,500

Saddlebag Lake

INYO NATIONAL FOREST

11,000

water taxi

11,500

11,000

10,500

10,500

South Water Taxi Dock

P

Saddlebag Campground

P

Alpine Lake

10,000

Lee Vining Cr.

SADDLEBAG LAKE RD.

10,500

© The Countryman Press

ELEVATION PROFILE

10,450 ft			
10,350 ft		Lake Helen	
10,250 ft			
10,150 ft			
10,050 ft	North Water Taxi Dock		North Water Taxi Dock
9,950 ft			

1   2   3   4 miles

NORTH PEAK REFLECTING IN STEELHEAD LAKE

in a clockwise direction around the loop, so turn left at the junction and pass the Hoover Wilderness boundary sign. In short order, Greenstone Lake appears in the distance, and at 0.3 mile you reach its shore. If the altitude doesn't take your breath away, the sublime scenery will.

As Mount Conness, North Peak, and

a host of other craggy, glacially scarred spires along the Sierra Crest command attention, you begin a 0.5-mile ascent past whitebark and lodgepole pines. Though the trail is rocky, the gradient is easygoing. Photographers will enjoy capturing the scenes reflected in the ponds and pools along the way. In the distance, the outlet for Conness Lakes splays somewhat erratically through chunky boulders in its downward course. The dark streaks staining the granite around the falls are caused by lichen.

Wander past sinuous, marshy drainages and a variety of wildflowers that add splashes of color to the dark, metamorphic terrain. Wasco Lake appears to the left, but you will stay high above it. The level trail parallels a verdant depression and passes an unofficial trail wandering left before arriving at Steelhead Lake, 1.4 miles from the boat landing. Excelsior Mountain and its rust-colored façade dominate the northern horizon, while a lovely cascade graces Steelhead's southernmost shore. Carefully cross the outlet creek at 1.8 miles and proceed 190 feet, at which point you will veer right and away from the lake to begin a short but steep ascent up its rocky bank. Topping the knoll above the creek, ignore the unofficial trail that veers right and stay straight. Wander between scrubby whitebark pines, clumps of willows, and possible patches of snow as you approach island-studded Shamrock Lake.

Traverse a talus slope lining the northern shore, its jumbled pieces spilling into the chilly waters below. Descend slightly, then mount a small ridge where Lake Helen comes into view. Red heather, Labrador tea, and shrubby cinquefoil line the trail, which becomes vague as you descend a multi-tiered rock slope. Cairns help somewhat, but you may also need to do a little navigating of your own. In this open country it isn't hard, and you can see the path below, a duff-colored streak parting a swath of grass.

Continuing on, travel across another expansive talus slope, this time around rockbound Lake Helen. As you look back, the drab granite of the Sierra Crest stands in stark contrast to the multihued metamorphic rock under your feet.

Carefully scramble down a steep 10-foot rock ledge, and at 2.75 miles cross Lake Helen's outlet (Mill Creek) on a pair of logs. Come to a signed T-intersection where Mill Creek exits left down Lundy Canyon, another fine destination worthy of exploration. Our described hike turns right, toward Saddlebag Lake. The endless talus slope, wonderfully adorned with Coleville's columbine, shows no sign of stopping as you skirt the edge of Lake Helen and clamber up a narrow ravine that ushers in the outlet for Odell Lake, next on our route. Crest the scree-filled chasm and take in the view of diminutive Lake Helen and the deeply etched ebony peaks behind it.

At 3.25 miles, you approach elongated Odell Lake and walk high above its rocky shore on your way toward Lundy Pass, a windswept saddle devoid of vegetation save the hardy grasses and sporadic whitebark pines that, at this elevation, generally take the form of low, densely matted shrubs rather than trees.

A couple of unofficial trails wander left near the outlet for Hummingbird Lake, the final gem on the circuitous route. Exit the Hoover Wilderness and spy Saddlebag Lake and Mount Dana in the distance. The trail gently descends along a trickling stream, which we later cross on our way back to the boat landing for our return trip across the water.

IV.

EASTERN SIERRA

Green Lake

TYPE: Day hike or overnight

SEASON: Mid-June to October

TOTAL DISTANCE: 6.2 miles round trip

RATING: Moderate

ELEVATION: 8,003 feet; +1,004 feet/-63 feet

LOCATION: Humboldt-Toiyabe National Forest, Hoover Wilderness

MAPS: USGS 7.5' Dunderberg Peak; Trails Illustrated Yosemite National Park No. 206

FEES AND PERMITS: A permit is not required for this day hike. Overnight trips into the Hoover Wilderness require a permit (fee) from Humboldt-Toiyabe National Forest.

CONTACT: Humboldt-Toiyabe National Forest, Bridgeport Ranger District (760-932-7070; www.fs.usda.gov/htnf).

Travelers along Green Creek Trail enjoy a profusion of trailside wildflowers, pass rushing streams, and wander through peaceful forests on their way to Green Lake, a scenic subalpine gem just outside the confines of Yosemite's northeast boundary. Like most other jaunts into the eastern Sierra, this hike gains a good bit of elevation in a relatively short distance. Don't worry though, the colorful peaks and pleasant vistas will keep your eyes occupied while you catch your breath. Make a day of it, or plan to overnight at Green or East Lake before returning.

GETTING THERE

From Bridgeport, drive 4.3 miles south on US 395 to the turnoff for Green Creek Road (FS Road 142). Allow 30 minutes to follow this unpaved road 8.6 miles to the trailhead parking area. Avoid several spur roads and stick to the main path toward Green Creek Campground. Near the 3.4-mile mark, you come to an intersection with unsigned Dunderberg Meadow Road heading southeast. Veer sharply right and continue 5.1 miles farther to the trailhead parking area near the campground.

THE HIKE

From the parking area, head southwest along a wide path through a mixed forest of lodgepole and Jeffrey pines, junipers, and aspens. Not far from the trailhead, enter a meadow filled with Richardson geranium and alpine lily. At 0.6 mile, veer right and join an old road that meanders along the north bank of willow-lined Green Creek. Heading left takes you to Green Creek Campground. Green Creek flows from its headwaters in the Hoover Wilderness into East

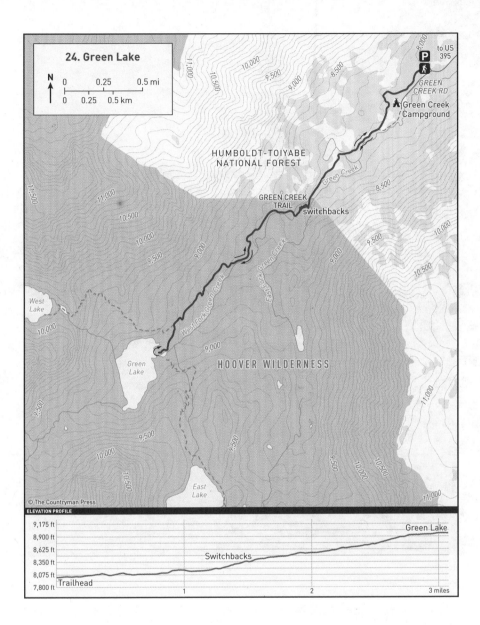

24. Green Lake

N

| 0 | 0.25 | 0.5 mi |
| 0 | 0.25 | 0.5 km |

ELEVATION PROFILE

Green Lake

Switchbacks

Trailhead

9,175 ft
8,900 ft
8,625 ft
8,350 ft
8,075 ft
7,800 ft

1 2 3 miles

Walker River, eventually spilling into Bridgeport Reservoir.

The landscape you now traverse is part of the Humboldt-Toiyabe Forest, the largest National Forest outside of Alaska, encompassing in excess of 6 million acres. Because the forest spans such a large swath of land, it includes a broad array of wildlife habitats, from arid desert to subalpine forest. Unfortunately, not unlike other regions of the globe, certain species here are in decline due to human influences and competition by nonnative species. Two local amphibians—mountain yellow-legged frog and Yosemite toad—which normally inhabit wet meadows, lakes, and streams, are struggling. The Forest Service has

GREEN LAKE

implemented a restoration program, but you can also help to minimize impacts to these and other species. Always practice the seven Leave No Trace principles, and if you plan on fishing, thoroughly disinfect all fishing gear if relocating to a different body of water to prevent the spread of disease. It's unlikely you will spot these critters during the hike, but if you do, consider yourself lucky.

The trail eventually narrows and you cross a small creek. A short climb and brief descent are followed by level walking. With the noisy creek still to your left, but mostly ensconced beneath thick vegetation, begin a steady ascent. The trail grade increases as you ascend a series of rocky, shadeless switchbacks. At the top of this zigzagging section, the grade mellows. Enjoy the shade now offered by a thickening canopy and cross a small creek at 1.8 mile, passing

aspens into their fiery autumnal palette. The trail dries out at the top of the incline, and you have the opportunity to admire the surrounding valley over the treetops before bisecting another lush area brightly adorned with fireweed's rose-colored flowers.

Continue your ascent, enjoying the expanded view down the valley toward the Bodie Hills and of the Monument Ridge, your western flank. The drab Kavanaugh Ridge rising to the east is punctuated by ochre Dunderberg Peak, a lovely contrast. At 2.9 miles, reach a junction and turn left to reach the east shore of Green Lake. The right fork heads to West Lake, a stiff climb that tacks on another 1.5 miles (one way) and 1,000 feet of elevation.

From the junction, Green Lake is an easy 0.25 mile farther. When you run into the West Fork of Green Creek, a difficult crossing in the early season, turn right, abandoning the main trail, and follow the creek upstream. Watch for cairns to show you the way. Green Lake's water is sparkling clear and, though it's a little chilly for swimming, angling for rainbow and brook trout can be fantastic. The lake is situated at the base of several colorful metamorphic pinnacles, the most notable being Gabbro Peak, which dominates the pine-dotted southern shore. Glines Canyon's forested valley stretches into the distance toward the saddle of Virginia Pass, beyond which lies Yosemite National Park. West Lake's outlet forms a thin cascade as it tumbles over chunky dark rock, accentuating the entire scene.

the entry sign for Hoover Wilderness not long after.

Look for the dark tip of Gabbro Peak poking above the greenery as you climb. Enter a wet, somewhat overgrown segment that puts on a dazzling wildflower display early in the season. Watch for cinquefoil, white-flowered bog orchid, paintbrush, and lupine. Fall is also a magical time to visit and experience the colorful transformation of quaking

Backpackers will find wonderful spots to set up camp near Green Lake or can continue on to East Lake, about 1.5 mile farther. Day hikers can take a relaxing respite before returning to the trailhead.

Virginia Lakes Basin

TYPE: Day hike	

SEASON: Mid-June to October

TOTAL DISTANCE: 6 miles round trip

RATING: Moderate to strenuous

ELEVATION: 9,843 feet; +1,282 feet/-1 feet

LOCATION: Humboldt-Toiyabe National Forest, Hoover Wilderness

MAPS: USGS Dunderberg Peak; USFS Toiyabe National Forest—Bridgeport Ranger District

FEES AND PERMITS: A permit is not required for this day hike. Overnight trips into the Hoover Wilderness require a permit (fee) from Humboldt-Toiyabe National Forest.

CONTACT: Humboldt-Toiyabe National Forest, Bridgeport Ranger District (760-932-7070; www.fs.usda.gov/htnf).

Beneath the watchful gaze of Dunderberg Peak and Black Mountain, glacially carved Virginia Lakes Basin is in a class by itself. This challenging hike explores a picturesque string of lakes and climbs the headwall of this vivid basin, to a windswept pass where you gain arresting views of Yosemite's barren high country and a new perspective of the valley you just traversed. Though steep in sections, the trail also enjoys its share of level walking in between climbs, so you have plenty of time to recover. Pack a windbreaker, as the pass can be breezy.

GETTING THERE

From Bridgeport, drive 13 miles south on US 395 to Conway Summit and the turnoff for Virginia Lakes. Drive 6.1 miles southwest on Virginia Lakes Road to the trailhead parking area at road's end. Find the trailhead behind a small restroom building at the far end of the parking lot.

THE HIKE

The Virginia Lakes Basin has some of the most beautiful scenery in all of the Sierra Nevada. What makes it so unique is that instead of the speckled gray granite so characteristic of the High Sierras, you get deep red volcanic rock, evidence of the Sierra Nevada's tumultuous volcanic past. When you consider the whole geologic package—glaciation, volcanism, uplift—you are left with a wonderland of sparkling lakes, polychromatic mountains, and sweeping vistas.

Begin by skirting the lodgepole-lined shore of Big Virginia Lake. Not long into the hike, a spur trail from the campground joins in from the right. Pass a small pond before the trail forks at the entry sign for Hoover Wilderness.

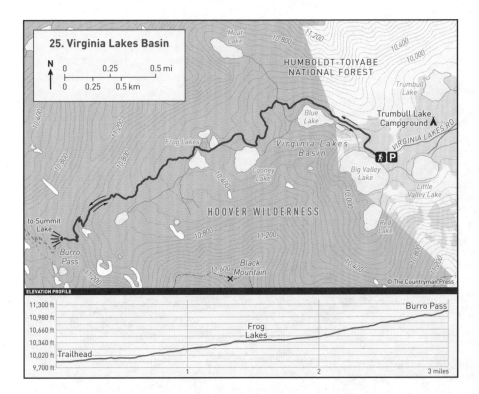

25. Virginia Lakes Basin

N
0   0.25   0.5 mi
0   0.25   0.5 km

Moat Lake
10,800
11,200
10,400
10,000
HUMBOLDT-TOIYABE NATIONAL FOREST
Trumbull Lake
10,400
Blue Lake
Trumbull Lake Campground
VIRGINIA LAKES RD
Frog Lakes
11,200
10,800
10,400
Virginia Lakes Basin
Cooney Lake
Big Valley Lake
Little Valley Lake
10,400
HOOVER WILDERNESS
10,000
to Summit Lake
Burro Pass
10,800
11,200
Black Mountain
11,600
11,200
10,400
10,800
Red Lake
© The Countryman Press

ELEVATION PROFILE

				Burro Pass
11,300 ft				
10,980 ft				
10,660 ft		Frog Lakes		
10,340 ft				
10,020 ft Trailhead				
9,700 ft	1	2		3 miles

Either path is fine, as they rejoin farther down the trail; however, the left fork stays along the shore and has a milder gradient.

Leave the forest behind as you ascend an open hillside of sage, mountain snowberry, and scattered wildflowers along the northern canyon wall. Reach Blue Lake and begin a gently ascending traverse across a talus slope spanning the toe of Dunderberg Peak. Across the way, Cooney Lake's outlet stream spills from the lip of the next terrace, through a red-tinged cleft, and disappears into the trees, reappearing just before plunging into Blue Lake's deep water.

Geographically speaking, the lakes in this chain are referred to as paternoster lakes. By eroding weak rock on the valley floor, glaciers often create a series of rock steps and excavated basins, resulting in a glacial stairway. When the ice recedes, rock-bound lakes may fill the basin, often appearing like beads on a string, connected by streams flowing down the glacial trough. At the valley's head is another glacial landform called a cirque, an oftentimes steep-sided amphitheater-shaped hollow formed at the head of an alpine valley by glacial erosion. This will all become very obvious once you reach your goal and can peer down on the landscape.

The trail grade increases as you ascend through a wet area filled with cinquefoil, aster, and arnica. The trail dries out briefly before an easy boulder hop over the outlet for unseen Moat Lake, situated high above. The streamlet is brimming with California corn lily and a profusion of lupine. Continue ascending the rooty, rocky trail and at 1 mile pass a dilapidated log miner's cabin. As you mount the next terrace,

VIRGINIA LAKES BASIN AS VIEWED FROM BURRO PASS

which corrals Cooney Lake, watch for pride of the mountain blooming from rocky crevasses and enjoy the view down the valley toward Mono Basin. To the west, your goal is in sight—the low point in the saddle at the head of the valley. (Though unnamed on the USGS topographic map, the pass is unofficially referred to as Burro Pass.)

Briefly follow the shore of Cooney Lake before climbing a series of switchbacks cut into the ochre-colored terrain. Approaching the 1.5-mile mark, use steppingstones to cross the creek that spills from a cluster of lakes collectively called Frog Lakes. Enjoy level walking as you meander through the trio and make another easy crossing of the stream linking them together. The largest of the Frog Lakes (the last one you come to) makes a pleasant picnic spot.

The ascent gently resumes, a warm-up for the steeper climb ahead, and you wind through clumps of weather-battered whitebark pine and a smattering of mountain hemlock. At 2.1 miles, rise above the first lake in the chain, a grassy, unnamed tarn situated at the foot of brooding Black Mountain and the headwall you are about to tackle. Later switchbacks slice through the scree-covered hillside, taking you higher. Watch your footing along the rocky path and look for red heather and Davidson's penstemon sprouting from the rocks. The views down canyon are nothing short of amazing and will hopefully keep your mind off the steady trudge.

Reach the broad bench of Burro Pass (11,125 feet) at 3 miles. Follow the trail a few yards beyond the actual crest and take in the stunning multicolored scene. To the west, the mountains and peaks of Yosemite's rugged northeast corner pitch and roll into the horizon. Stark and

VIBRANT PINK PENSTEMON SPROUTING ALONG THE TRAIL

barren but fantastically beautiful, this is a panorama you won't soon forget. The vista to the east is no less impressive. From your lofty saddle, the Virginia Lakes Basin is on full display, its lake-filled terraces stretching toward the dry expanse of Mono Basin. If the elevation on this hike doesn't take your breath away, the vistas will.

When you're done admiring the scene, return to Frog Lake for a picnic out of the wind before descending back to the trailhead.

Mono Lake

TYPE: Day hike

SEASON: May through October

TOTAL DISTANCE: 2-mile loop (Panum Crater)/0.75-mile loop (South Tufa)

RATING: Easy/easy

ELEVATION: 6,842 feet; +357 feet/-357 feet (Panum Crater)/6,413 feet; +31 feet/-31 feet (South Tufa)

LOCATION: Mono Basin National Forest Scenic Area, Inyo National Forest

MAPS: USGS 7.5' Lee Vining; USFS Inyo National Forest; Mono Lake Tufa State Natural Reserve brochure map

FEES AND PERMITS: A permit is not required for these day hikes. There is a day-use fee of $3 per person charged at the South Tufa area (children 16 and under are free).

CONTACT: Mono Lake Tufa State Natural Reserve (760-647-6331; www.parks.ca.gov/?page_id=514).

While not technically "in" the Sierra Nevada, Mono Lake lies in the Great Basin along the eastern margin of this massive range. The exposed high desert terrain makes it easy to explore the surrounding volcanic landscape and the unusual tufa towers of the ancient landlocked lake. Two hikes are detailed here. If you find yourself limited on time and can choose only one, definitely head for the South Tufa area. There is no shade along either trail, and during summer the region can be extremely hot, so an early morning start is best.

GETTING THERE

From the Mono Lake Visitor Center just north of Lee Vining, drive 5.8 miles south on US 395 and turn left onto CA 120 east toward Benton. Drive 3 miles and turn left onto the signed turnoff for Panum Crater. Follow the narrow, unpaved road 0.8 mile to the parking area with no facilities. To get to the South Tufa Area from US 395, drive 4.7 miles along CA 120 east toward Benton (passing the turnoff for Panum Crater) and turn left onto the signed turnoff for Mono Lake South Tufa. Pass the unpaved road leading to Navy Beach at 0.1 mile and proceed straight. Continue along the now unpaved road 0.8 mile to the large parking area with pit toilets.

THE HIKE

The Mono Basin visitor center is a great place to start your visit, and includes a variety of exhibits explaining the natural and human history of the area.

The first hike explores Panum Crater, one of the northernmost plug-dome volcanoes in a chain stretching north from Long Valley Caldera near Mammoth Lakes, some 30 miles to the south.

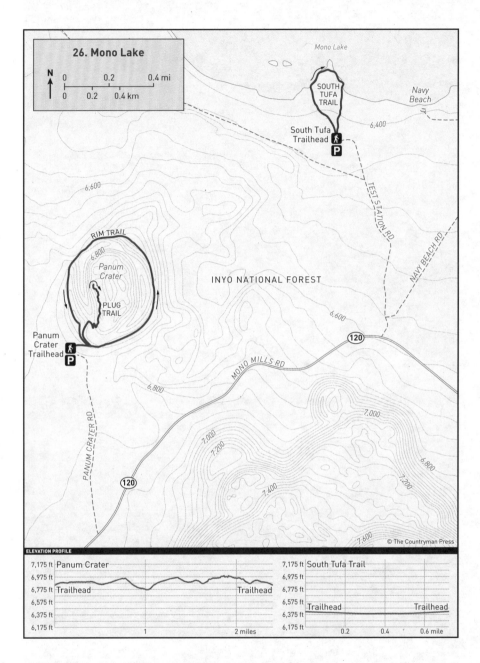

ELEVATION PROFILE

Panum Crater

7,175 ft	
6,975 ft	
6,775 ft	Trailhead ... Trailhead
6,575 ft	
6,375 ft	
6,175 ft	1 ... 2 miles

South Tufa Trail

7,175 ft	
6,975 ft	
6,775 ft	
6,575 ft	Trailhead ... Trailhead
6,375 ft	
6,175 ft	0.2 ... 0.4 ... 0.6 mile

© The Countryman Press

The Mono Craters, as the chain is collectively called, represent the youngest mountain range in North America, having erupted into existence within the last 40,000 years. (Panum Crater is the youngest, having erupted around 650 years ago.) After the eruption, cooled lava created a domelike structure that now "plugs" the volcanic vent beneath the dormant—not extinct—crater.

From the parking area, ascend a wide, pumice-laden trail lined with bitterbrush and desert peach to the rim of the crater. From here you can see the rocky plugged

TUFA TOWERS POKING OUT OF MONO LAKE

dome (you'll walk inside later). Follow the Rim Trail in a counterclockwise direction (the open terrain makes it difficult to get lost). As you make your way around the rim, enjoy splendid views of the eastern Sierra Nevada, notice the Mono Craters extending south, and garner a bird's-eye view of Mono Lake. The entire trail is rather sandy and there are a couple of steep sections, but for the most part it's easy going.

Watch for butter-colored blazing star and sulphurflower along the trail, adding splashes of color to the otherwise drab desert palette. You might also spot obsidian, a shiny black rock that has extremely sharp edges when broken, making it a favorite of Native Americans for spear and arrow points. Circumnavigate the rim after 1.5 miles and then head toward the center of the crater via the Plug Trail, which climbs 0.25 mile to the top of the dome. Follow all trail signs and avoid cutting or collecting.

The shore of Mono Lake and the South Tufa area is our next stop. The 60-square-mile lake is one of the oldest lakes in North America (more than one million years old). Because the lake has no outlet, water's only means of escape is through evaporation, a process that leaves behind a profuse amount of dissolved salt, making the lake two and a half times as salty and eighty times as alkaline as seawater. Once referred to as a dead sea, Mono Lake is actually a productive ecosystem, albeit a fragile one, that supports a variety of bird species including grebes, phalaropes, and gulls.

Our walk begins near several information boards that detail the flora and fauna that have adapted and thrive in this saline-rich environment. The paved trail heads north through a landscape covered in Russian thistle and sage. Interpretive signs guide you along the way. Take note of the lake-level signs signifying the lake's historic elevation. In 1941, the City of Los Angeles began diverting four of the five major streams that empty into Mono Lake, causing the lake to drop more than 40 feet. Concerns over the lake's fragile ecosystem, health risks associated with airborne alkali dust, and aesthetics led to a long-running political and judicial battle that finally ended in 1994 when the State Water Resources Control Board issued an order protecting the lake and its tributary streams.

Approaching the lake, the path turns into a boardwalk and you begin to see the peculiar tufa formations sprouting about. Tufa is formed when underwater springs rich in calcium mix with lake water rich in carbonates, resulting in a chemical reaction that creates calcium carbonate, or limestone. Over time, the limestone accumulates, forming the towers and spires that decorate Mono Lake's shoreline. On a calm day, photographers will enjoy the chance to capture the otherworldly reflection of tufa towers and the distant Sierra Nevada Mountains in Mono Lake's brackish water.

The boardwalk ends at the beach, where you will undoubtedly notice the carpet of black alkali flies near the water's edge and perhaps clouds of tiny brine shrimp swimming in the water. Both serve as the main course for more than eighty species of migratory birds that depend on the lake for food and refuge.

Turn right at the end of the boardwalk and follow the shore 0.15 mile to a trail sign and a narrow single-track trail that leads to a second beach. The trail then meets a junction heading east toward Navy Beach, which, if you have time, creates a longer loop. We stay straight and return to the parking area.

San Joaquin Ridge

TYPE: Day hike

SEASON: Mid-June to mid-October

TOTAL DISTANCE: 4.5 miles round trip

RATING: Moderate

ELEVATION: 9,255 feet; +1,044 feet/-51 feet

LOCATION: Inyo National Forest

MAPS: USGS Mammoth Mountain; Trails Illustrated Mammoth Lakes Mono Divide No. 809

FEES AND PERMITS: A permit is not required for this day hike.

CONTACT: Inyo National Forest, Mammoth Ranger District (760-924-5500; www.fs. usda.gov/inyo).

This hike traverses a high-altitude ridgeline that serves as the boundary between the Ansel Adams Wilderness and Inyo National Forest. The trail climbs steadily along a wide four-wheel-drive road toward Deadman Pass and our goal, a lofty unnamed knoll (10,248 feet) along the summit ridge. Along the way, enjoy breathtaking vistas of the Ritter Range jutting to the west and the docile White Mountains rising on the eastern horizon. If the climb is too rigorous, simply walk for as long or as short as you like, and the views all along the trail won't disappoint. The limited canopy (which gradually dwindles the higher you climb and eventually become nonexistent) can make this jaunt rather warm in the afternoon, so get an early start and pack plenty of water and sun protection.

GETTING THERE

From Bishop, drive 39 miles north on US 395. Exit to CA 203 and drive west 3.8 miles toward Mammoth Lakes/Devils Postpile. Turn right onto Minaret Road (still designated CA 203) and continue 5.4 miles to Minaret Summit, passing Mammoth Mountain Ski Area along the way. Turn right just before the Minaret Vista Entrance Station to Devils Postpile National Monument and follow the paved road 0.3 mile to the small trailhead parking area.

THE HIKE

Start at the stone overlook, where a helpful display will allow you to familiarize yourself with the jagged peaks of the Ritter Range dominating your field of view. Mount Ritter, the most prominent peak, rises 13,157 feet on this imposing skyline of granite. Immediately north of Ritter is

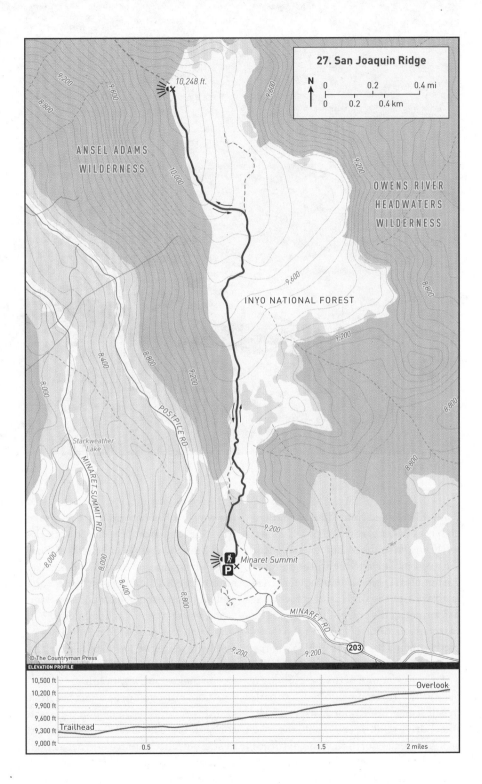

27. San Joaquin Ridge

N

| 0 | 0.2 | 0.4 mi |

| 0 | 0.2 | 0.4 km |

10,248 ft.

ANSEL ADAMS
WILDERNESS

9,200

9,600

8,800

10,000

8,400

8,800

POSTPILE RD

Starkweather
Lake

MINARET SUMMIT RD

8,000

8,400

9,200

OWENS RIVER
HEADWATERS
WILDERNESS

9,200

8,600

INYO NATIONAL FOREST

9,600

9,200

8,800

8,800

Minaret Summit

8,800

9,200

MINARET RD

9,200

9,200

203

© The Countryman Press

ELEVATION PROFILE

10,500 ft				Overlook
10,200 ft				
9,900 ft				
9,600 ft				
9,300 ft	Trailhead			
9,000 ft				
	0.5	1	1.5	2 miles

THE RITTER RANGE

Banner Peak, and immediately south of both is a cluster of serrated peaks collectively known as the Minarets, named for their resemblance to the spires on Muslim temples. Their sawtooth appearance is a result of the expansion of ice that has formed in the cracks of the rock. The seasonal repetition of freezing and thawing fragments the granite, chiseling the mountains' jagged appearance.

From the far end of the parking area, behind the restrooms, join a footpath that descends briefly northeast to a four-wheel-drive road. Veer left onto the road as it heads due north through a diffuse mixed conifer forest. Take note of where you joined the road—sans signs pointing

the way, it's easy to miss on the return trip. Not long after you merge with the road, a narrower trail branches left. Continue along the wider road and emerge onto a dry hillside covered with sage and mountain snowberry and speckled with Brewer's lupine, nude buckwheat, woolly mule's ears, and mountain pennyroyal. Without trees blocking the view, you can peer both east and west as you make your way uphill.

At 0.4 mile, you get a short breather as the grade eases, but don't get too comfortable. The level stretch covered in sun-bleached pumice and occasional sprouting sulphurflower is short-lived, and the climb resumes less than 0.5 mile

At 1.6 miles, stay left at another junction and once again head steeply uphill. Gnarled and weather-battered whitebark pines dot the hillside. These hardy pines can eke out an existence in the most unforgiving environments. You will also spot sporadic wildflowers such as ranger's buttons, lupine, and Sierra penstemon. Spot your goal up ahead, the views taking your mind off the trudge still remaining.

Though it may seem illogical, the ridge beneath your feet is where High Sierra waters divide. From west to east, the Sierras take the form of a non-equilateral triangle—the altitude gradually increases as you travel east toward the crest, beyond which the altitude swiftly decreases, resulting in the abrupt eastern Sierra escarpment. Precipitation falling on the western slope of this ridge feeds the San Joaquin River, eventually emptying into the Pacific Ocean. Precipitation dropping on the eastern slope flows into the Owens River, which ultimately provides water to parched southern California, little of it reaching the ocean.

Attain the knoll at 2.25 miles and bask in the 360-degree panorama. Views north expand toward Deadman Pass, the Two Teats, and countless distant peaks poking toward the sky. To the west, the forested valley gives way to barren granite pinnacles and shady crevasses that harbor lingering snow. The tempered topography of the White Mountains and the Great Basin stretches east and Mammoth Mountain, with Mammoth Crest behind it, bulges to the south.

later. The higher you climb, the sparser the trees and ground cover become. Lose the view briefly as you enter a swath of pines and a miniature field of aster.

Past the occlusive vegetation, on the now shadeless path, don't forget to turn around and take in the view of Mammoth Mountain at your back. Its slopes, devoid of snow, are rife with unseen mountain bikers sprinting down its ski-run-scarred face. A fork at 1.3 miles calls for a decision. Stay left here and slowly advance along the steepening ridge. As you attain the crest of this challenging hump, the grade eases and your views expand south and east to include Lake Crowley and the White Mountains.

Experienced hikers can continue another 3.5 miles along the challenging ridge to San Joaquin Mountain (11,600 feet). For now, be content to savor the views before returning to your vehicle.

28

Devils Postpile to Rainbow Falls

TYPE: Day hike

SEASON: Mid-June to mid-October

TOTAL DISTANCE: 3.5 miles one way

RATING: Easy

ELEVATION: 7,564 feet; +455 feet/-347 feet

LOCATION: Devils Postpile National Monument, Ansel Adams Wilderness, Inyo National Forest

MAPS: USGS Mammoth Mountain, Crystal Crag; Trails Illustrated Mammoth Lakes Mono Divide No. 809

FEES AND PERMITS: A permit is not required for this day hike. To reduce congestion in Devils Postpile National Monument, from mid-June into September, day-use visitors must ride a shuttle bus. Purchase tickets and board buses at Mammoth Mountain Adventure Center ($7 for adults, $4 for children ages 3 to 15, and children 2 and under are free).

CONTACT: Devils Postpile National Monument (760-934-2289; www.nps.gov/depo).

Explore a fantastic columnar basalt formation and watch the Middle Fork of the San Joaquin River plunge over a volcanic cliff on this easy hike through Devils Postpile National Monument. By disembarking the shuttle bus at stop 6 (Devils Postpile) and boarding at stop 9 (Rainbow Falls Trailhead) you can do this hike one way and only retrace your steps for about 0.5 mile.

GETTING THERE

From Bishop, drive 39 miles north on US 395. Exit CA 203 and drive west 3.8 miles toward Mammoth Lakes/Devils Postpile. Turn right onto Minaret Road (still designated CA 203) and continue 4.2 miles to Mammoth Mountain Main Lodge and Adventure Center. Park in the lot (if you arrive early) or along Minaret Road. Buy tickets for the shuttle bus at the Adventure Center.

THE HIKE

Find the trailhead on the south side of the ranger station at the Devils Postpile shuttle stop (#6). The wide trail begins by bisecting verdant Soda Springs Meadow. The Middle Fork San Joaquin River flows lazily to your right. Enter a lodgepole forest and, after a gentle climb, come to a trail fork at 0.2 mile. Veer left and continue your ascent toward Devils Postpile. Nearing the Postpile, come to the northern junction of a loop trail that climbs to the top of this unusual geologic formation. Stay straight and explore Devil's Postpile from below before backtracking to this junction and venturing atop the columns.

Devils Postpile is one of the finest examples of columnar basalt in the world. About 100,000 years ago, lava erupted some 2 miles upstream from

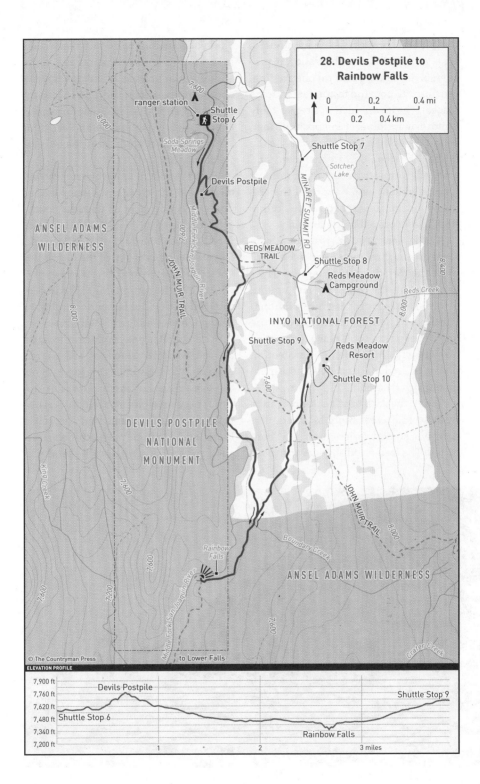

28. Devils Postpile to Rainbow Falls

N

| 0 | 0.2 | 0.4 mi |
| 0 | 0.2 | 0.4 km |

ranger station

Shuttle Stop 6

Soda Springs Meadow

7,600

8,000

Devils Postpile

MIDDLE FORK SAN JOAQUIN RIVER

JOHN MUIR TRAIL

ANSEL ADAMS WILDERNESS

7,600

8,000

MINARET SUMMIT RD

Shuttle Stop 7

Sotcher Lake

REDS MEADOW TRAIL

Shuttle Stop 8

Reds Meadow Campground

Reds Creek

8,400

INYO NATIONAL FOREST

8,000

Shuttle Stop 9

Reds Meadow Resort

Shuttle Stop 10

7,600

DEVILS POSTPILE NATIONAL MONUMENT

7,600

King Creek

7,600

7,200

Rainbow Falls

Middle Fork San Joaquin River

JOHN MUIR TRAIL

8,000

Boundary Creek

ANSEL ADAMS WILDERNESS

7,600

Crater Creek

© The Countryman Press

to Lower Falls

ELEVATION PROFILE

7,900 ft	Devils Postpile		
7,760 ft			Shuttle Stop 9
7,620 ft			
7,480 ft	Shuttle Stop 6		
7,340 ft		Rainbow Falls	
7,200 ft			

1   2   3 miles

the current location of the monument. As lava flowed down the valley, it presumably ran into a natural obstruction, causing it to pool (up to 400 feet in some places). The lava, which was remarkably uniform in its mineral composition, then began to cool at a very slow rate. As the molten lava cooled, it contracted and cracked, forming hexagonal columns. Later, a glacial event exposed the columns and polished the top of the formation, which looks like tile flooring.

In the early 1900s, pressure from local mining interests who wanted to blast the formation and dam the river won out briefly, and the monument, originally part of Yosemite National Park, lost its park status. Luckily, before any devastation took place, conservationists pushing for federal protection prevailed, and in 1911 the 798-acre monument was created.

Today, the dark basalt columns range from 40 to 60 feet high. Most are vertical but some are irregular and contorted. The formation appears as a giant chain of volcanic rock dominoes frozen in mid-topple—the warped northern fringe in the process of collapsing, the southern end erect and poised. Many of the columns, felled by natural processes such earthquakes and erosion, lie in a fragmented heap at the base of the formation.

Past the monument, the trail moves away from the river and climbs again. You eventually meet up with the southern junction of the loop trail to the top of Devil's Postpile near the 0.5-mile mark. (If you climb to the top of the formation and complete the loop, this is where you will rejoin the main trail.) From here, the trail generally descends through a lodgepole pine and red fir forest.

Although it is geographically located on the western slope of the Sierra Nevada, the monument's proximity to the eastern escarpment puts it at the nexus of several climatic regions, resulting in a rich and unusual mix of species. Flora includes both the wetter western species (red fir, mountain hemlock,

DEVILS POSTPILE

alder, and gooseberry) and drier eastern species (quaking aspen, Sierra juniper, sagebrush, and Jeffrey pine).

At 0.75 mile, reach the junction with the Reds Meadow Trail. Stay straight and shortly thereafter navigate an easy log crossing of Reds Creek. Our trail, which generally follows the eastern boundary of the park, continues in a southward direction, meeting up with the river once again. Carefully walk to the edge of the ravine to spy it coursing below.

Pass an intersection with the John Muir Trail at 1.25 miles. You have undoubtedly noticed the thinning forest and the plethora of downed and fire-scarred trees since leaving Devil's Postpile, all the unfortunate result of the lightning-ignited Rainbow Fire in 1992, which destroyed the thickly forested slopes near the monument, taking away the shady canopy and leaving only singed stumps in its wake.

Enjoy mostly level walking with some mellow ups and downs on the now shadeless and sandy path as you approach the junction with the Rainbow Falls Trail. Take note of this intersection, as you will turn right here on the return trip to reach the Rainbow Falls Trailhead.

Cross Boundary Creek via a wooden footbridge and you'll soon pass a sign announcing your entry into Ansel Adams Wilderness. Veer right at the junction with Fish Creek Trail and descend a log-lined stairway to an overlook directly across from the falls. From a cliff of volcanic rock, watch the wide San Joaquin River plummet 101 feet into a pool of green water at the base of a dark, vertical-walled canyon. When the sun is just right, you can watch rainbows dance in the billowing mist.

From the viewpoint, you have the option of continuing along the east bank

RAINBOW FALLS

of the river to Lower Falls, about 0.7 mile farther, and a stairway that leads down to river level (this mileage is not considered in the total given above). When you are done admiring the falls, retrace your steps to the Rainbow Falls Trail junction, where you take the right fork and head uphill 0.75 mile to the trailhead. The gradient is easy and there are several shady spots to rest. Along the way you will pass a junction leading to Reds Meadow Resort, and later the Pacific Crest Trail will cross your path. From the trailhead sign, proceed 100 yards up the unpaved road to the Rainbow Falls shuttle stop (#9).

29

Little Lakes Valley to Gem Lakes

TYPE: Day hike or overnight

SEASON: June through October

TOTAL DISTANCE: 7.1 miles round trip

RATING: Moderate

ELEVATION: 10,264 feet; +760 feet/-73 feet

LOCATION: Inyo National Forest, John Muir Wilderness

MAPS: USGS Mount Morgan, Mount Abbot; Trails Illustrated Mammoth Lakes Mono Divide No. 809

FEES AND PERMITS: A permit is not required for this day hike. Overnight trips into the John Muir Wilderness require a permit (fee) from Inyo National Forest.

CONTACT: Inyo National Forest, White Mountain Ranger District (760-873-2500 general information, 760-873-2483 wilderness permits; www.fs.usda.gov/inyo).

Little Lakes Valley is one of the most scenic areas in the entire eastern Sierra. With a paved roadway ready to deposit you at the over 10,000-foot altitude trailhead, it's the easiest way to experience High Sierra splendor with the least amount of effort. This ease of arrival is both a blessing and a curse, and you should be prepared to share the trail with everyone from young families to 70-somethings, but don't let that stop you. This trail meanders past a delightful chain of lakes into a wonderland of exposed granite, and with the mellow gradient and variety of turnaround options this out-and-back hike is one to add to your must-do list.

GETTING THERE

From Mammoth, drive 14.8 miles south on US 395 and turn right (southwest) onto Rock Creek Road (near Tom's Place). The roadway is two lanes and paved for 8.8 miles. Past the pack station, the road becomes a single lane with turnouts for the final 1.6 miles to the road's end at Mosquito Flat, where you will find the trailhead parking area.

THE HIKE

The starting elevation of this hike is undoubtedly higher than most of us are accustomed to, so take precautions to avoid the effects of altitude sickness by drinking plenty of fluids and taking it slow.

From the southern end of the parking area, past the restroom, begin by gently ascending the west bank of willow-lined Rock Creek. The sandy trail is brightly trimmed with lupine, cinquefoil, larkspur, and Indian paintbrush. A short distance from the trailhead, pass a sign indicating entry into the John Muir

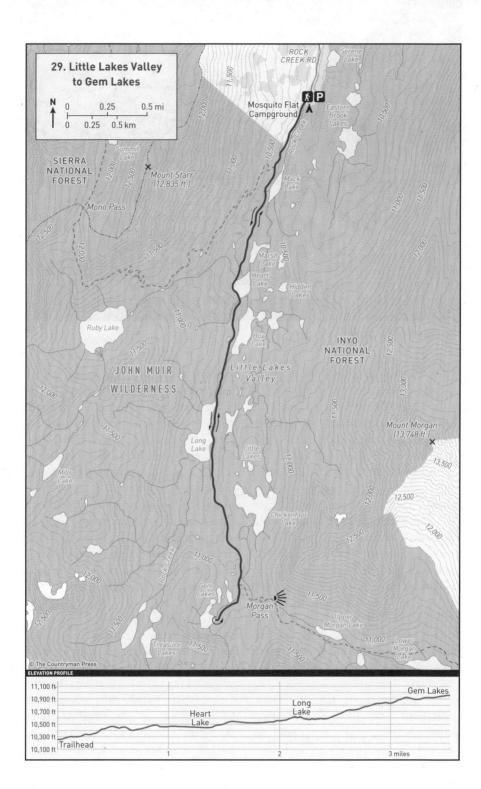

29. Little Lakes Valley to Gem Lakes

N
0   0.25   0.5 mi
0   0.25   0.5 km

ROCK CREEK RD
Serene Lake
Mosquito Flat Campground
Eastern Brook Lakes
Rock Creek
Summit Lake
SIERRA NATIONAL FOREST
Mount Starr [12,835 ft.]
Mono Pass
Mack Lake
Marsh Lake
Heart Lake
Hidden Lakes
Ruby Lake
Box Lake
Little Lakes Valley
INYO NATIONAL FOREST
JOHN MUIR WILDERNESS
Long Lake
Little Lakes
Mount Morgan [13,748 ft.]
Mills Lake
Chickenfoot Lake
Rock Creek
Gem Lakes
Morgan Pass
Upper Morgan Lake
Lower Morgan Lake
Treasure Lakes

© The Countryman Press

ELEVATION PROFILE

11,100 ft			Gem Lakes
10,900 ft		Long Lake	
10,700 ft	Heart Lake		
10,500 ft			
10,300 ft			
10,100 ft	Trailhead		

1   2   3 miles

TRAIL THROUGH LITTLE LAKES VALLEY

Wilderness and climb a series of widely spaced rock steps.

Take the left fork at the Mono Pass trail junction and continue toward Morgan Pass. Cresting a short climb, gain a magnificent view of Little Lakes Valley and a host of 13,000-foot snow-clad peaks standing sentinel at its helm— Mount Mills (13,451 feet), Mount Abbot (13,704 feet), Mount Dade (13,400 feet), and Bear Creek Spire (13,713 feet). Along much of the trail, the lodgepole and whitebark pine forest is open, allowing full appreciation of the ever-changing vistas as you delve deeper into this glacially sculpted valley.

The trail descends into a small meadow and crosses the inlet for Mack Lake, which is somewhat shrouded to the left. This process repeats a few times—gentle climb, fabulous view, descend to flower-filled meadow. Pass a footpath heading east to Marsh Lake and, at 1.2 miles, an easy boulder hop— and later a wooden footbridge—take you across an inlet to Heart Lake. Skirt the western shore of this popular fishing hole, admiring the small cascade on the opposite side where Rock Creek spills in.

Leave Heart Lake and begin another brief ascent, which crests high above Box Lake. Its sparkling blue-green water is like a mirror reflecting the pines, granite, and sky that encircle it.

Rejoin the western bank of Rock Creek and use steppingstones to cross it at 1.8 miles. Look for Coleville's columbine sprouting from the cracks and crevasses in a talus slope to the left. Opposite, Rock Creek, pacified for the moment, meanders through a grass-filled meadow. Traverse a somewhat shady section and arrive at Long Lake's boulder-strewn shore just past the 2-mile mark. Bear Creek Spire and Mount Abbot dominate the southern horizon. The trail is hemmed by a sheer cliff to the left and Long Lake's clear, trout-filled waters to the right. At the far end of the lake there is a broad grassy area, ideal for spreading out a picnic or casting a line.

Past Long Lake, the largest lake of

the chain, the trail gradient increases as you climb to a junction headed for Chickenfoot Lake, which lies in the shadow of Mount Morgan (13,748 feet). Oddly enough, the lake looks like a chicken's foot on the topographic map. The lake is 0.2 mile from the main trail, and backpackers will enjoy excellent camping near its shore. Forgoing this side trip, continue up the rocky path which rolls up and down through the narrowing valley and its imposing granitic terrain. Cross the outlet for Gem Lakes at 3.25 miles, and immediately bear right at the Morgan Pass junction to head toward Gem Lakes.

Morgan Pass, at just over 11,000 feet, is a relatively easy conquest at this point. Vertically ascend 225 feet over 0.35 mile and you're there. From the rocky saddle, you have fantastic views down Little Lakes Valley and of the Morgan Lakes extending southeast.

For now, follow the verdant single-track trail along the outlet's southern bank. The level trail is dotted with red heather, water-loving willows, and swamp onion. Gem Lakes is comprised of a trio of peaceful alpine ponds. Passing the two smaller ones first, notice Mount Dade's hulking presence in the background. The trail culminates at the largest lake, which is framed by steep, striated granite walls and a monstrous talus slope. Trout are found in all three lakes, and if you've packed a rod, now's the chance to test your mettle against the resident wild brookies, which are delightfully hungry. Campsites near Gem Lakes are limited due to the marshy, rocky nature of the terrain.

Linger as long as you like before backtracking along the same trail and enjoying the scenery all over again in reverse.

GEM LAKES

Blue Lake

TYPE: Day hike or overnight
SEASON: Late June to mid-October
TOTAL DISTANCE: 6.3 miles round trip
RATING: Moderate to strenuous
ELEVATION: 9,080 feet; +1,383 feet/-76 feet
LOCATION: Inyo National Forest, John Muir Wilderness
MAPS: USGS Mount Thompson; Trails Illustrated Mammoth Lakes Mono Divide No. 809
FEES AND PERMITS: A permit is not required for this day hike. Overnight trips into the John Muir Wilderness require a permit (fee) from Inyo National Forest.
CONTACT: Inyo National Forest, White Mountain Ranger District (760-873-2500 general information, 760-873-2483 wilderness permits; www.fs.usda.gov/inyo).

This moderately challenging hike near the Sierra Crest is chock full of fantastic vistas and austere alpine scenery. Throw in a few splashing cataracts, superb trout fishing, and a fine picnic spot, and you've got the makings for a perfect day in the backcountry.

GETTING THERE

From US 395 in Bishop, head west on CA 168 toward Lake Sabrina and South Lake. At 15 miles, the road to South Lake veers left. You stay straight and continue toward Lake Sabrina and the trailhead 3.7 miles farther. The road narrows past the Sabrina Campground. Early birds can find parking in the small roadside turnouts nearest the trailhead; otherwise park in the designated hiker parking area near the intersection with North Lake Road (0.4 mile northeast of the actual trailhead). Walk along the road and find the trailhead on the left-hand side.

THE HIKE

Long before Samuel Addison Bishop drove herds of cattle into the Owens Valley in 1861 to support miners and business owners in the booming city of Aurora, Nevada (now a ghost town) some 80 miles to the north, the area was inhabited by resourceful Paiute people. Like other Native Americans of the Sierra Nevada, the Paiute were nomadic. As seasons changed, they moved throughout the region harvesting pine nuts and other vegetation, fishing, and hunting game such as deer and desert bighorn sheep.

The winter of 1861–62 was especially severe for the Paiute, and traditional food sources became scarce. When the recently transplanted cattle began

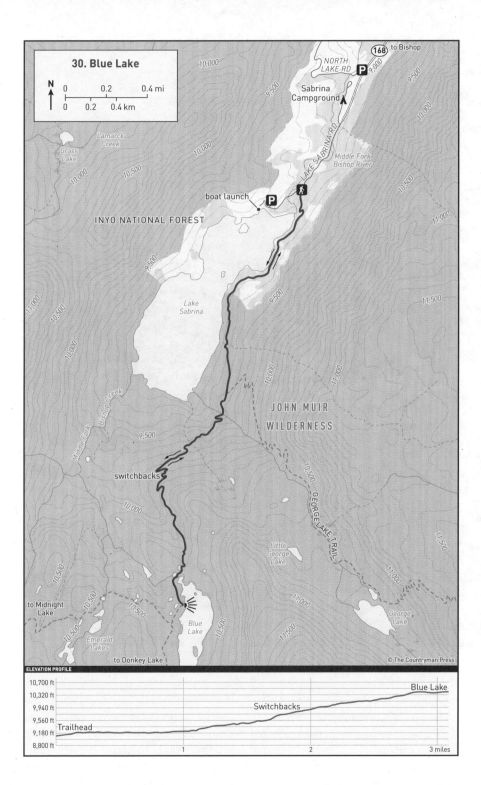

30. Blue Lake

N

| 0 | 0.2 | 0.4 mi |
| 0 | 0.2 | 0.4 km |

to Bishop

168

NORTH LAKE RD

P

9,000

9,500

Sabrina Campground

LAKE SABRINA RD

Middle Fork Bishop River

10,000

10,500

11,000

11,500

Lamarck Creek

Grass Lake

10,000

10,500

INYO NATIONAL FOREST

boat launch

P

9,500

Lake Sabrina

Middle Fork Bishop Creek

9,500

JOHN MUIR WILDERNESS

10,000

11,000

10,500

GEORGE LAKE TRAIL

switchbacks

10,000

Little George Lake

11,500

11,000

to Midnight Lake

10,500

Blue Lake

10,500

George Lake

Emerald Lakes

to Donkey Lake

11,500

© The Countryman Press

ELEVATION PROFILE

10,700 ft	Blue Lake
10,320 ft	
9,940 ft	Switchbacks
9,560 ft	
9,180 ft	Trailhead
8,800 ft	

1   2   3 miles

GRANITE-BOUND BLUE LAKE

foraging on vegetation they depended on for survival, it seemed only natural to the Paiute that the cattle could be killed for their own use. This sparked a period of fierce fighting, which ultimately ended a little over two years later with the surrender of hundreds of Paiute. The Owens Valley Paiute Shoshone Cultural Center-Museum in downtown Bishop is a great place to gain a better understanding of their culture and traditions before hitting the trail.

Begin by heading uphill above the dam confining the trout-filled waters of Lake Sabrina. As quaking aspens are tickled by the breeze, look for mountain pennyroyal, Indian paintbrush, and fireweed burgeoning in the cracks between boulders. The first mile of this hike is relatively level as it traverses high above the eastern shore of the lake. Initially, you meander through lush areas decorated with brightly colored wildflowers, but soon leave that behind for dry slopes littered with sage, mountain mahogany, and bush chinquapin. Enjoy fantastic views of the Sabrina basin and at 0.8 mile, cross the boundary for the John Muir Wilderness.

Just past the 1-mile mark, climb a series of switchbacks and pass a junction heading steeply east toward George Lake, then up and over the Table Mountains to Tyee Lakes. Continue straight and boulder-hop across the outlet for George Lake. Not long after, spot a lovely sheet of water sliding down a rock face to the left and cross another small stream it creates. Navigate a series of switchbacks, and at 1.7 miles catch your breath and take in the view from a rocky overlook. The lake, flanked by talus- and sage-covered slopes, appears as glass, unbroken except for the ripples cast by fishing boats as they troll the sapphire waters in search of Alpers trout, rainbows, and big browns.

Under the sporadic shade of lodgepole pines, a granite stairway takes you higher. A thin ribbon of water slices down the opposite canyon wall, the outlet for a collection of unseen alpine lakes. At 2.3 miles, views expand to include a ridge of imposing peaks stretching out along the western skyline. Follow the boulder-lined trail over an exposed granite slab and descend ever so briefly back into the forest.

Climb another series of rock stairs before emerging at the base of a dry streambed with a handy set of switchbacks festooned with two varieties of showy columbine. The most common and most widely distributed of the native western columbines has five elongated red petals that stretch backward toward the sky while the forward portions are yellow. Coleville's columbine has large yellow to white flowers. Where the two are found in close proximity, they tend to hybridize.

As you ascend the jumble of rocks and close in on your goal, don't forget to turn around and take in the views. Also notice the dikes (vertical) and sills (horizontal) streaking through the granite walls. These white lines are formed by igneous intrusions that create rock masses after molten material has been forced between rock layers and subsequently cools.

Crest the dry ravine, pass a muddy pond to your right, and spy Blue Lake through the trees. Level walking brings you to Blue Lake's outlet stream at 3 miles. Cross the wide outlet using rocks and logs and continue along the western shore for 0.15 mile to a granite rise. From here you have a fine view of the lake's clear waters peacefully nestled beneath the snow-clad peaks of the rugged Thompson Range. If you've packed along a pole, keep heading south along the trail where you will gain shoreline access.

Backpackers will find excellent campsites near Blue Lake or a host of other picturesque lakes farther along the trail with clever names like Dingleberry, Drunken Sailor, and Hungry Packer. With the hard climbing behind you, the trail past Blue Lake has an easy gradient, and the scenery improves with every step.

Long Lake

TYPE: Day hike or overnight	

SEASON: Late June to mid-October

TOTAL DISTANCE: 4.2 miles round trip

RATING: Moderate

ELEVATION: 9,833 feet; +955 feet/-43 feet

LOCATION: Inyo National Forest, John Muir Wilderness

MAPS: USGS Mount Thompson; Trails Illustrated Mammoth Lakes Mono Divide No. 809

FEES AND PERMITS: A permit is not required for this day hike. Overnight trips into the John Muir Wilderness require a permit (fee) from Inyo National Forest.

CONTACT: Inyo National Forest, White Mountain Ranger District (760-873-2500 general information, 760-873-2483 wilderness permits; www.fs.usda.gov/inyo).

Mere minutes from Bishop, you can trade the arid Owens Valley for a more pleasant world of rushing streams, pine forests, and deep-blue lakes. The well-used South Lake trailhead offers a multitude of desirable destinations for day hikes or extended overnights. Photographers, anglers, and nature lovers alike will find something to love about this fine Eastern Sierra jaunt bursting with resplendent alpine scenery and a collection of picturesque lakes.

GETTING THERE

From US 395 in Bishop, head west on CA 168 toward Lake Sabrina and South Lake. At 15 miles, turn left onto South Lake Road. Continue another 7 miles to the road's end and the ample trailhead parking area with pit toilets.

THE HIKE

This hike begins near South Lake, one of the many manmade lakes created in the early 1900s as a means of corralling Sierra runoff and producing hydroelectric power. The lake is home to several species of trout, making it a popular destination with anglers.

From the parking area, head south into a willowy meadow and immediately cross two wood-plank footbridges. Look for ranger's button, fireweed, and Sierra lily along this brief section. Mere minutes from the trailhead, a postcard panorama of South Lake's forest-ringed shores and the Sierra Crest rising in the distance fill your view. Hurd Peak, Mount Gilbert, and Mount Thompson all vie for your attention. Continue along the aspen-lined trail as it climbs above the eastern shore. Intermingled amid the aspens is a hodgepodge of sun-loving species, including mountain

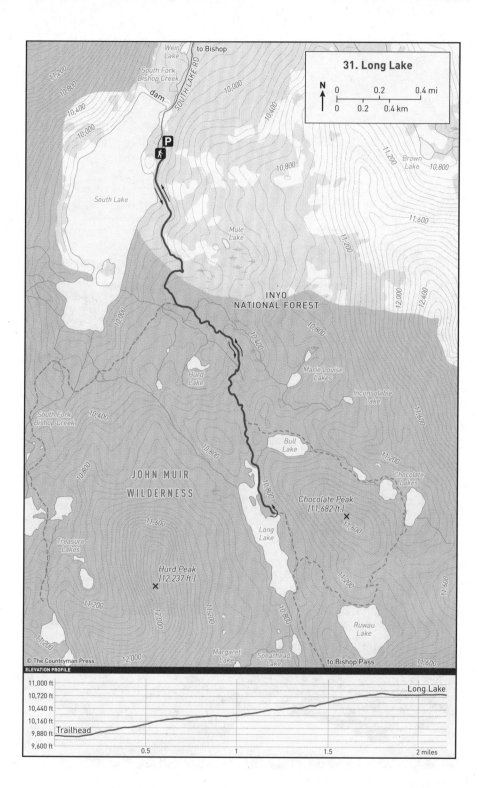

31. Long Lake

N

| 0 | 0.2 | 0.4 mi |
| 0 | 0.2 | 0.4 km |

to Bishop

Weir Lake

South Fork Bishop Creek

SOUTH LAKE RD.

dam

P

South Lake

Mule Lake

INYO NATIONAL FOREST

Brown Lake

10,000

11,200

10,800

10,400

10,000

10,400

10,800

11,200

11,600

12,000

12,400

10,800

Hurd Lake

Marie Louise Lakes

Inconsolable Lake

South Fork Bishop Creek

10,400

10,800

JOHN MUIR WILDERNESS

11,600

Treasure Lakes

Hurd Peak (12,237 ft.)
×

11,200

12,000

11,200

Margaret Lake

Spearhead Lake

Bull Lake

Long Lake

Chocolate Peak (11,682 ft.)
×

Chocolate Lakes

11,200

Ruwau Lake

to Bishop Pass

11,600

11,600

11,200

10,800

© The Countryman Press

ELEVATION PROFILE

11,000 ft			Long Lake
10,720 ft			
10,440 ft			
10,160 ft			
9,880 ft	Trailhead		
9,600 ft	0.5	1	1.5	2 miles

LONG LAKE IN REPOSE BENEATH BISHOP PASS

mahogany, sage, and their wildflower brethren—nude buckwheat, mountain pennyroyal, and fiery red penstemon.

At 0.5 mile, curve away from the lake and ascend a narrow ravine sprinkled with shooting star and columbine. Underneath the shade of lodgepole pines, switchback up the rocky trail and enter the John Muir Wilderness. The trail alternates between somewhat level walking and moderate climbs. Arrive at a junction with a trail heading to Treasure Lakes at 0.8 mile. Proceed left toward Bishop Pass and cross a shallow creek via a wooden footbridge. Below and to your right the creek drains into a grassy meadow. Shortly, the hulking mass of Hurd Peak is front and center and we arrive at another junction, this time heading to Mary Louise Lakes. Keep right and continue ascending to another willow-filled glen, crossing it via wooden footbridge at 1.4 miles.

Negotiate a series of short switchbacks and glimpse pine-encircled Hurd Lake below. At 1.8 miles, come to the northern end of a semi-loop trail that circumnavigates Chocolate Peak, passing Bull, Chocolate, and Ruwau lakes in the process. This spur eventually rejoins the main trail toward the southern end of Long Lake. Maintain your course toward Bishop Pass as you make the final push toward your goal. Reach the crest after traversing yet another willow-laden

ROCKY TRIAL TO LONG LAKE

section of trail and get a good look at Chocolate Peak—its anomalous brown hue a vivid contrast to the surrounding sea of ashen granite.

Begin a gentle descent, reaching the north shore of Long Lake at 2.1 miles. The elongated lake, cradled between Chocolate and Hurd Peaks, is riverine looking as it snakes into the distance. In the background, Bishop Pass and Mount Goode frolic on an enormous granite teeter-totter—Bishop Pass, the low point on the horizon, holding the contraption down, allowing weary hikers passage to points beyond.

There is a healthy population of rainbow, brook, and brown trout swimming in Long Lake's cool water and an equally healthy number of anglers attempting to catch them. The trail continues along the lake's edge for a little over 0.5 mile, so continue as long as you like before turning around. Campers can stake out a spot here or continue on toward Saddlerock Lake, which sits in repose at the foot of Mount Goode.

32

Big Pine Lakes Basin to Second Lake

TYPE: Day hike or overnight

SEASON: June through September

TOTAL DISTANCE: 9 miles round trip

RATING: Moderate to strenuous

ELEVATION: 7,820 feet; +2,314 feet/-22 feet

LOCATION: Inyo National Forest, John Muir Wilderness

MAPS: USGS 7.5′ Coyote Flat, Split Mountain; USFS John Muir Wilderness

FEES AND PERMITS: A permit is not required for this day hike. Overnight trips into the John Muir Wilderness require a permit (fee) from Inyo National Forest.

CONTACT: Inyo National Forest, White Mountain Ranger District (760-873-2500 general information, 760-873-2483 wilderness permits; www.fs.usda.gov/inyo).

First, Second, and Third Lakes, although mundanely named, are anything but ordinary. In a range famous for deep-blue waters, this stunning trio of glacially fed lakes, their brilliant turquoise water hemmed by pine-studded shores and granite spires, is sure to grab your attention. The climb is rather unrelenting as you follow Big Pine Creek upstream to these unique High Sierra gems. A good part of the trail traverses a shadeless sagebrush landscape, so carry plenty of water and sun protection.

GETTING THERE

From Bishop, drive 15 miles south on US 395 to Big Pine and turn right (west) onto Crocker Street, which eventually becomes Glacier Lodge Road. Signs on US 395 direct you toward Big Pine Creek Recreation Area. Follow the paved road 10.6 miles to the road's end, where you will find the day-use parking area with pit toilets. If the lot is full, return to the backpacker parking area farther back along the road near the pack station.

THE HIKE

Walk around a closed gate and begin by strolling up an old roadbed as birch- and willow-enshrouded Big Pine Creek tumbles to your left. Wander past some private cabins and follow the painted trail signs (no doubt put in place by residents tired of hikers accidentally traipsing onto their property) and cross raucous Big Pine Creek on a wooden footbridge at 0.3 mile.

Reach a junction, turn right up the North Fork Trail, and ascend the sagebrush- and mountain mahogany-covered hillside via a series of switchbacks. The South Fork Trail heads to Brainerd and Finger Lakes, which lie tucked

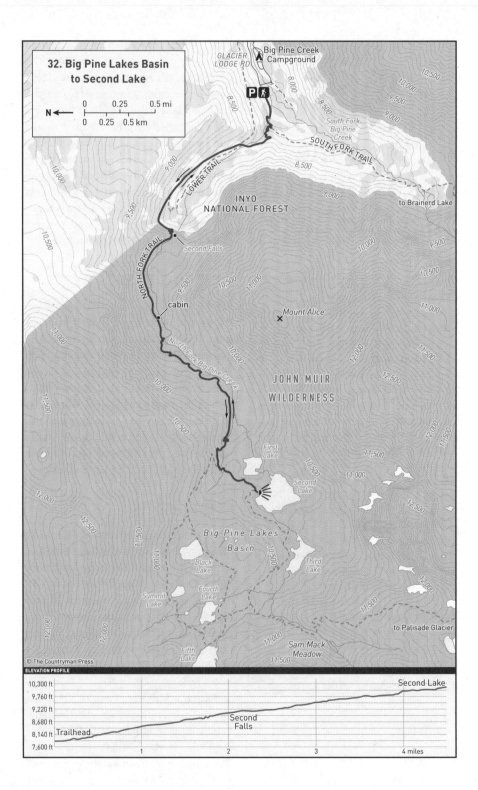

32. Big Pine Lakes Basin to Second Lake

N ←

| 0 | 0.25 | 0.5 mi |
| 0 | 0.25 | 0.5 km |

GLACIER LODGE RD

Big Pine Creek Campground

P 🚶

South Fork Big Pine Creek

SOUTH FORK TRAIL

to Brainerd Lake

LOWER TRAIL

INYO NATIONAL FOREST

NORTH FORK TRAIL

Second Falls

cabin

North Fork Big Pine Creek

Mount Alice ×

JOHN MUIR WILDERNESS

First Lake

Second Lake

Big Pine Lakes Basin

Black Lake

Third Lake

Summit Lake

Fourth Lake

to Palisade Glacier

Fifth Lake

Sam Mack Meadow

© The Countryman Press

ELEVATION PROFILE

10,300 ft	Second Lake
9,760 ft	
9,220 ft	
8,680 ft	Second Falls
8,140 ft	Trailhead
7,600 ft	

1   2   3   4 miles

beneath the Middle Palisade Group, a collection of peaks that attract technical climbers.

Beyond the switchbacks, rejoin the old road and turn right. Shortly thereafter, recross the creek on another sturdy footbridge. From here you can follow the Lower Trail (the old road) upstream along the creek or walk across the road and head briefly uphill to connect with the Upper Trail, which begins at the backpacker parking area. Either way is fine; however, the Lower Trail is slightly longer. We choose the shorter path and head uphill. After a steep but brief climb, join the Upper Trail by veering left. The sandy trail steadily ascends the northeastern canyon wall. Watch for mountain pennyroyal, sulphurflower, and the occasional cactus interspersed among the sagebrush and scrub. By getting an early start, you can walk in the shade cast by the canyon wall before the sun gets high enough to drench it with sunlight.

Continue to a four-way intersection with Baker Trail (bending sharply right) and the Lower Trail (joining us on the left). Your current goal is the top of Second Falls, which is visible in the distance. Mount a series of rocky switchbacks and pass the John Muir Wilderness boundary sign near the top of the falls at 1.8 miles. Climb a rock staircase adjacent the noisy creek before leaving the scattered shade of Jeffrey and lodgepole pines to cross a field of bushy manzanita.

Enter a peaceful meadow filled with ranger's buttons, Sierra lily, Indian paintbrush, and monkshood and arrive at the Big Pine Creek Wilderness Ranger Camp cabin at 2.6 miles. The rustic stone domicile was originally built in the 1920s by silent film star Lon Chaney, best known for his roles as

creepy, deformed monsters like Quasimodo and the Phantom of the Opera.

The trail continues its ascent, alternating between dry segments and wildflower-filled meadows. Round a bend at 3.3 miles and behold Temple Crag (12,975 feet). Don't be surprised to encounter helmet- and rope-toting climbers along the trail, many of whom plan on scaling this sheer rock face (I think I'll just watch). Farther along the trail, the view expands down canyon to include Mount Sill (14,163 feet), Thunderbolt Peak (14,003 feet), Mount Winchell (13,893 feet), and Mount Agassiz (13,893 feet).

The trail levels somewhat until you step across the willow-lined outlet for Black Lake and ascend a series of stone steps and ensuing switchbacks. Later, recross the stream, wider now, with the aid of steppingstones. At 4.1 miles, reach the Black Lake Trail junction. Backpackers or strong hikers prepared for a long day can veer right and complete a loop that travels past Black, Fourth, Third, Second, and First Lakes, ultimately returning to this junction (this semiloop is 13 miles round trip from the trailhead).

Take the left fork and continue toward the unimaginatively named Lakes First through Seventh, crossing Black Lake's outlet for the final time. Glimpse First Lake's stunning aquamarine water through the trees and pass an excellent campsite in a small depression beneath the trail. This is an excellent base camp for backpackers planning to further explore Big Pine Canyon.

First through Third Lakes are fed by streams formed by the melting Palisade Glacier. Their characteristic turquoise color comes from light being dispersed by finely ground glacial silt suspended in the water. The Palisade Glacier holds

TEMPLE CRAG AND THE MILKY WATERS OF SECOND LAKE

the distinction of being the largest glacier in the Sierra and the southernmost in the United States.

Continue 0.25 mile farther to Second Lake. Look for a small footpath between some boulders leading to a rocky perch high above the lake. Second Lake is definitely the most scenic of the trio, and from the overlook you will understand why. The lake sits in a deep granite bowl, Temple Crag's steeples towering above the southern shore. To the west, Third Lake's milky water tumbles through a rocky cleft, forming a lovely cascade.

Take time to explore the shore as far as you wish, keeping in mind that you eventually have to return to your starting point. If time allows, venture 0.7 mile farther to Third Lake. Being first in line for the glacier's runoff, it has the milkiest appearance.

33

Lone Pine Lake

TYPE: Day hike

SEASON: June through October

TOTAL DISTANCE: 5.5 miles round trip

RATING: Moderate to strenuous

ELEVATION: 8,296 feet; +1,852 feet/-195 feet

LOCATION: Inyo National Forest, John Muir Wilderness

MAPS: USGS Mount Langley, Mount Whitney; USFS John Muir Wilderness

FEES AND PERMITS: A permit is not required for this day hike. Day hikers going beyond Lone Pine Lake and overnight users entering the Mount Whitney Zone must obtain a permit (fee) from Inyo National Forest. There are strict quotas and a specific application process for this trailhead.

CONTACT: Inyo National Forest, Mount Whitney Ranger District (760-876-6200 general information, 760-873-2483 wilderness permits; www.fs.usda.gov/inyo).

At 14,496 feet, Mount Whitney is the highest mountain in the continental United States. As you can imagine, with that lofty distinction, the trail to its summit is one of the most heavily traveled in all of the Sierra Nevada—so much so that the United States Forest Service has instituted a strict quota system and random lottery process as a means of divvying out permits. Day hikers can experience a slice of this magnificent trail without a permit by staying outside the Mount Whitney Zone and turning around at Lone Pine Lake, a photogenic destination and perfect picnic spot in its own right. Granted, solitude is not one of the virtues of this wildly popular trail, but the phenomenal scenery more than makes up for it.

GETTING THERE

From US 395 in Lone Pine, turn west onto Whitney Portal Road and drive 13 miles to road's end. The trailhead is located on the north side of the roadway near the store. Park in the lot closest to the trailhead if possible; if not, backtrack to one of the other lots farther down the road.

THE HIKE

In 1860, under the direction of Josiah Dwight Whitney, the California Geological Survey was created. Its establishment directly correlated to California's exploding population due to the Gold Rush and the need for reliable maps and geologic data. In 1864, a small survey team, including Clarence King, one of the High Sierras' most famous explorers, entered the region and discovered a cluster of high peaks, naming the tallest in honor of Whitney.

King attempted to climb Mount Whitney twice during their trip but was

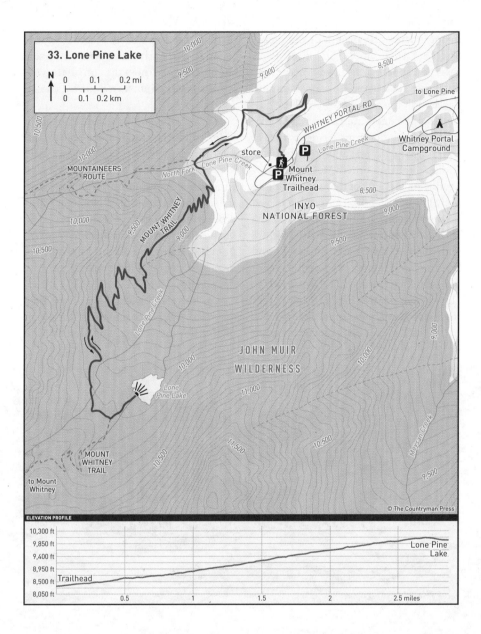

33. Lone Pine Lake

N

| 0 | 0.1 | 0.2 mi |
| 0 | 0.1 | 0.2 km |

to Lone Pine

WHITNEY PORTAL RD

Lone Pine Creek

Whitney Portal
Campground

store

Mount
Whitney
Trailhead

INYO
NATIONAL FOREST

MOUNTAINEERS
ROUTE

North Fork   Lone Pine Creek

MOUNT WHITNEY TRAIL

Lone Pine Creek

JOHN MUIR
WILDERNESS

Lone
Pine Lake

Mexican Creek

MOUNT
WHITNEY
TRAIL

to Mount
Whitney

© The Countryman Press

ELEVATION PROFILE

10,300 ft
9,850 ft
9,400 ft
8,950 ft
8,500 ft
8,050 ft

Trailhead

Lone Pine
Lake

0.5   1   1.5   2   2.5 miles

unsuccessful. He later returned, in 1871, to summit what he believed to be Mount Whitney, but which was in actuality Mount Langley farther south. By the time the error was discovered two years later, the first ascent had already been made in 1873 by three local fishermen. King eventually made the fourth ascent.

John Muir, who made his first ascent in 1873 as well, was the first person to climb Mount Whitney from the east via what is today known as the Mountaineers Route.

None of these early explorers could have possibly imagined that 136 years later this mountain would attract peak baggers from all corners of the globe, and that they would be required to reserve a spot months in advance for the chance to set foot on its craggy summit.

Though the hike described here culminates at Lone Pine Lake, a good distance from the summit, we get a taste of the many sights and sounds the trail has to offer. From the signed Mount Whitney Trailhead, just east of the store, immediately begin ascending through a mixed conifer forest. The trail initially heads in a northeastward direction before sharply bending back on itself and heading west along the northern canyon wall. The forest thins, giving way to slopes covered in chinquapin, mountain mahogany, and manzanita. This section of trail can be especially hot on summer afternoons, so an early start is recommended. An early start also gives you the chance to witness the sun fill the valley with warm light as it makes its daily round.

At 0.5 mile, enter a lush thicket of alder and ferns and boulder-hop across an unnamed creek. Off to your left, locked in its rocky confines, spy Lone Pine Creek putting on a display as it crashes down the valley. Not long after, cross wider North Fork Lone Pine Creek via a combination of rocks and logs. At 0.9 mile, enter the John Muir Wilderness and begin switchbacking up, and up, and up.

Looking eastward, you have fine views of the Alabama Hills, the floor of the Owens Valley, and the distant

MOUNT WHITNEY AS VIEWED FROM TRAIL CAMP   CRYSTAL WEST

White Mountains, all neatly framed by Whitney Portal Canyon's sheer granite walls. Cross willow-choked Lone Pine Creek at 2.5 miles by traversing a series of wooden logs expertly assembled to avoid soggy toes. Come to the junction with a spur trail descending left to Lone Pine Lake a short distance farther.

From the shore, granite-hemmed Lone Pine Lake appears to be dangling at the edge of the world—a natural infinity pool of sorts. Walk around its edge to the natural dam that confines it and peer up at Lone Pine Peak towering to the south while Thor Peak and Wotans Throne loom to the north. In the distance, with Mount Whitney just out of sight, serrated peaks invite us farther, but alas, without a permit we must return to the trailhead.

Permit-carrying travelers can continue along the main trail to Mirror Lake, Trail Camp, and finally the apex of Mount Whitney. If you've set your sights on the summit, do your research on the application process and know the rules. The hike to the top is 11 miles one way and gains upwards of 3,700 feet from its starting point at Whitney Portal. This is a nontechnical climb, and any person in good physical condition can complete the hike. There are super-hikers who ascend in one day, starting in the wee hours of the morning by flashlight and hoofing it all day, but I don't recommend it. For the best possible experience and to better your chances of reaching the

MOUNT WHITNEY TRAILHEAD   CRYSTAL WEST

summit, I suggest acclimating at Whitney Portal for one night before commencing, and then taking two to three days to summit and descend (day one, overnight at Trail Camp; day two, climb to summit and return to Trail Camp; day three, descend to Whitney Portal).

V.

YOSEMITE NATIONAL PARK AREA

Wapama Falls

TYPE: Day hike

SEASON: April through October

TOTAL DISTANCE: 5 miles round trip

RATING: Easy

ELEVATION: 3,805 feet; +581 feet/-515 feet

LOCATION: Yosemite National Park

MAPS: USGS 7.5' Lake Eleanor; Trails Illustrated Yosemite NW—Hetch Hetchy Reservoir No. 307

FEES AND PERMITS: A permit is not required for this day hike. Passenger vehicles entering the park are charged a $30 admission fee, which is good for seven days.

CONTACT: Yosemite National Park (209-372-0200; www.nps.gov/yose).

While much of the Sierra Nevada remains blanketed in snow, this low-elevation hike in Yosemite's peaceful northwest corner is a perfect primer for those itching to lace up their lug soles. The gentle trail to thunderous Wapama Falls follows the northern shore of 8-mile-long Hetch Hetchy Reservoir, passes Tueeulala Falls, and offers spectacular views of the valley along the way. The region is best experienced in the spring, when flows are abundant and temperatures are mild. Summer tends to be quite warm, often reaching 90–100 degrees Fahrenheit, and although autumnal temperatures are pleasant, the valley's waterfalls aren't nearly as impressive as they are in spring.

GETTING THERE

From the Big Oak Flat Entrance, exit the park and drive 1 mile west on CA 120, following signs for Hetch Hetchy Reservoir. Turn right on narrow Evergreen Road and travel 7.4 miles. (No vehicles over 25 feet long or 8 feet wide are allowed in the Hetch Hetchy area.) At Camp Mather, turn right on Hetch Hetchy Road and proceed 1 mile, where you will reenter the park at the Hetch Hetchy Entrance. Hetch Hetchy Reservoir and the day-use parking lot are 8 miles farther. The road to Hetch Hetchy is open to passenger vehicles during daylight hours only.

THE HIKE

John Muir (1838–1914), a man indelibly linked to Yosemite and the Sierra Nevada, was one of America's most influential naturalists and conservationists. Although Muir is most widely known for his involvement in the creation of Yosemite and other national parks,

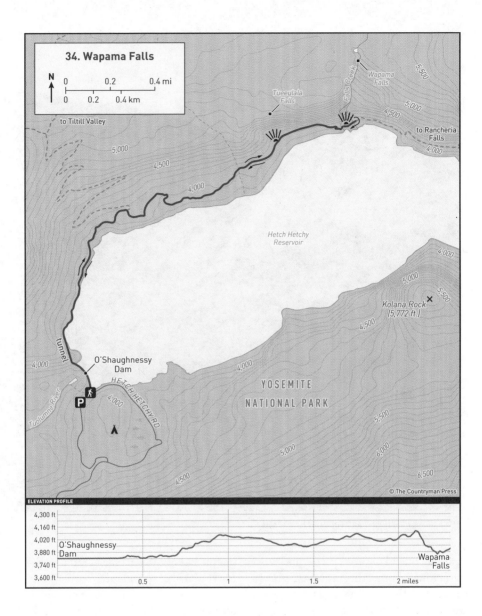

affording him the patriarchal moniker "father of our national parks," one of his most challenging battles involved the proposed damming of Hetch Hetchy Valley, said to rival Yosemite Valley itself, in an effort to supply water to the City of San Francisco.

In 1901, Muir led the Sierra Club, a group he formed in 1892, and a coalition of civic and conservation organizations in a campaign to protect the Hetch Hetchy Valley from being flooded. His lengthy and contentious battle unfortunately failed. In 1913, Congress passed the Raker Act, granting the City of San Francisco the right to dam the Hetch Hetchy Valley as a reservoir.

One of Muir's famous quotes underscores his passion for this beautiful valley: "Hetch Hetchy is a grand landscape

HETCH HETCHY RESERVOIR AND THE DISTANT WAPAMA FALLS

garden, one of nature's rarest and most precious mountain temples. As in Yosemite, the sublime rocks of its walls seem to glow with life . . . while birds, bees, and butterflies help the river and waterfalls to stir all the air into music. . . . These temple destroyers, devotees of ravaging commercialism, seem to have a perfect contempt for Nature, and, instead of lifting their eyes to the God of the mountains, lift them to the Almighty Dollar. . . . Dam Hetch Hetchy! As well dam for water-tanks the people's cathedrals and churches, for no holier temple has ever been consecrated by the heart of man."

Muir's battle wasn't all for naught. It ultimately resulted in a greater awareness and widespread conviction that our national parks are sacrosanct. Subsequent attempts to dam our national parks have been stopped because of Muir's earlier environmental campaign. Incidentally, the restoration of Hetch Hetchy still remains at the forefront of the Sierra Club's agenda.

From the parking area, walk across O'Shaughnessy Dam, named for the

an old roadbed, lies above and parallel to the northern shore of the reservoir. Lined with manzanita, gray pines, California black oak, and California bay trees, the trail is mostly exposed, although there are intermittent sections of shade. Carry plenty of water and sun protection, and be aware that poison oak and rattlesnakes exist in this area of the park.

At 1 mile, you reach a left-branching trail to Tiltill Valley. Bear right, following the sign to Wapama Falls. The trail narrows past the junction and gently rises and falls as you make your way through small meadows sprinkled with purple brodiaea, monkey flower, and farewell-to-spring. As butterflies flutter about and you make several seasonal stream crossings, watch for California newts making their slow spring migration to ponds for mating season. If you encounter them along the trail, as we did, be sure to give them plenty of space.

Leaving the meadows, come to a polished granite slab where the trail becomes vague for about 150 feet. Just keep heading east and easily pick up the trail. At 1.5 miles, arrive at the base of seasonal Tueeulala Falls. Though Tueeulala and Wapama Falls are both fed by Falls Creek, Wapama siphons a majority of the water, and the feeder creek to Tueeulala is usually bone dry by July. In spring, when flows are heavy, Tueeulala Falls plunge gracefully into the valley from 1,000 feet above.

Crossing a footbridge at the base of the falls, continue along the trail where views around Kolana Rock unfold and the boisterous spray of Wapama Falls rises into the air in the distance. The trail gets increasingly rocky as you approach, and at 2.5 miles you come to the first of a series of wooden footbridges that span the base of the falls.

chief engineer, pausing atop the 312-foot-high structure to take in the view of the Poopenaut Valley and Tuolumne River to the west. To the east lies Hetch Hetchy Reservoir. The sheer face of Kolana Rock, an active breeding area for peregrine falcons, stands sentinel along the southern shore. Along the north shore, Tueeulala and Wapama Falls tumble into the reservoir, and Hetch Hetchy Dome reposes in the distance.

Once across the dam, walk through a 500-foot-long granite tunnel to a trail sign at 0.3 mile. This section of trail,

WATER-LOGGED TRAIL SECTION

During peak spring flows, water can cover the bridges, making passage dangerous. For the most part, though, if you aren't afraid of getting wet, crossing is well worth the drenching.

Viewing the falls from all angles as the frothy water of Falls Creek spills over the cliff edge, crashing down on the boulder-strewn landscape below, and experiencing the power of this vigorous cataract is refreshing and exhilarating. If you want to cross, but can do without the deluge, pack along a poncho and some water sandals. When you've had your fill, return via the same trail.

Those looking for a more challenging hike can continue past Wapama Falls to Rancheria Falls (13 miles round trip).

35

Panorama Trail

TYPE: Day hike

SEASON: Late May to October

TOTAL DISTANCE: 8.2 miles one way

RATING: Moderate to strenuous

ELEVATION: 7,135 feet; +900 feet/-4,000 feet

LOCATION: Yosemite National Park

MAPS: USGS 7.5' Half Dome; Trails Illustrated Yosemite SW—Yosemite Valley & Wawona No. 306

FEES AND PERMITS: A permit is not required for this day hike. Passenger vehicles entering the park are charged a $30 admission fee, which is good for seven days. One-way bus tickets from Yosemite Valley Lodge to Glacier Point cost $27 for adults, $17 for children ages 5-12, and nothing for children under 5.

CONTACT: Yosemite National Park (209-372-0200 general information; 888-413-8869 bus reservations; www.nps.gov/yose).

Panorama Trail isn't named Panorama Trail for nothing. From your starting point perch atop Glacier Point, the Yosemite Valley unfolds before you, a life size relief map at your feet. Glacier Point is one of the most easily accessed vantage points in the entire Sierra Nevada, as evidenced by the hordes of summertime visitors filling the parking lot. Leave the masses behind and descend 3,100 vertical feet along a well-graded, well-marked trail, where the jaw-dropping views only get better as each bend in the trail offers a new perspective on the glacially carved grandeur below. Though the hike is mostly downhill, there is a moderate climb after crossing Illilouette Creek before the trail continues its descent to Happy Isles.

GETTING THERE

This point-to-point hike requires a little coordination. Arrange to have someone drop you off at Glacier Point and meet you in the Valley or, even better, purchase a one-way bus ticket to Glacier Point through the Yosemite tour desk. Reservations are required, and you should make them far in advance, as seating is limited. The bus leaves Yosemite Valley Lodge daily and takes a little over an hour to get to Glacier Point. I recommend leaving early so you have all day to ooh and aah as you make your way into the Valley. At the end of the hike, ride the free Yosemite Valley shuttle back to your vehicle. If you are driving, from Chinquapin (10 miles south of Yosemite Village on CA 41) follow the signs to Glacier Point. Drive 16 miles along Glacier Point Road (open seasonally) to its terminus, where you will find restrooms, water, and a gift shop.

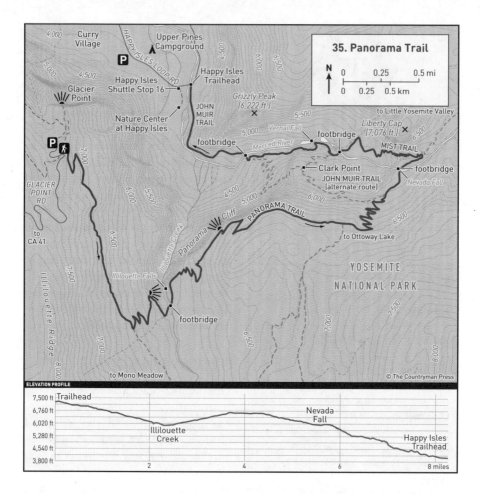

ELEVATION PROFILE

THE HIKE

Glacier Point was once the stage for the after-dark "firefall" spectacle—a bonfire of red fir bark shoved over the cliff's edge. To spectators gathered below, the veil of burning embers appeared as a flaming waterfall plunging into Yosemite Valley. The practice was halted in 1968 when the National Park Service began deemphasizing manmade attractions within the park. Who needs manmade attractions when you're in Yosemite?

Once atop Glacier Point, take the short walk to the viewpoint before commencing this hike. The commanding view of the Valley floor and the High Sierra landscape in the distance won't soon be forgotten.

The signed trailhead is located at the eastern end of the Glacier Point parking area near the amphitheater. Mere seconds after stepping onto the trail, reach a junction with the Pohono Trail. Stay left and follow the sign to Illilouette Falls.

The exposed trail gently switchbacks downhill through the open, fire-scarred landscape where manzanita and deerweed proliferate. These low-lying shrubs thrive after fire has devastated an area, quickly covering exposed slopes and reducing erosion.

As you descend through sparse stands of mixed pines and charred stumps, you get a fantastic view of Liberty Cap standing sentinel over Nevada and Vernal Falls, while Half Dome looms defiantly, back turned on the whole scene.

Look closely and you can spot the trail zigzagging below along Panorama Cliff. Come to a trail fork at 1.5 miles leading to Mono Meadow. Stay left and continue toward Illilouette Falls, which comes into view not long thereafter. A short spur trail leads to an overlook directly across from the falls that isn't for the faint of heart. Carefully maneuver to the edge for a view of the entire falls as they spill 370 feet from a narrow opening in the canyon wall. Continue

along the trail to the bank of Illilouette Creek, a perfect spot to take a break before heading uphill for the first time.

At 2.2 miles, cross the Illilouette Creek footbridge just upstream from the falls and begin ascending 765 feet through a forest of red fir, lodgepole, and Jeffrey pine. After a short distance, Upper Yosemite Falls and later Lower Yosemite Falls come into view across the Valley. Yosemite Creek plunges over the edge of what geographers call a hanging valley to create these impressive falls. While the huge mass of ice that sculpted the main Yosemite Valley was at work, smaller glaciers filled the Valley's feeder streams and tributaries. These smaller glaciers weren't able to carve as deeply as the large Valley glacier, so when the ice finally retreated, tributary valleys were left "hanging" precariously above

TRAILHEAD SIGN POINTING THE WAY

YOSEMITE VALLEY AS VIEWED FROM GLACIER POINT

the Valley floor. For those visual learners out there (myself included) this vantage suddenly makes it all crystal clear.

Come to a junction at 4.1 miles leading to Ottoway Lake, among other backcountry destinations. Stay straight on the main trail to Yosemite Valley where the downhill begins in earnest again. In the spring, as you pass through the shaded boulder-strewn landscape, watch for the unmistakable red snow plant emerging from the duff-covered forest floor, its fiery leaves a stark contrast to the earth tones surrounding you.

At 5.1 miles, the Panorama Trail intersects the John Muir Trail. From here you can either turn left (west) and proceed 2.3 miles to the base of Vernal Falls along the John Muir Trail, or turn right (east) and proceed 0.2 mile to the top of Nevada Falls and eventually descend via Mist Trail. Even if your preference is to take the John Muir Trail, continuing on to Nevada Falls is definitely worth the extra mileage. The trail opens onto a broad flat expanse of granite atop the falls that funnels the swift Merced River and sends it plummeting 594 feet into

head down the longer but less steep John Muir Trail, or cross the footbridge spanning the Merced River and continue 0.2 mile to the Mist Trail junction. There are pit toilets here, but expect a line. Turn left at the junction to head down extremely popular Mist Trail. Continuing straight takes you to Little Yosemite Valley.

Carefully make your way down the steep granite stairway alongside thundering Nevada Falls, being mindful of ascending hikers. Follow the trail along the frothy Merced River until you reach the edge of Nevada Falls' downstream neighbor—317-foot Vernal Falls. At this point, I recommend slipping into rain gear before embarking down the next 0.5 mile of soggy trail, especially during spring and early summer, when billowing spray and mist can be a real drencher. Follow the procession of people through a rock opening and down a wet granite staircase to the western junction with the John Muir Trail.

If your knees and ankles are too fatigued, avoid Mist Trail and instead take the John Muir Trail. It affords outstanding views of Nevada Falls just past the Panorama Trail junction, but you won't see Vernal Falls until you reach the footbridge at the base of the falls 2.3 miles beyond. A convenient 0.4-mile cutoff trail at Clark Point leads to just above Vernal Falls, providing a connection between the John Muir and Mist Trails and allowing you to experience both trails if you choose.

At 7.2 miles (via Mist Trail), cross the Merced River again via a footbridge and enjoy the paved walkway back to the Happy Isles trailhead, where you can catch the free Yosemite Valley shuttle back to your vehicle.

the abyss. It's a perfect spot to rest your legs and have a snack, but keep a vigilant eye for fearless critters looking for an easy meal.

Don't expect solitude, as this is a popular rest stop for hikers making the trek from the Valley to the top of Nevada Falls and points beyond. Expect a significant amount of company from here on out.

After absorbing the sights and sounds, you can either turn back and

36

Half Dome

TYPE: Day hike or overnight

SEASON: The cables are usually up by mid-June and removed in October

TOTAL DISTANCE: 14 miles round trip via Mist Trail; 16.4 miles round trip via John Muir Trail

RATING: Very strenuous

ELEVATION: 4,053 feet; +4,953 feet/-216 feet

LOCATION: Yosemite National Park

MAPS: USGS 7.5' Half Dome; Trails Illustrated Yosemite SW—Yosemite Valley & Wawona No. 306

FEES AND PERMITS: A permit (fee) is required to day hike to the top of Half Dome when the cables are up. A limited number of permits are available each day via a pre-season lottery or daily lottery. To apply for a permit, visit www.recreation.gov or call 877-444-6777. Overnight trips into the Yosemite backcountry require a wilderness permit (fee). A trailhead quota system is in effect, so if you plan on camping, reserve as early as possible. Space is limited and disappears quickly. Passenger vehicles entering the park are charged a $30 admission fee, which is good for seven days.

CONTACT: Yosemite National Park (209-372-0200 general information; 209-372-0740 wilderness permits; www.nps.gov/yose).

If Yosemite has an icon, Half Dome is it. Climbing to the top of this monolith is an amazing experience, but it's not for everyone. It's a grueling journey, and you should expect to share the trail with hordes of other hikers trudging to the summit alongside you. The final push to the top is especially demanding. If any part of two metal cables, 400 feet of sheer rock face, and no safety net sounds overly unnerving, then sit this one out. Otherwise, be prepared to experience some of the most resplendent scenery Yosemite Valley has to offer and add an impressive peak to your bag. A few must-haves for this trip: ample water (or a water filter), a poncho, a pair of work gloves, and a good attitude.

GETTING THERE

From the Arch Rock Entrance Station on CA 140, drive 12 miles east into Yosemite Valley. Just past Curry Village, turn right into the backpacker parking area. From here, walk along a paved pathway 0.6 mile farther east to the Happy Isles Trailhead. Alternatively, board the free Yosemite Valley Shuttle from any location in the park and get off at Happy Isles (Stop #16).

THE HIKE

The overwhelming majority of permit-wielding hikers tackle the summit of Half Dome as a day hike, but I think an overnight is the way to go. You can take your time and savor every step of this epic journey. A good option is to camp at Little Yosemite Valley (3.2 miles from the summit), but an even better one is to set up camp on the forested saddle just below Half Dome's northeast shoulder (a little less than a mile from the summit). This does mean you'll have

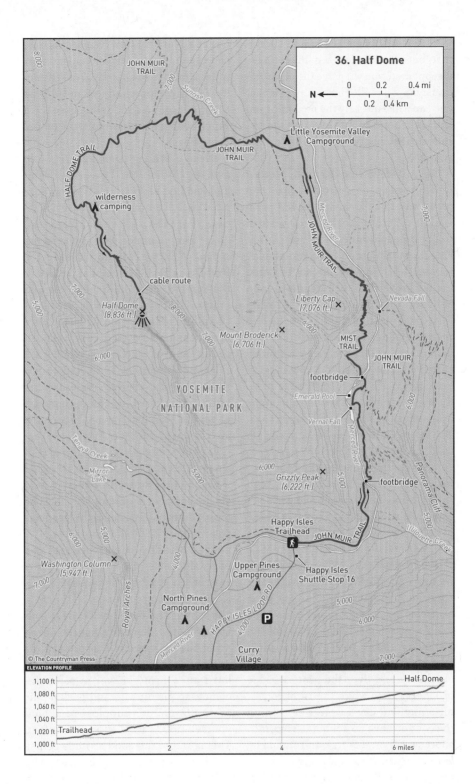

36. Half Dome

N ◄—

| 0 | 0.2 | 0.4 mi |
| 0 | 0.2 | 0.4 km |

8,000

JOHN MUIR TRAIL

7,000

Sunrise Creek

Little Yosemite Valley Campground

HALF DOME TRAIL

JOHN MUIR TRAIL

wilderness camping

JOHN MUIR TRAIL

Merced River

7,000

cable route

Liberty Cap (7,076 ft.) ×

Nevada Fall

Half Dome (8,836 ft.) ×

5,000

7,000

8,000

6,000

MIST TRAIL

7,000

Mount Broderick (6,706 ft.) ×

JOHN MUIR TRAIL

6,000

footbridge

Emerald Pool

6,000

YOSEMITE NATIONAL PARK

Vernal Fall

Merced River

Tenaya Creek

Mirror Lake

5,000

6,000

Grizzly Peak (6,222 ft.) ×

5,000

footbridge

Panorama Cliff

5,000

Happy Isles Trailhead

JOHN MUIR TRAIL

Illilouette Creek

Washington Column (5,947 ft.) ×

7,000

Royal Arches

4,000

Upper Pines Campground

Happy Isles Shuttle Stop 16

North Pines Campground

HAPPY ISLES LOOP RD.

5,000

6,000

P

Merced River

Curry Village

7,000

© The Countryman Press

ELEVATION PROFILE

1,100 ft					Half Dome
1,080 ft					
1,060 ft					
1,040 ft					
1,020 ft	Trailhead				
1,000 ft		2	4		6 miles

to schlep your backpack that much farther, but once the last day hikers have disappeared, you will have the place gloriously to yourself. The best part is that you can wake up early the next morning and make the final push to the summit, sans crowd, just in time to watch the sunrise.

Begin by following the rowdy Merced River upstream on a dirt path that soon gives way to a pleasantly paved pathway. At 0.8 mile, cross a sturdy wooden footbridge spanning the river. Vernal Falls is putting on a fantastic display to your left. Now on the south bank, the trail reverts to dirt. Bear left, soon reaching the John Muir Trail (JMT)–Mist Trail junction. Both paths lead to the top of Nevada Falls, the difference being that the JMT ascends via a series of well-engineered switchbacks, making it longer, while the Mist Trail is more direct, climbing a massive rock staircase alongside Vernal and Nevada Falls. The staircase is steep, wet, and slick (a rain poncho will keep you from getting completely drenched by the billowing mist). The choice is yours. Since both trails are incredibly scenic and you don't want to miss either one, I advise ascending Mist Trail while your legs and mind are fresh and descending via the JMT.

From where the JMT and Mist Trail reunite (2.4 miles from the trailhead), continue following the Merced River upstream on the wide, sandy trail. Come to a Y-junction just before Little Yosemite Valley. Either path is fine as they eventually rejoin, however, the left fork climbs up and over the eastern ridge of Liberty Cap, while the right fork is blissfully flat. Level trail is something that, as you have no doubt realized, is in short supply on this trek and should be savored. Bearing right also gives you the chance to replenish your water supply from the Merced River, your last reliable source, and to use the convenient solar toilet near the overused Little Yosemite Valley campground (3.8 miles from the trailhead). As with all backcountry water sources, be sure to treat before drinking.

Head north out of the campground and rejoin the JMT by veering right and heading steeply uphill along Sunrise Creek. Continue 1.2 miles to a junction, where the JMT veers right (east) on its long-distance trek to the top of Mount Whitney. You go left onto the Half Dome Trail for the final 2 miles to the summit. The trail bends west and crests a saddle along the northeast shoulder of Half Dome. Though there is no designated campground, you can set up camp as long as you follow park rules and regulations. Dispersed wilderness camping is allowed 2 miles beyond Little Yosemite Valley campground (at or beyond Moraine Dome or beyond the Half Dome/John Muir Trail junction). Camping is not permitted on top of Half Dome. This is a good time to note that if thunderstorms are threatening, you should scrap your summit attempt. The top of this exposed dome is the last place you want to be if lightning strikes.

With blue skies overhead, zigzag up a rocky slope. The gradient progressively steepens as you creep higher, the incredible views taking your mind off the arduous climb. The switchbacks soon end and you drop down to the base of the infamous cable route. There is usually a pile of gloves at the base of the cables, but I am a firm believer in self-sufficiency, so play it safe and pack a pair of your own. Don your gloves and haul yourself up the final 400 vertical feet. This is where the good attitude comes in. The slow procession of people can be frustrating, and passing isn't exactly an

POLISHED BACKSIDE OF HALF DOME AND PRECIPITOUS CABLE ROUTE TO THE SUMMIT

option. Take your time and be patient—you will get there. Temper the off-the-charts crowd factor by overnighting as I recommended earlier.

From the broad summit of Half Dome (8,836 feet), the views are phenomenal. Looking west, several of Yosemite Valley's notable features are on display: Glacier Point, the Merced River, and El Capitan. Behind you, Quarter Domes, Clouds Rest, and the distant Cathedral Range fill the horizon, creating a sublime scene. This sanctuary of forested valleys, granite domes, and plummeting waterfalls seems to radiate from this single point, making you feel as though you are at the center of something magical—well, you are!

When ready, carefully descend the cables and retrace your steps. When you make it back to the JMT–Mist Trail junction, stay straight on the JMT and continue toward Nevada Falls. The top of the falls is a fantastic spot to take a break. Scout out a nice boulder and drop your pack, but watch out for fearless varmints ready to abscond with your grub. Bid farewell to the falls and continue your descent, passing a junction with the Panorama Trail (left) that heads to Glacier Point and later a junction at Clark Point (right) that cuts across to Mist Trail. Follow the endless series of switchbacks downhill, eventually meeting up again with the paved walkway you started on.

37

Clouds Rest

TYPE: Day hike

SEASON: June to October

TOTAL DISTANCE: 14.4 miles round trip

RATING: Strenuous

ELEVATION: 8,170 feet; +2,355 feet/-696 feet

LOCATION: Yosemite National Park

MAPS: USGS 7.5' Tenaya Lake; Trails Illustrated Yosemite National Park No. 206

FEES AND PERMITS: A permit is not required for this day hike. Passenger vehicles entering the park are charged a $30 admission fee, which is good for seven days.

CONTACT: Yosemite National Park (209-372-0200; www.nps.gov/yose).

If you've got a day at your disposal, this demanding trek to Clouds Rest (9,926 feet) is definitely one to add to your list. As its lofty name implies, Clouds Rest is where the clouds go to rest—well, not really, but it sure feels that way from atop this precipitous pinnacle, where 360-degree views are yours for the taking. Because Clouds Rest lacks the notoriety of Half Dome (although I'm not sure why), you won't have to do as much elbowing along the way. Acrophobes may want to sit this one out, as the final stretch to the summit is a little precarious. Get an early start and don't attempt the climb if a storm is threatening. Ambitious hikers might even consider an early morning moonlight hike to reach the top before dawn—watching the sun's rays illuminate the valley from this airy summit is a magical experience.

GETTING THERE

From the Tioga Pass Entrance Station along CA 120, drive 15.6 miles west to the Sunrise Lakes Trailhead (Stop #10). There is limited parking in the lot, so make use of the wide roadside shoulder.

THE HIKE

Two major trails emanate from this trailhead, so don't get confused. You want to follow the signs toward Sunrise High Sierra Camp (HSC), which means you start out on a paved pathway that meanders through a thick forest of lodgepole pines on its way toward Tenaya Creek. Just when you're wishfully envisioning a paved walkway all the way to the top, you trade the pavement for dirt and make a long but simple boulder hop across shallow Tenaya Creek (a tricky crossing during times of high water).

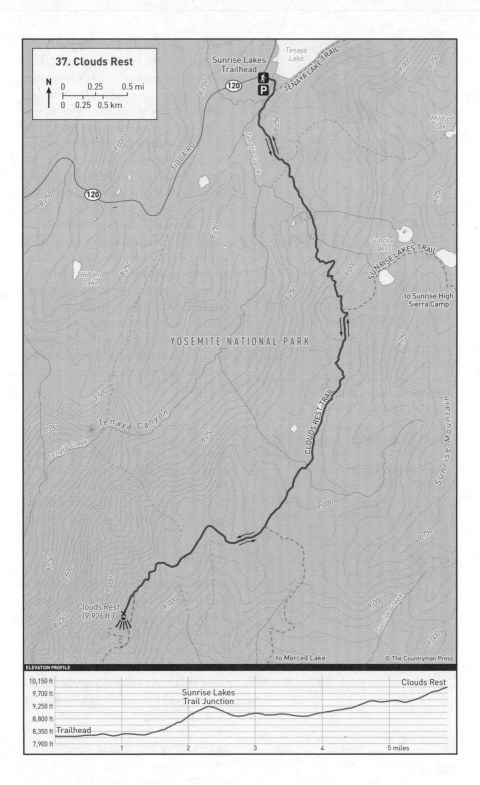

37. Clouds Rest

N

| 0 | 0.25 | 0.5 mi |
| 0 | 0.25 | 0.5 km |

Sunrise Lakes
Trailhead

Tenaya
Lake

120

TENAYA LAKE TRAIL

9,000

9,750

Mildred
Lake

8,250

TIOGA RD

Tenaya Creek

120

8,250

8,250

Hidden
Lake

8,250

Sunrise
Lakes

SUNRISE LAKES TRAIL

9,000

9,750

to Sunrise High
Sierra Camp

YOSEMITE NATIONAL PARK

8,250

7,500

CLOUDS REST TRAIL

9,750

Tenaya Canyon

6,750

8,250

Sunrise Mountain

Tenaya Creek

9,000

9,000

9,750

6,750

7,500

9,000

9,000

Sunrise Creek

9,000

Clouds Rest
(9,926 ft.)

8,250

9,000

to Merced Lake

© The Countryman Press

ELEVATION PROFILE

10,150 ft						Clouds Rest
9,700 ft		Sunrise Lakes				
9,250 ft		Trail Junction				
8,800 ft						
8,350 ft	Trailhead					
7,900 ft						

1   2   3   4   5 miles

Veer right at a junction on the opposite bank. The trail is pleasantly flat for the first mile and a half as you stroll alongside the peaceful creek and past flowering meadows filled with California corn lily, arrowleaf butterweed, and alpine lily. The trail descends slightly to cross Mildred Lake's outlet creek, beyond which you ascend a short hill. Navigate a dry cobble-strewn creekbed as red firs and mountain hemlocks join the forest mix and mountain spirea's hot pink flower clusters decorate the trail.

The trail gradient increases and you head up a rocky slope of seemingly unending switchbacks that rise 1,000 vertical feet. Climbing higher, enjoy views of the pine-scattered granite landscape punctuated by dramatic Mount Hoffman and Tuolumne Peak to the north.

Just when you thought you should have taken the elevator instead of the stairs, reach the ridgetop at 2.5 miles and a trail leading left toward Sunrise High Sierra Camp. Stay straight and unfortunately zigzag steeply down the drier, south-facing slope, forfeiting some of the precious elevation you just fought so valiantly for.

Lose the view toward the bottom where the trail levels and you pass through a verdant meadow, stepping over a couple of small streamlets as you go. Climb above the meadow and across a jumbled pile of boulders at the base of Sunrise Mountain. Sun-seeking aspens poke through the rocky crevices, coloring the chunks of pale granite with clumps of green. Reenter the forest and entertain Yosemite's characteristic boulder-strewn landscape before coming to a verdant pocket and the shore of a small unnamed lake.

The now sandy trail wanders through a densely forested section before intersecting a small creek, which you easily cross. Begin a mild ascent and reach a trail fork at 4.7 miles heading toward Merced Lake. Stay straight and continue the steady uphill trudge. Off to your left, catch glimpses of Bunnell Point, Cascade Cliffs, and Mount Starr King between gaps in the trees.

Cresting the climb, enjoy relatively level walking as you traverse a broad ridgeline before dipping down along its right shoulder to a low saddle at the base of Clouds Rest. From here the grade significantly increases as you close in on your goal. Steep switchbacks carry you uphill, affording spectacular views back toward Tenaya Lake sitting serenely in a bowl of granite. As you approach the summit, the rocks begin to change and appear layered like a stack of pancakes.

Clouds Rest is a perfect example of an arête, a thin, almost knifelike ridge of rock typically formed when two glaciers erode parallel U-shaped valleys. The word arête is actually French for edge.

The trail isn't particularly clear, but the goal is obvious. If there is any doubt, a sign identifying the Clouds Rest Foot Trail points you in the right direction. Carefully make your way up and along a narrow spine of disjointed rocks. This final push to the summit can be unnerving due to the steep drop-offs on either side of the ridge. Just take it slow and you'll reach the broad summit in no time, where you can savor the well-earned, 360-degree panorama.

Lording some 5,900 feet over Yosemite Valley, suspended between two granite chasms, the view from Clouds Rest is nothing short of amazing. Yosemite Valley's forested floor and the hunched backside of Half Dome dominate your southern vista. Sharp eyes will spot

STEADY CLIMB TO CLOUDS REST

the famous cable trail draped along its shoulder. Peer down Merced and Tenaya Canyons and behold the fantastic landscape of domes, spires, and sheer granite faces that undulate into the limitless horizon.

Perhaps John Muir was perched atop Clouds Rest when he wrote: "Glaciers, back in their cold solitudes, work apart from men, exerting their tremendous energies in silence and darkness. Outspread, spirit-like, they brood above the predestined landscapes, work on unwearied through immeasurable ages, until, in the fullness of time, the mountains and valleys are brought forth, channels furrowed for the rivers, basins made for the lakes and meadows, and long, deep arms of the sea, soils spread for the forests and the fields—then they shrink and vanish like summer clouds."

When you're ready, silent reverie complete, begin the long descent back to the trailhead.

TRAIL ALONG NARROW ARÊTE NEAR THE SUMMIT OF CLOUDS REST

38

Cathedral Lakes

TYPE: Day hike

SEASON: Mid-June to early October

TOTAL DISTANCE: 6.5 miles round trip to Lower Cathedral Lake (add 1.2 miles round trip if you tack on a visit to Upper Cathedral Lake)

RATING: Moderate

ELEVATION: 8,577 feet; +1,010 feet/-294 feet

LOCATION: Yosemite National Park

MAPS: USGS 7.5' Tenaya Lake; Trails Illustrated Yosemite NE—Tuolumne Meadows & Hoover Wilderness No. 308

FEES AND PERMITS: A permit is not required for this day hike. Passenger vehicles entering the park are charged a $30 admission fee, which is good for seven days.

CONTACT: Yosemite National Park (209-372-0200; www.nps.gov/yose).

This hike along a portion of the John Muir Trail visits a pair of liquid gems tucked amid the Yosemite backcountry. Easy access and splendid scenery make this a popular destination and almost guarantee you won't be alone. Nonetheless, this pleasant day hike is a worthy venture. Though camping is allowed at the Cathedral Lakes, I recommend doing this as a day hike due to the sheer numbers of people passing through the area—not the most ideal overnight backcountry experience.

GETTING THERE

From the Tioga Pass Entrance Station along CA 120, drive 8.7 miles west to the Cathedral Lakes Trailhead located on the south side of the road. Park along the shoulder. The trailhead has sparkling clean portable toilets (at least when I visited). For a bit of luxury, however, stop off at the Tuolumne Meadows Visitor Center just minutes east, where you can peruse the exhibits and use a "real" bathroom before hitting the trail.

THE HIKE

The John Muir Trail (JMT) is one of the Sierra's eminent long-distance trails. It is 211 miles long and stretches from Yosemite Valley south to Mount Whitney (mostly in conjunction with the much longer Pacific Crest Trail). The segment this hike follows serves as the primary footpath between Tuolumne Meadows and Yosemite Valley.

A few steps from the trailhead, come to a four-way junction—left heads toward Tuolumne Meadows Campground, right toward Tenaya Lake. Stay straight and begin a steady uphill trudge through a thick forest of lodgepole pines and red

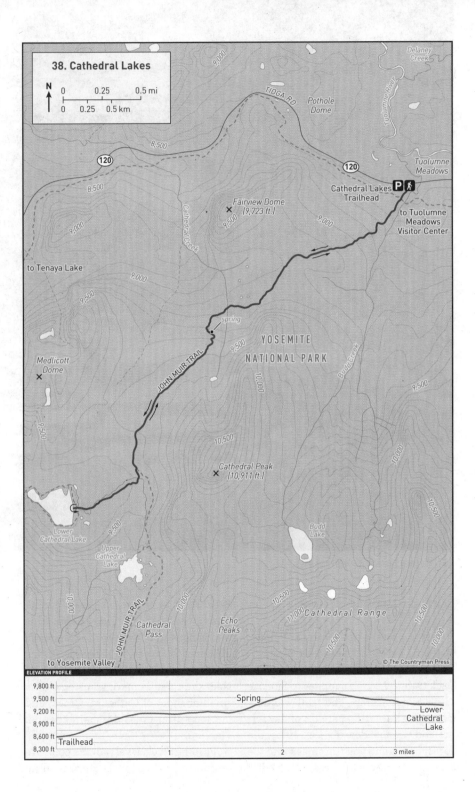

38. Cathedral Lakes

N

| 0 | 0.25 | 0.5 mi |
| 0 | 0.25 | 0.5 km |

Delaney
Creek

TIOGA RD

Pothole
Dome

Tuolumne River

120

Tuolumne
Meadows

Cathedral Lakes
Trailhead

P

to Tuolumne
Meadows
Visitor Center

8,500

120

8,500

Fairview Dome
(9,723 ft.)

9,000

Cathedral Creek

to Tenaya Lake

9,000

9,500

spring

YOSEMITE
NATIONAL PARK

9,500

Budd Creek

Medlicott
Dome

JOHN MUIR TRAIL

10,000

9,500

9,500

10,500

Cathedral Peak
(10,911 ft.)

Budd
Lake

10,000

10,500

Lower
Cathedral Lake

9,500

Upper
Cathedral
Lake

JOHN MUIR TRAIL

10,000

Cathedral
Pass

Echo
Peaks

11,000 Cathedral Range

10,500

10,500

10,000

to Yosemite Valley

© The Countryman Press

ELEVATION PROFILE

9,800 ft			
9,500 ft		Spring	
9,200 ft			Lower
8,900 ft			Cathedral
8,600 ft			Lake
8,300 ft	Trailhead		
	1	2	3 miles

PINE-STUDDED TRAIL TO CATHEDRAL LAKES

firs. Budd Creek tumbles to your left for a time.

After a rather uneventful 0.75 mile, the trail levels off and gets sandy in spots, most likely due to heavy usage by pack trains ferrying supplies to Sunrise High Sierra Camp. The trail wanders between alternating patches of dry forest and wet meadow. At 1.25 miles, the forest opens and you run smack into the domelike northern buttress of Cathedral Peak. For now, the peak's jagged pinnacles are concealed from view behind this imposing wall of granite. To the north, obscured by trees, is Fairview Dome. Nodding hemlocks join the forest mix. Near the 1.5-mile mark you step over a small offshoot of Cathedral Creek, and not long after cross the main channel via a log.

Past the creek, level walking comes to an abrupt end and you begin ascending

Lower Cathedral Lake. Medlicott Dome is visible to the right while Cathedral Peak, the pulpit in Nature's temple of granite, rises to the left.

Cathedral Peak is a geographic anomaly in this landscape of smooth, glacially rounded rock. It is believed that when glaciers covered the area, the peak's uppermost tip remained above—and therefore out of–the sculpting path of the moving mass of ice. The peak has many different personalities, depending on your perspective.

Reach the junction for Lower Cathedral Lake at 2.7 miles and veer right. The trail narrows and you step across the outlet creek flowing from Upper Cathedral Lake. Continue on a general descent along the creek's southern bank, admiring California corn lily and arrowleaf butterweed as you go. Follow a boulder-lined path over a rock slab and break out of the forest and into a broad meadow lushly carpeted with verdant grasses.

From here, a host of narrow footpaths cut across the meadow—none of them straight. When the flowing creek hits the flat meadow it splays in several directions, creating a web of snaking channels. Early in the season, this area can be quite muddy, so expect to get a little dirty and maybe even get your toes wet as you make a couple of giant leaps over the sinuous creek. Try your best to follow an existing footpath rather than blazing your own trail and carving the landscape up any further.

From the lengthy granite lip corralling Lower Cathedral Lake, the views are splendid. Southwest, prominent Tresidder Peak juts above the sparkling blue water. Across the lake, Mount Hoffman and Polly Dome appear above the tree tops, and behind you, the spiky spires

via a series of switchbacks. As the creek playfully splashes to the left, follow it upstream to its origin—an effluent spring that seeps from the ground. Looking north, views of Fairview Dome improve, its rounded cap framed by erect red firs. At 2.1 miles, the trail tops out onto a broad saddle (the high point of the journey). Enjoy level walking for a spell before leaving the dry ridgetop and descending toward the junction for

LOWER CATHEDRAL LAKE WITH TRESIDDER PEAK IN THE BACKGROUND

of Cathedral Peak pierce the sky. From the lake's outlet on the far western end (an approximately 0.5-mile walk), you can gaze across Tenaya Canyon, taking in the expanded southwestward vistas. Some will be quite content spending the day here admiring the scene and exploring the shoreline. Or, better yet, slip into the chilly water for a refreshing dip and then recline on a sun-warmed slab of granite—nothing could be more sublime.

If time allows, return to the junction with the JMT and turn right to proceed to Upper Cathedral Lake 0.6 mile farther. The trail loosely follows the lake's outlet stream. When you arrive at a small pond (no, this isn't the lake) turn right along a narrow unofficial path to a granite bench, beyond which lies smaller, but no less scenic, granite-hemmed Upper Cathedral Lake.

Spend as much time as you like before retracing your steps to the trailhead.

Waterwheel Falls

TYPE: Overnight

SEASON: June through October

TOTAL DISTANCE: 16.4 miles round trip

RATING: Moderate to strenuous

ELEVATION: 8,584 feet; +592 feet/-2,375 feet

LOCATION: Yosemite National Park

MAPS: USGS 7.5' Tioga Pass, Falls Ridge; Trails Illustrated Yosemite NE—Tuolumne Meadows & Hoover Wilderness No. 308

FEES AND PERMITS: Overnight trips into the Yosemite backcountry require a wilderness permit (fee). A trailhead quota system is in effect, so if you plan on camping, reserve as early as possible. Space is limited and disappears quickly. Passenger vehicles entering the park are charged a $30 admission fee, which is good for seven days.

CONTACT: Yosemite National Park (209-372-0200 general information; 209-372-0740 wilderness permits; www.nps.gov/yose).

If you're looking for waterfalls, this trail's got them—five major ones in fact, not to mention a multitude of delightful unnamed pools and cascades in between the big drops to keep you oohing and aahing the whole way. Last, but certainly not least, in this procession of cataracts is Waterwheel Falls. Keep in mind that the descent comes first on this hike, quite steeply toward the end, and you climb on the way back out. Strong hikers can make the trek in a day, but it's considerably more enjoyable to do as an overnight.

GETTING THERE

From the Tioga Pass Entrance Station along CA 120, drive 7 miles west to the Lembert Dome parking area on the north side of the road (also signed for Soda Springs, Dog Lake, and Glen Aulin). Turn right onto the gravel road and park on the left-hand side, where space allows. The trail begins past a gate blocking vehicular traffic 0.3 mile from the turnoff, where the road bends right toward the stables.

THE HIKE

Begin by walking 0.5 mile along a wide dirt road (actually part of the Pacific Crest Trail) as it skirts the northern fringe of Tuolumne Meadows to the official trailhead. Follow the signs to Glen Aulin as you pass several interpretive plaques. Soda Springs and historic Parson's Lodge are nearby and worth quick exploration before forging on.

Leaving the road, the path narrows. Although it is sandy, the trail is level and easy going for the first 2 miles as it winds through a rocky lodgepole forest. Pass a

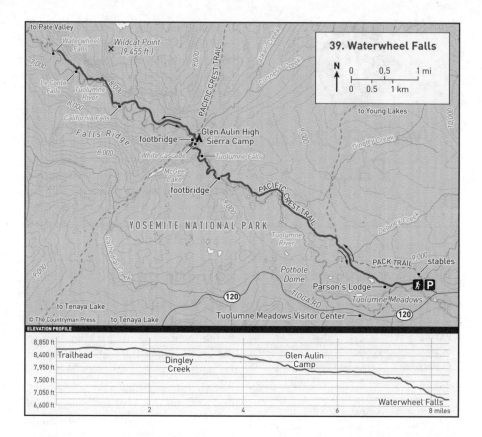

ELEVATION PROFILE

8,850 ft
8,400 ft — Trailhead
7,950 ft
7,500 ft
7,050 ft
6,600 ft

Dingley Creek

Glen Aulin Camp

Waterwheel Falls

2   4   6   8 miles

trail from the stables merging in on the right and carefully cross Delaney Creek on steppingstones at 1.3 miles. This section of trail is rather uneventful as you alternate between thick forest and open meadows that offer occasional views of the surrounding domes and peaks poking above the treetops.

At 1.6 miles the trail forks; stay left and soon cross a granite slab, guided by cairns (there are several of these along the route). Reach a broad meadow and spot the lazy Tuolumne River snaking peacefully to your left, no doubt saving its energy for the downstream extravaganza. Traverse several dry branches of Dingley Creek, round a granite outcrop, and gain your first view down the Grand Canyon of the Tuolumne, a spectacular

chasm that stretches all the way to Hetch Hetchy Valley.

At 4 miles, cross twin bridges spanning the river, which is starting to liven up a bit. The river's awakening also signifies changes in elevation, and you begin a more noticeable descent along the rocky western bank to Tuolumne Falls. Pass a left-branching trail heading toward Tenaya Lake at 4.9 miles and soon reach White Cascade, its frothy water funneled through a narrow cleft of granite before plunging erratically into a pool of emerald water.

A short distance farther, recross the river via footbridge and arrive at a junction leading to Glen Aulin High Sierra Camp (HSC). Turn right and cross a second bridge spanning Conness Creek and follow signs to the backpacker campground, where you can drop your gear and have a snack before continuing on. The backpacker camp has two metal bear boxes, but you should definitely carry your own canister, as they fill up fast and are quite a distance from some of the upper campsites. There is also a pit toilet, potable water, and a community fire ring for campers to share.

If your idea of a backcountry experience doesn't include sleeping on the ground and noshing on freeze-dried delicacies, you're in luck. Glen Aulin HSC is one of five outposts spaced 5.7–10 miles apart along a magnificent loop in Yosemite's backcountry. The only way to reach the camps is by foot or on horseback. The HSCs were originally built by the National Park Service in an effort to attract people to the park's high country. Now they are a wildly popular way to visit the wilderness without having to schlep a heavy pack and food. For a fee, and with a little luck (reservations are made by lottery), you can luxuriate in a dormitory-style tent cabin, eat hot meals, and, best of all, take a shower (at some locations).

Back on the main trail, ignore a junction heading to Virginia Canyon and

TUOLUMNE RIVER AND THE DISTANT GRAND CANYON OF THE TUOLUMNE

WHITE CASCADE NEAR GLEN AULIN HIGH SIERRA CAMP

climb up and over a small knoll, where the distant panorama unfolds. The river, peaceful again, slices through the forested floor, while bare walls of sculpted granite, the stone heart of the Sierra, hold it captive.

Generally following the northeastern bank of the river, the trail is pleasantly flat for 1.3 miles as it wanders through fire-scarred areas of young forests and meadows bursting with lupine. The seemingly still river is all but begging you to take a swim. If you are looking for a bit more solitude than Glen Aulin can offer, there are several fine campsites here along the river.

At 6.5 miles, reach California Falls, first in the upcoming string of impressive cataracts. The views along this nonstop series of cascades are from the side and can be somewhat obscured by the forest. You will notice several spur trails wandering closer for a better look. Take great caution if you approach, as the smooth granite underfoot is unbelievably slick, even if it isn't wet.

Under the sparse shade of a mixed conifer forest, begin a steep, stair-stepping descent past gigantic boulders that reverberate the river's pandemonium. At 7.7 miles, Le Conte Falls, caught in the throes of gravity, lurches and heaves as it slips through a maze of boulders beneath the watchful eye of Wildcat Point looming to the right.

Waterwheel Falls soon comes into view through the trees. An unsigned spur trail at 8.2 miles takes you closer (about midway down the falls). Rather than plunging, the falls are created when the Tuolumne River spills over a water-honed lip and races down a smooth granite incline, diving into deep holes sculpted into the rocky riverbed, then blasting out so fast that it curls back on itself, creating its signature "waterwheels." Several waterwheels are visible, and they are most impressive during the spring and early summer when flows are high. Linger a while, being mindful of the 1,100 vertical feet that stand between you and your tent at Glen Aulin.

40

Gaylor Lakes

TYPE: Day hike

SEASON: Late June through October

TOTAL DISTANCE: 3.5 miles round trip

RATING: Moderate to strenuous

ELEVATION: 9,945 feet; +1,039 feet/-198 feet

LOCATION: Yosemite National Park

MAPS: USGS 7.5' Tioga Pass; Trails Illustrated Yosemite NE—Tuolumne Meadows & Hoover Wilderness No. 308

FEES AND PERMITS: A permit is not required for this day hike. Passenger vehicles entering the park are charged a $30 admission fee, which is good for seven days.

CONTACT: Yosemite National Park (209-372-0200; www.nps.gov/yose).

Often overlooked by tourists dashing to more notable destinations like Tuolumne Meadows and Tenaya Lake, this short hike into Yosemite's alpine environs is an eminently worthwhile excursion. Enjoy relative solitude as you marvel at the sweeping vistas above Tioga Pass, ramble past a pair of picturesque alpine lakes, and explore the remnants of the Great Sierra Mine. If you can make it past the initial butt-kicking climb, you're home free, and the wonders of this lightly visited region are all yours.

GETTING THERE

From the Tioga Pass Entrance Station along CA 120, proceed through the gate and immediately turn right into a small parking area adjacent to the trailhead. If the lot is full, exit Yosemite, park along the shoulder just outside the gate, and make the short walk to the trailhead.

THE HIKE

Set out on the well-defined path and immediately begin a stiff climb through the lodgepole pine forest. Aster, Sierra penstemon, and monkey flower brighten the grassy understory. You will rise upwards of 600 feet over the next 0.5 mile, but if you can make it past this demanding section, I promise you won't be disappointed. Your lungs and legs will soon forget their recent travail when you take in the expansive panorama that awaits.

The trail begins to level off near the top of a broad, open saddle where views of Lee Vining Canyon unfurl. Opposite, red-tinted Mount Dana casts shadows upon Dana Meadows, appearing almost like a golf course spreading out below. To the southwest, the meadow gives way to forest before colliding with the

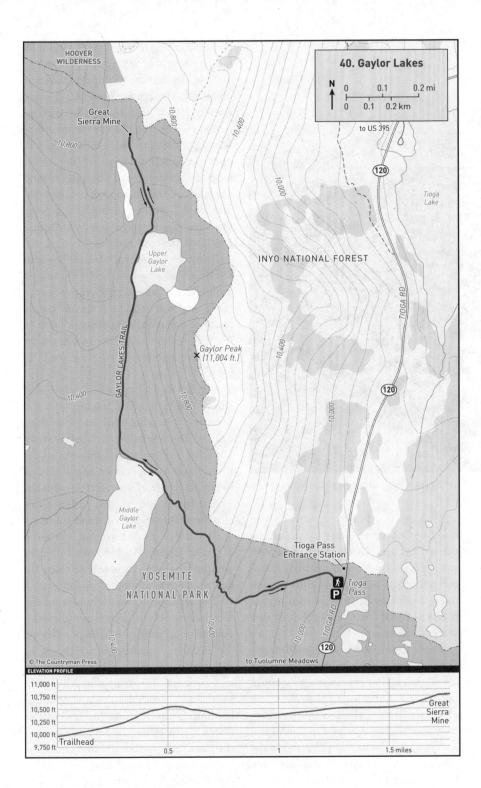

GAYLOR LAKES TRAIL WITH VIEWS OF DANA MEADOW BELOW

anglers looking to hook up with its small but feisty wild brook trout.

I've decided that "Gaylor" apparently means "lake of many insects" in some ancient forgotten language. If you happen to visit during their seasonal proliferation and don't want to be bombarded, consider packing along a bug net for the most infested parts of the trail (around the lakes). Granted, though not the most fashionable outdoor attire, it will keep the little buggers out of your mouth, and that's worth something.

The now single-track trail adheres to the northern shore as it cuts through a high-altitude grassland. Easily cross the lake's inlet, beyond which the trail bends north and continues upstream. Stick to the trail, as the subalpine meadow that gloriously surrounds you is especially fragile.

Begin a short, gradual ascent toward Upper Gaylor Lake. A variety of wildflowers color the trail as you skirt around the backside of Gaylor Peak. Look for yellow-bellied marmots sunning themselves along the trail, or listen for their characteristic whistle. These fuzzy, jumbo-size rodents are closely related to both ground squirrels and prairie dogs. At 1.3 miles, attain the shore of Upper Gaylor Lake, slightly smaller though more scenic than its downstream companion.

The level trail meanders around the west shore before ascending toward a collection of dilapidated rock edifices, the remnants of the town of Dana, an 1800s mining settlement full of hopes and dreams. The trail officially ends past several crumbling cabins. Wander farther up the hillside to explore the Great Sierra Mine, the impetus behind the town and another ill-fated endeavor by the Great Sierra Consolidated Silver Mining Company (see Hike 22).

massive Cathedral Range rising on the distant horizon. Continue up and over the saddle, littered with chunky metamorphic rock, and spot Middle Gaylor Lake, Gaylor Peak, and a host of jagged pinnacles that form the crown of this stark landscape.

From here, begin a steep descent through scraggly whitebark pine to the lakeshore, losing precious elevation in the process. At 0.7 mile, reach the shore of Middle Gaylor Lake. Lacking perspective, the pointy tips of the Cathedral Range appear to barely poke above the lake's southern fringe. Though too cold for swimming, the lake is frequented by

MIDDLE GAYLOR LAKE AND GAYLOR PEAK

Take care when exploring the area, as there are open shafts that are extremely dangerous.

The views in this alpine wonderland are stunning, and if you're up for some more reconnoitering, the seldom-visited Granite Lakes sit just over the low rise immediately west of Gaylor Peak. This will require some freelancing over the alpine countryside, but with a good map it shouldn't be difficult. Upper and Lower Granite Lakes sit gracefully at the bottom of a large rocky bowl, a classic glacial cirque. When you are ready, retrace your steps to the trailhead.

41

Chilnualna Falls

TYPE: Day hike

SEASON: April to November

TOTAL DISTANCE: 8 miles round trip

RATING: Strenuous

ELEVATION: 4,183 feet, +2,257 feet/-165 feet

LOCATION: Yosemite National Park

MAPS: USGS 7.5' Wawona, Mariposa Grove; Trails Illustrated Yosemite SW–Yosemite Valley & Wawona No. 306

FEES AND PERMITS: A permit is not required for this day hike. Passenger vehicles entering the park are charged a $30 admission fee, which is good for seven days.

CONTACT: Yosemite National Park (209-372-0200; www.nps.gov/yose).

Since Wawona, a Miwok word for "big trees," is located at an elevation of 4,000 feet, this makes a fantastic early season jaunt to the top of one of Yosemite's lesser-known but no less spectacular waterfalls. Views of this reclusive cataract, however, come at a cost—four miles of steep, relentless uphill climbing—that deters all but the brave few. If you choose to be one of the few, and I hope you do, the relatively quiet trail will reward you with outstanding views of Wawona Dome, the Chowchilla Mountains, and the South Fork Merced River coursing below. Pack along plenty of water, as the trail can get warm as summer approaches, and remember to watch for rattlesnakes. Water displays are best during the spring when Chilnualna Creek is gushing with snowmelt.

GETTING THERE

From the South Entrance on CA 41, drive 7.4 miles north through Wawona to Chilnualna Falls Road and turn right (0.25 mile north of the Wawona Hotel). Proceed 1.7 miles past the Wawona stables, where the road narrows through a private residential area before reaching the trailhead parking lot, where there are pit toilets.

THE HIKE

With most tourists heading straight for Yosemite Valley, other equally transcendent regions of the park often get overlooked. One such place is Wawona, a small, quiet community located in southern Yosemite. This somewhat isolated and less visited (by Yosemite standards) area of the park is home to the historic Wawona Hotel, Pioneer History Center, Mariposa Grove of giant sequoias, and our trailhead to Chilnualna Falls.

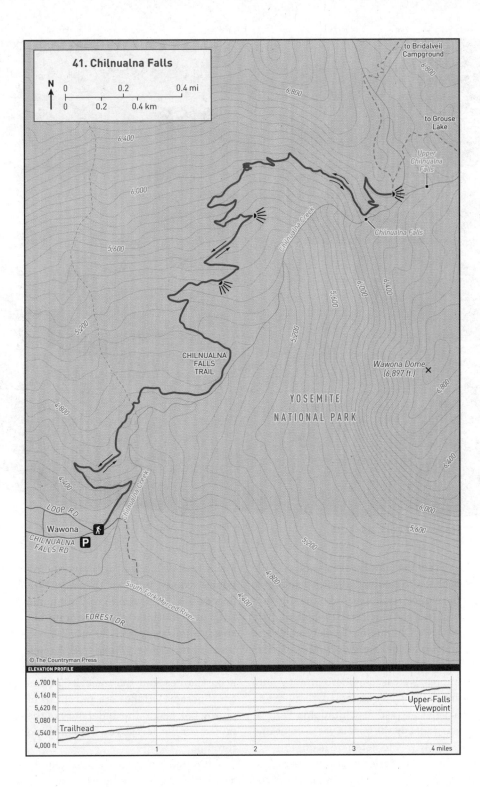

41. Chilnualna Falls

N
0   0.2   0.4 mi
0   0.2   0.4 km

to Bridalveil
Campground

6,900

6,800

to Grouse
Lake

6,400

Upper
Chilnualna
Falls

6,000

Chilnualna Creek

Chilnualna Falls

5,600

6,000

6,400

5,600

5,200

5,200

Wawona Dome
(6,897 ft.)

6,800

CHILNUALNA
FALLS
TRAIL

YOSEMITE
NATIONAL PARK

4,800

6,400

6,000

5,600

4,400

Chilnualna Creek

5,200

LOOP RD

Wawona

CHILNUALNA
FALLS RD

P

4,800

4,400

South Fork Merced River

FOREST DR

© The Countryman Press

ELEVATION PROFILE

6,700 ft				Upper Falls
6,160 ft				Viewpoint
5,620 ft				
5,080 ft				
4,540 ft	Trailhead			
4,000 ft				
	1	2	3	4 miles

RAINBOW OVER CHILNUALNA FALLS

From the parking area, walk 0.1 mile back to Chilnualna Falls Road and up to the signed trailhead. Take the dirt foot trail (not the stock trail), which quickly narrows. Chilnualna Creek tumbles and crashes to your right as it stair-steps its way over gigantic boulders, creating an impressive cascade mere minutes into your hike. Don't be fooled, though: you haven't arrived at Chilnualna Falls at warp speed—the best is yet to come and the only way to get there is up.

Ascend a series of granite steps, and at 0.3 mile, arrive at a junction with the stock trail and a placard announcing your entrance into the Yosemite Wilderness. Follow the sign to Chilnualna Falls and continue your moderate but steady climb away from the creek, along the mountain misery-lined trail. A thick carpet of this fernlike flowering shrub accompanies you the majority of the trip. Sporadic wildflowers and sprigs of poison oak add to the understory of the mixed conifer forest you are traveling through.

Although your lungs are acutely aware of the effort being exerted, your eyes aren't fully rewarded until 2 miles into the hike, when you come to a granite overlook with views of Wawona Dome directly across from you, and the forested slopes of the Chowchilla Mountains in the distance. Catch your breath and listen for the rumble of Chilnualna Falls beckoning you to disregard your aching quadriceps and forge on.

About 0.5 mile past the overlook, get your first glimpse of Chilnualna Falls tucked in a narrow granitic chasm high on the ridge. Your view is limited from this vantage and continuously changes to include more of the falls as you switchback higher through the forest. Despite your sideways view, it is the most complete view of the largest drop in the falls.

At 3.1 miles, cross a small seasonal stream as you make your way through a shady forest of black oaks, incense cedar, and red fir offering peek-a-boo views of the valley below. The trail then opens as you make a final push to the top of the falls along a granite staircase.

From your perch atop the brink of the free-fall you admired on the way up, watch Chilnualna Creek plunge from the edge into a water-darkened chasm of rock, mist, and rainbows. Though this is not the most photogenic part of the falls (since you are on top and not in front of them) don't despair—just turn your attention upstream to upper Chilnualna Falls. A cascading wall of water tumbles hundreds of feet down the boulder-lined creek channel as it courses its way to the lower free-fall and ultimately the Merced River below.

Find a comfy spot and take a well-deserved rest along the rushing creek, or, if you still want more, continue along the trail 0.5 mile farther to the top of the upper cascade. The trail will begin rising above and parallel to the creek, then veer sharply away and into a forest of manzanita before turning back toward the upper tiers. From a signed junction, walk to the waterfall's edge and enjoy a whole new set of cascades and pools before returning via the same trail.

At the junction, 0.3 mile from the trailhead, avoid the temptation to descend via the stock trail. It takes you on a circuitous route that only increases your mileage. Opt to take the foot trail and see Chilnualna Creek from a whole new vantage.

If time allows, the popular Mariposa Grove of giant sequoias, the largest inside park boundaries and just south of Wawona, is fascinating to visit. Several easy trails crisscross the grove, which was discovered in 1857 by Galen Clark, the first guardian of Yosemite and the original proprietor of the Wawona Hotel. With fanciful names like Bachelor and Three Graces, Faithful Couple, Grizzly Giant, and Clothespin Tree, how can you resist a walk among these stately giants?

42

Hite Cove

TYPE: Day hike

SEASON: Typically, November through May. The trail is closed during periods of high fire danger.

TOTAL DISTANCE: 2 to 4 miles round trip for wildflower viewing; 7.4 miles round trip to Hite Cove

RATING: Moderate

ELEVATION: 1,414 feet; +524 feet/-341 feet

LOCATION: Sierra National Forest

MAPS: USGS 7.5' Kinsley, El Portal

FEES AND PERMITS: A permit is not required for this day hike.

CONTACT: Sierra National Forest, Bass Lake Ranger District (559-877-2218; www.fs.usda.gov/sierra); Yosemite Redbud Lodge (209-379-2301).

This hike has historic beginnings and endings, and with the right timing, a bounty of spring wildflowers in between. Touted by some as the best wildflower hike in California, the first couple miles have the most dense and lively displays. The single-track trail parallels the South Fork Merced River as it rushes to join the main stem of the Merced River near the trailhead. The trail is narrow, exposed, and has a precarious downhill drop-off along a significant portion, so is no place for the inattentive. The sub-2,000-foot elevation means warmer temperatures and limited shade. Pack along plenty of water, sun protection, and a wildflower identification field guide. Keep a keen eye for poison oak, rattlesnakes, and slow-footed newts along the trail.

GETTING THERE

From Mariposa, drive 22 miles north on CA 140 toward Yosemite National Park, or about 11 miles west of the Arch Rock Entrance to Yosemite. Park on the north shoulder of the highway (river side) and find the well-marked trailhead on the opposite side.

THE HIKE

The trail begins at the site of historic Savage's Trading Post. James D. Savage, a miner, established a trading post here in 1849, shortly after gold was discovered at Sutter's Mill, to trade gold for goods with local Native American tribes. The store was eventually attacked, pillaged, and burned by tribes rebelling against the scourge of miners descending upon their land. Later Savage was appointed to lead the Mariposa Battalion to search for tribal leaders responsible for raiding American settlements. During their

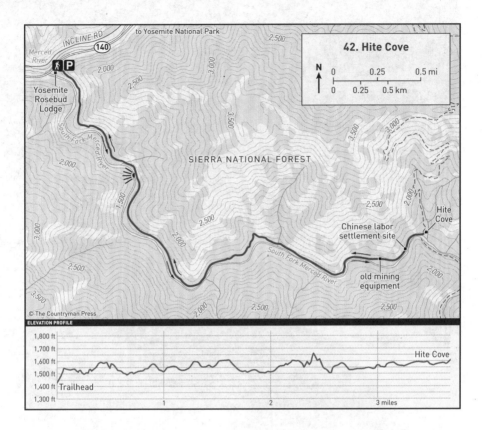

42. Hite Cove

ELEVATION PROFILE

search, the Battalion entered Yosemite Valley in 1851, and in doing so, became the first group of non-indigenous discoverers of the Yosemite Valley.

The hike culminates at the remnants of Hite Cove, a mining camp named after John Hite, who discovered one of the richest quartz-gold veins in the Central Sierra here in 1862. Hite ran the mine for 17 years and built a small town on the site that included a hotel, saloon, and even a post office at one point to support laborers working the mine. By 1874, the facility had increased from a crude, circular stone arrastra pulled by mules to a 20-unit stamp mill that pulverized rock to extract the gold. The historical value of the gold removed is estimated at $3,000,000. While the

buildings burned down in 1924, many foundations and remnants still exist.

To begin the hike, find the signed trailhead behind the Yosemite Redbud

MARIPOSA LILY

HITE COVE TRAIL AND SOUTH FORK MERCED RIVER

Lodge. Proceed up the paved driveway and immediately turn right onto a dirt path. The first 0.75 mile of this hike crosses private property. An initial short climb takes you past a few buildings and water tanks associated with the lodge. The South Fork Merced River quickly comes into view coursing some 150 feet below and rarely leaves your side the rest of the way, although it's well out of reach during the first 2 miles. The rolling trail cuts across the eastern canyon wall, which is swathed in species commonly found in an arid chaparral community: manzanita, scrub oak, buckeye, chamise, and hardy grasses and forbs.

With John Hite's mining operation long gone, the new "gold" hikers seek

of blossoms, including poppy, redbud, blazing star, Chinese houses, Indian pink, and Mariposa lily, to name but a few. As you ogle the blooms, keep an eye out for Sierra newts crossing the trail. They lumber more than scurry out of the way so watch your footing to avoid stepping on them.

Pass a sign indicating that you are entering Sierra National Forest at 0.75 mile. Shortly thereafter, a rock outcrop offers nice views overlooking the river. The generally parched trail crosses several trickling creeks lined with a lush mix of riparian vegetation. Keep a vigilant eye for poison oak, which likes to encroach upon the trail, and for ticks looking for a ride. At approximately 2 miles the trail descends to a sandy bar along the river and there are several spur trails that will deposit you closer to the water. At about 2.5 miles, pass a cluster of sedimentary rocks with an intricate swirling pattern. This is a perfect spot to take a break and enjoy the river's raucous serenade.

Continuing upstream, still near to the river, the trail flattens and enters a broad sandy section with a denser forest canopy. At 3.4 miles, the first evidence of a mining operation comes into view. Scattered along the north side of the trail, explore the rusty remains of a Pelton wheel, cone grinders, and an arrastra. A bit farther, come upon the remains of a small Chinese labor settlement and what's left of a suspension bridge that once spanned the river. Cross the ravine to explore the overgrown vestiges of the once bustling Hite Cove. Return via the same path back to the trailhead.

comes in the form of spring wildflowers. Depending on the water year, there is a narrow window sometime between March and early May when the canyon slopes come alive in a vibrant palette

VI.

SEQUOIA AND KINGS CANYON NATIONAL PARKS

43

Mist Falls

TYPE: Day hike

SEASON: May to November

TOTAL DISTANCE: 8 miles round trip

RATING: Easy to moderate

ELEVATION: 5,025 feet; +638 feet/-0 feet

LOCATION: Kings Canyon National Park

MAPS: USGS 7.5' The Sphinx; Trails Illustrated Sequoia Kings Canyon National Parks No. 205

FEES AND PERMITS: A permit is not required for this day hike. Wilderness permits are required year-round for all overnight trips. During the peak season a trailhead quota system is in effect and there is a fee; the remainder of the year permits are free. If you are planning an overnight in this area, be advised that camping is not allowed along this stretch of trail until you reach Lower Paradise Valley, which is 1 mile past the falls. Passenger vehicles entering the park are charged a $30 admission fee, which is good for seven days.

CONTACT: Sequoia and Kings Canyon National Parks (559-565-3341 general information; 559-565-3766 wilderness permits; www.nps.gov/seki).

Where the blacktop ends, the adventure begins. At Roads End in Kings Canyon National Park, that couldn't be truer. The terminus of CA 180 near Cedar Grove is the farthest your car can take you into this playground, where glaciers scoured and rivers sculpted the earth into a natural masterpiece. Roads End, a widely used springboard for backpackers into the deep reaches of Kings Canyon, is where our trail to Mist Falls begins. Chaperoned by the vigorous South Fork Kings River, this popular hike to one of the canyon's most impressive cataracts is a relatively easy jaunt. Proximity to the Kanawyer Loop Trail also gives you an option for a whole different perspective on the return trip.

GETTING THERE

From the Kings Canyon National Park Big Stump Entrance Station, follow CA 180 for 35 miles to Roads End (5 miles past the turnoff for Cedar Grove Village), where you will find ample parking, water, and pit toilets. The trailhead is located near the ranger station at the east end of the parking lot.

THE HIKE

Sequoia and Kings Canyon National Parks are not endowed with a plethora of stunning waterfalls like their northerly neighbor, Yosemite. Nonetheless, what the parks lack in quantity is made up in quality.

Walk past the ranger station and join the wide, sandy trail that parallels the South Fork Kings River through an open, mixed forest of oaks, pines, and cedars. Quickly come to a wooden footbridge that carries you across Copper Creek. The nearly level trail wanders past fire-scarred trees and boulders that

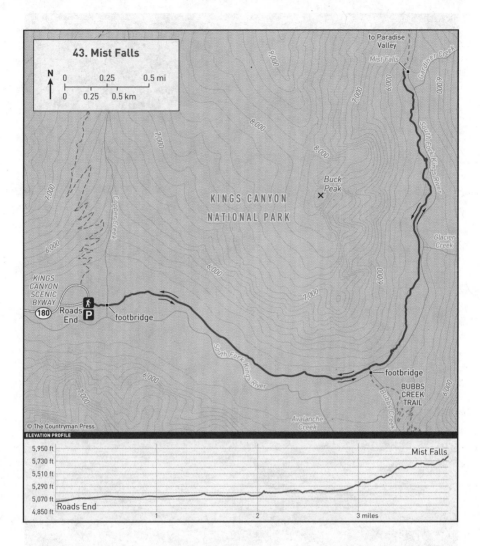

43. Mist Falls

ELEVATION PROFILE

gravity brought crashing down from the granite cliffs above. Look for mule deer foraging on grasses and black-crested Steller's jays zipping about. The area also sees its share of rattlesnakes and bruins, so use caution.

The forest is open enough to grant views of the upright granite walls that form Kings Canyon, one of the deepest and most dramatic gorges in North America. Just outside the boundary of the park, near the confluence of the South and Middle Forks of the Kings River, Spanish Peak (10,051 feet) towers over the meandering river some 8,000 feet below. Like much of the Sierra, the upper reaches of the canyon were glacially sculpted (U-shaped valleys) with the lower reaches being carved by rivers (V-shaped valleys).

After bisecting a dense pocket of manzanita shrubs, the trail descends slightly into a cool forest, its understory blanketed with ferns. Trade the sandy trail for hard-packed dirt and reach a trail fork at 1.9 miles, where you veer

MIST FALLS PUTTING ON A DISPLAY

left toward Mist Falls and Paradise Valley. The Bubbs Creek Trail is to the right and crosses the South Fork Kings River via a steel footbridge. Take note of this junction. On the return trip you have the option of crossing the river here and following the southern bank back to the trailhead.

From the junction, the trail begins to climb via a series of stone steps, rising above the turbulent river. Incense cedars, ponderosa pines, and black oaks provide shade. Bend away from the river momentarily into a peculiar stand of invasive bamboo, then cross an exposed mini-avalanche of boulders before heading back into the shady forest. Rendezvous with the frothy river once again and ascend another longer granite staircase to the top of a rocky outcrop, 3 miles from the trailhead, where views downstream unfold. The Kings River courses below, flanked by imposing granite walls on both sides. Standing sentinel in front of you is the Sphinx, an irregularly shaped granite peak that (if you squint a little and the light is just right) looks remotely like its Egyptian namesake.

Continue your ascent, passing several smaller cataracts clogged with boulders and downed logs as you close in on your goal, but don't mistake them for the real thing—you haven't reached the falls yet. At 4 miles, a sign, dispelling any doubts, marks your arrival at spectacular Mist Falls. A short spur trail takes you close to the base of the raucous cataract. As the name implies, Mist Falls is misty, so use caution on the slippery rocks if you do venture closer. Although the falls are only 45 feet high, the immense flow of water in early spring creates a frothy, white, tumbling torrent that sends a cooling spray billowing into the air. As the season wears on and flows diminish, the raging torrent is tamed, and the subtle details of the cascade can be seen. You can hike to the top of the falls by following the main trail less than 0.5 mile, but undoubtedly the best vantage is from below.

When ready, retrace your steps and enjoy the views of the canyon all over again. When you reach the Bubbs Creek Trail junction (1.9 miles from the trailhead), bear left and cross Bailey Bridge. Shortly after crossing, bear right at a trail fork and head west along the south bank of the river toward Roads End.

Early in the season, when flows from Avalanche Creek are high, the trail may be underwater just past the fork, and crossing can be dangerous. If that's the case, turn around and head back the way you came.

Though this is a slightly longer option (2.6 miles versus 2 miles back to the trailhead from the Bubbs Creek Junction), the trail is less traveled and offers a new perspective. You will need to walk slightly downstream of the trailhead to reach a footbridge where you can re-cross the river and head back to the parking lot at Roads End.

If you are looking to delve deeper into the backcountry, from short weekend trips to long-distance treks, there is a plethora of backpacking opportunities out of Roads End. Backpackers can complete the breathtaking 42-mile Rae Lakes Loop, cross the Sierra via Kearsarge Pass, join up with the Pacific Crest Trail and hike to Canada, or simply overnight in Paradise Valley.

On your drive to Roads End, you may have noticed Boyden Caverns along the south bank of the Kings River. To date, more than 200 caves have been found in Sequoia and Kings Canyon. Most are in the western third of the parks, along a narrow bank of marble paralleling the Sierra. If you are looking for a fun diversion, stop in at privately owned Boyden Caverns, which is just outside the park. Although it's highly commercialized, a 45-minute tour, suitable for children, takes you into the cavern, where you can marvel at the amazing underground formations. Crystal Cave (in Sequoia) is the only commercialized cavern within the boundaries of the park. Note that both Boyden Caverns and Crystal Cave charge separate admission fees.

44

Redwood Mountain Grove

TYPE: Day hike or overnight

SEASON: Mid-May through November

TOTAL DISTANCE: 7.2-mile loop

RATING: Moderate

ELEVATION: 6,218 feet; +1,465 feet/-1,465 feet

LOCATION: Kings Canyon National Park

MAPS: USGS 7.5' General Grant Grove; Trails Illustrated Sequoia Kings Canyon National Parks No. 205

FEES AND PERMITS: A permit is not required for this day hike. Wilderness permits are required year-round for all overnight trips. During the peak season a trailhead quota system is in effect and there is a fee; the remainder of the year permits are free. Passenger vehicles entering the park are charged a $30 admission fee, which is good for seven days.

CONTACT: Sequoia and Kings Canyon National Parks (559-565-3341 general information; 559-565-3766 wilderness permits; www.nps.gov/seki).

Redwood Mountain Grove is the largest concentration of giant sequoias left in the world. Partly because of its obscurity and partly because of the dirt road you take to get there, Redwood Mountain Grove has remained off the grid for the majority of Sequoia and Kings Canyon visitors, who would rather flock to the manicured trails within Giant Forest. This loop hike takes you into the very heart of the grove, where you can walk among the soaring monarchs in blissful solitude. The lightly used trail wanders past lush meadows, along trickling creeks, and under a shady canopy that offers fleeting vistas of the surrounding peaks.

GETTING THERE

From the Kings Canyon National Park Big Stump Entrance Station, continue along CA 180 for 0.9 mile and turn right onto CA 198 (General's Highway). Proceed 3.5 miles to Quail Flat, and turn right onto a dirt road signed for Redwood Canyon (opposite the paved road to Hume Lake). Reach a Y-junction at 1.7 miles and veer left, following the sign to Redwood Canyon Trailhead. Find the spacious parking area with pit toilets 0.1 mile farther. The signed Hart Tree trailhead is at the southeast corner of the parking area.

THE HIKE

There are two loop trails that start here, Hart Tree Trail and Sugar Bowl Trail. We take the Hart Tree Trail, which passes through Redwood Mountain Grove's eastern side. Later, I discuss how to combine the two trails to create a slightly longer loop.

Descend the wide trail (once a roadbed) into a beautiful forest where giant

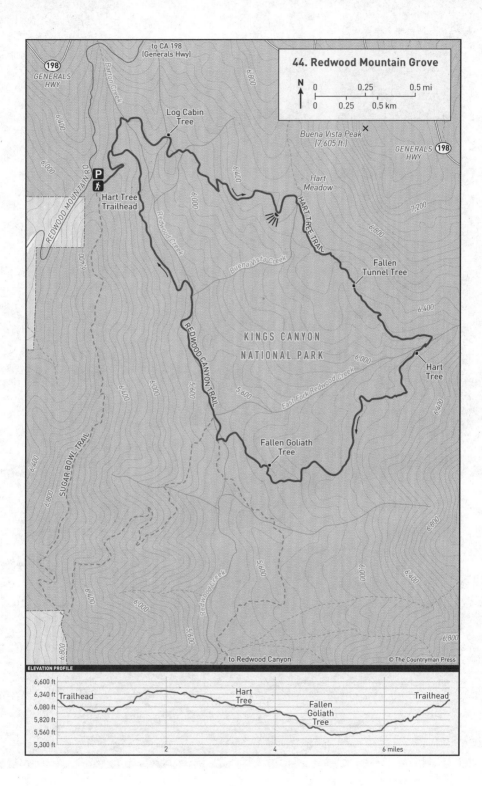

44. Redwood Mountain Grove

N

| 0 | 0.25 | 0.5 mi |
| 0 | 0.25 | 0.5 km |

to CA 198
(Generals Hwy)

198
GENERALS
HWY

Barton Creek

Log Cabin
Tree

Buena Vista Peak ×
(7,605 ft.)

GENERALS 198
HWY

Hart
Meadow

7,200

REDWOOD MOUNTAIN RD

P

Hart Tree
Trailhead

Redwood Creek

HART TREE TRAIL

Fallen
Tunnel Tree

Buena Vista Creek

REDWOOD CANYON TRAIL

KINGS CANYON

NATIONAL PARK

East Fork Redwood Creek

Hart
Tree

SUGAR BOWL TRAIL

Fallen Goliath
Tree

Redwood Creek

to Redwood Canyon

© The Countryman Press

ELEVATION PROFILE

Trailhead — Hart Tree — Fallen Goliath Tree — Trailhead

| 6,600 ft | 6,340 ft | 6,080 ft | 5,820 ft | 5,560 ft | 5,300 ft |
| 2 | 4 | 6 miles |

GIANT SEQUOIAS FLANKING THE TRAIL

sequoias intermingle with other conifers and shade a rich understory of dogwood, California rose, and broadleaf lupine. Pure stands of sequoias are rarities. Most often, they are found growing alongside white firs, sugar pines, and red firs. Ponderosa pines and California black oaks often occupy drier sites within the grove boundaries. Pass an interesting cluster of four sequoias in perfect alignment, and at 0.3 mile come to a trail fork. Bear left and continue along Hart Tree Trail. The right fork will be our return leg.

Enjoy the melodious, fluty warble of the hermit thrush as you descend toward Barton Creek. Easily cross the lush, fern-choked rivulet and begin a mild climb to the next creek crossing just before Log Cabin. The "cabin" is actually a downed giant sequoia that was hollowed out, partially by fire, and transformed into a rudimentary domicile by an enterprising human during the first half of the twentieth century, when the grove was unfortunately logged (prior to it falling under the purview of the National Park Service).

Past the cabin, you climb above the creek to a manzanita-covered saddle where the forest opens briefly, offering limited views of the tree-covered slopes to the west. Sequoias are scant along this section of trail, but will reappear later. Pass a swath of singed trees and charred stumps, but notice how nature heals itself as grasses and wildflowers quickly reemerge on the forest floor.

You cross two more seasonal creeklets and climb to a granite outcrop at 1.75 miles, from which you have views of Redwood Mountain to the west and Big Baldy to the south. From here, enjoy level walking before meeting Hart Meadow, which is bursting with slender grasses and elegant ferns. At the southwestern end of the meadow, easily cross the double channels of Buena Vista Creek and follow the trail on a general descent. The sequoias reappear, and you bisect a small stand of about six of them, giving a little perspective to their enormity. The trail then passes through Fallen Tunnel Tree, a fire-gutted sequoia (watch your head), and your descent steepens for about 0.2 mile. Walk through and along fallen sequoias, crossing East Fork Redwood Creek 3 miles from the trailhead. This crossing can be slightly difficult when flows are high.

From the creek, ascend along the southern bank and shortly thereafter reach a junction with a short, steep trail leading to fire-scarred Hart Tree, the largest tree in the grove. Fire is a critical factor in the growth and vigor of giant sequoia forests. Their unusually thick bark is fire-resistant, allowing them to survive while other species perish. They actually depend on the intense heat of fire to open their small cones, allowing seeds to be released. Once released, the tiny seeds require contact with bare soil to germinate, and this is only possible when fire has cleared leaf litter and other debris from the forest floor. Fire also thins out other species that compete with sequoia seedlings for light and moisture, and it cycles nutrients back into the soil. A century's worth of fire suppression has taken its toll on sequoia populations. Realizing the role fire plays in the lifecycle of these giant trees, the National Park Service now routinely sets prescribed fires, allowing sequoia forests to reproduce and as a tool for fuel management.

After admiring Hart Tree, return to the main trail and watch for Hartweg's iris as the descent continues to a lushly lined, unnamed creek with a lovely ribbon waterfall that glides between moss-covered rocks into a small pool. Easily cross via steppingstones and continue through the mixed forest to the bottom of the canyon, crossing one more seasonal creek. Nearing the 4.5-mile mark, the descent steepens, and you should watch for the small, ankle-twisting sequoia cones that litter the trail. You would think such a massive tree would have equally massive cones, but the opposite is true.

At 4.6 miles, a spur trail leading to Fallen Goliath makes a small loop off the main trail and rejoins it after passing along the enormous trunk of this downed giant. Reach the low point of the journey at 5.1 miles and cross alder-lined Redwood Creek. Fortunately, a fallen tree spans the creek, creating a natural bridge—otherwise crossing might prove difficult in the early season.

On the other side of the creek, you come to a signed junction with Redwood Canyon Trail. Turn right and travel upstream along the western bank of Redwood Creek, arriving at a second junction at 5.2 miles with Sugar Bowl Trail. You have the option of turning left here and creating a longer loop of 9 miles. Stay straight and follow signs to the parking area. With the creek pleasantly trickling beside you, make your way through a lush understory of dogwood, thimbleberry, and a smattering of wildflowers, the most prolific being broadleaf lupine, which grows in thickets beneath the towering sequoias. At 5.9 miles, the gently ascending trail turns away from the creek and begins a steeper climb, passing around and through the decaying corpses of several fallen giants. The main cause of death among mature sequoias is toppling, due to their shallow, wide-spreading lateral root system.

Reach the junction with Hart Tree Trail at 6.9 miles, closing the loop. From here, turn left (south), retracing your steps to the parking area.

45

Little Baldy

TYPE: Day hike

SEASON: June through October

TOTAL DISTANCE: 3.4 miles round trip

RATING: Moderate

ELEVATION: 7,360 feet; +764 feet/-110 feet

LOCATION: Sequoia National Park

MAPS: USGS 7.5' Giant Forest; Trails Illustrated Sequoia Kings Canyon National Parks No. 205

FEES AND PERMITS: A permit is not required for this day hike. Passenger vehicles entering the park are charged a $30 admission fee, which is good for seven days.

CONTACT: Sequoia and Kings Canyon National Parks (559-565-3341; www.nps .gov/seki).

Rise above the treetops on this pleasant hike to the top of one of Sequoia's uncharacteristic exposed granite domes. The well-defined trail climbs moderately along wildflower-laden hillsides to a broad outcrop with expansive views in every direction. In fact, the view from Little Baldy's summit is so extensive that it was once used as a fire lookout. There are no facilities at the trailhead, nor is there any water along the trail. Little Baldy's exposed nature is an invitation for lightning, so be mindful of changing weather and descend immediately if storms threaten.

GETTING THERE

From the Kings Canyon National Park Big Stump Entrance Station, continue along CA 180 for 0.9 mile and turn right onto CA 198 (General's Highway). Proceed 17.7 miles south to Little Baldy Saddle and park in the roadside pullout. The trail begins near a large sign on the east side of the highway.

THE HIKE

Mount a series of steps and enter a mixed forest of stately red firs and Jeffrey pines. The trail steadily rises, parallel to the highway, past hillsides adorned with scattered ferns, bitter cherry, thimbleberry, and a cornucopia of wildflowers. The hum of vehicles quickly recedes the higher you climb, and you enjoy slivers of view through periodic breaks in the trees of Chimney Rock (frequented by rock climbers) and the protruding round face of Big Baldy to the northwest.

In late spring and early summer, wildflower enthusiast will enjoy the fantastic array of blooms. The path is mottled with blue-eyed Mary, monkey flower, groundsel, penstemon, Coulter's

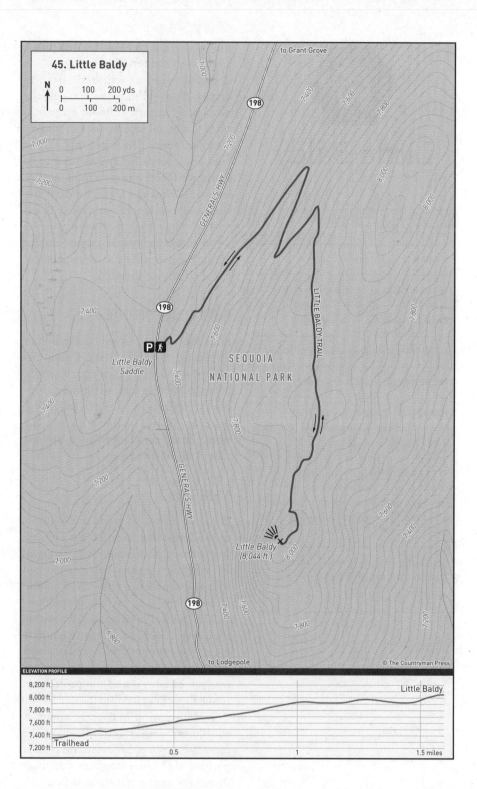

45. Little Baldy

N
0   100   200 yds
0   100   200 m

to Grant Grove

198

GENERALS HWY

198

P 🚶

Little Baldy
Saddle

LITTLE BALDY TRAIL

SEQUOIA
NATIONAL PARK

GENERALS HWY

Little Baldy
(8,044 ft.)

198

to Lodgepole

© The Countryman Press

ELEVATION PROFILE

8,200 ft
8,000 ft
7,800 ft
7,600 ft
7,400 ft
7,200 ft

Little Baldy

Trailhead

0.5   1   1.5 miles

ASCENDING THE TRAIL TO LITTLE BALDY SUMMIT

HAZY VIEW OF THE GREAT WESTERN DIVIDE FROM THE LITTLE BALDY SUMMIT

daisy, wallflower, Indian paintbrush, and larkspur, to name just a few. In addition to the wildflowers, watch for marmots, chipmunks, butterflies, and birds on your quest for the summit. We even had to pause while a sooty grouse and her brood of youngsters crossed the trail.

Continue uphill via a series of long, easy switchbacks, and at the 1-mile mark reach the crest of the hillside. Enjoy level walking along a fire-scarred ridge littered with downed logs and dense clusters of saplings vying for survival. The flat path comes to an end a short 0.2 mile farther, and you make a small climb, passing a rocky knoll to your right. Lose 100 feet of the precious elevation you worked so hard to attain before

the final climb to the summit. From the base of Little Baldy, a short, rocky climb leads to the top and the panoramic view.

From the broad granite summit (8,044 feet), Spanish Mountain and Obelisk are visible to the north. To the east, the Great Western Divide dominates the landscape. This small side range of the Sierra Nevada separates the Kaweah and Kern River watersheds. Southward you can see the top of Moro Rock and the jutting spires of Castle Rocks. Westward, you now have an unobstructed view of Big Baldy and Chimney Rock, and in the distance, through the haze, the San Joaquin Valley. When you are done admiring the view, return to your vehicle via the same path.

46

Tokopah Falls

TYPE: Day hike

SEASON: May through October

TOTAL DISTANCE: 3.8 miles round trip

RATING: Easy

ELEVATION: 6,762 feet; +683 feet/-3 feet

LOCATION: Sequoia National Park

MAPS: USGS 7.5' Lodgepole; Trails Illustrated Sequoia Kings Canyon National Parks No. 205

FEES AND PERMITS: A permit is not required for this day hike. Passenger vehicles entering the park are charged a $30 admission fee, which is good for seven days.

CONTACT: Sequoia and Kings Canyon National Parks (559-565-3341; www.nps.gov/seki).

This hike up glacially carved Tokopah Valley culminates at the base of 1,200-foot-high Tokopah Falls. This impressive cataract along the Marble Fork of the Kaweah River originates high above in alpine environs, and you get a front row seat as it slides, plunges, tumbles, and careens over smooth granite faces in its quest for the valley floor. Tokopah Falls is without a doubt the most spectacular falls in Sequoia National Park. The easy trail and its proximity to Lodgepole, one of the park's major hubs of activity, negates any chance of solitude. However, by starting early you can avoid much of the crowd.

GETTING THERE

From CA 198 (General's Highway), head east at the signed Lodgepole junction. Proceed 0.7 mile, passing the visitor center and campground entrance station to a large parking area. Walk up the campground access road, passing the Walter Fry Nature Center and restrooms to a fork in the road. Veer left and cross a bridge spanning the Marble Fork of the Kaweah River and immediately find the trailhead on the right.

THE HIKE

Your course follows the north bank of the Marble Fork of the Kaweah River. Throughout the hike, you will notice several unofficial trails leading down to the river's edge. If your plans call for fishing or a chilly soak for trail-worn toes, take care on slippery rocks and near swift-moving sections of the river, especially during peak flows.

The falls lie at the east end of U-shaped Tokopah Valley, which was formed in much the same way as Yosemite Valley. As the powerful Tokopah Glacier moved

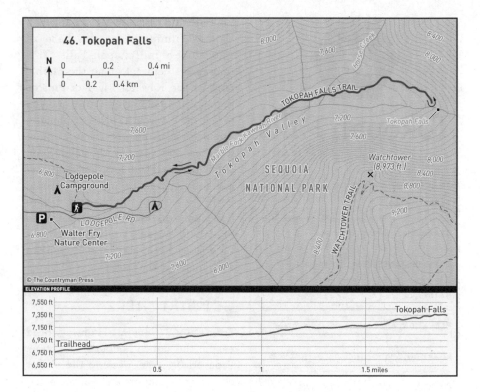

across the land, it carved, scoured, and scraped, leaving in its wake towering cliffs of smooth, bare granite marred by rock fragments and boulders carried by the moving sheet of ice. At the head of the valley lie the Tablelands, a lofty plateau of stark granite flanked by Mount Silliman to the north and Alta Peak to the south.

Begin by gently climbing through a mixed forest of red firs, incense cedars, and ponderosa and Jeffrey pines. A variety of wildflowers like golden brodiaea, lupine, cinquefoil, and mustang clover soften the boulder-strewn path and fill trailside meadows. Though the trail meanders near and far from the splashing river, its soothing melody is never far from earshot. There are many spots to stop and admire the pleasing pools, cascades, and ripples created by the streambed's changing terrain. Cross

a verdant meadow on a narrow path trimmed with stones and, as you move farther into the valley, garner glimpses of its towering southern flank.

At 1.3 miles, an easy boulder hop takes you across a small tributary clogged with boulders and downed limbs, and you get your first good view of the Watchtower, an island of granite rising 1,600 feet above the river. Views of this hulking monolith only improve as you continue farther, and if you look closely, you might even be able to spy the trail to Heather and Pear Lakes clinging to the cliff's edge (see Hike 47).

Traverse the first of three wooden footbridges over Horse Creek and continue across a dry wash. At 1.6 miles, as you leave the forest, the trail grade increases, and you get your first glimpse of Tokopah Falls as it stair-steps and spills down the valley's headwall. Over

TOKOPAH FALLS MAKING ITS STAIR-STEPPING PLUNGE INTO TOKOPAH VALLEY

the last 0.25 mile, shady conifers are replaced by drier, sun-loving shrubs, and the trail becomes increasingly rocky. Watch your footing and your noggin as you cross a talus slope, occasionally passing beneath head-banging boulders. A flat bench at the base of the falls signifies the end of the trail. A sign warns hikers not to continue farther, as steep cliffs make travel extremely dangerous.

Now up close, you can only see the final cascade. Like most Sierra waterfalls, these are best viewed in spring and early summer when the rivers are swollen with snowmelt. From the falls you have amazing views of the pointy Watchtower knob jutting from the striated southern wall, you can watch the pacified river disappear into the forested valley downstream, and gaze up at the chunky granite wall directly behind you (north).

Watch for yellow-bellied marmots sunning themselves on boulders or listen for their distinctive whistle. Marmots, relatives of ground squirrels and prairie dogs, are commonly called "whistle pigs." Their whistle is typically used to notify other marmots of approaching predators; however, I think it also serves to let the group know of incoming hikers lugging backpacks loaded with tasty vittles. Guard your food and don't give them any handouts, no matter how cute they appear. After enjoying the falls, return the way you came.

Lakes Trail to Heather Lake

TYPE: Day hike or overnight

SEASON: Mid-June through October

TOTAL DISTANCE: 8.2 miles round trip

RATING: Moderate to strenuous

ELEVATION: 7,281 feet; +2,210 feet/-229 feet

LOCATION: Sequoia National Park

MAPS: USGS 7.5′ Lodgepole; Trails Illustrated Sequoia Kings Canyon National Parks No. 205

FEES AND PERMITS: A permit is not required for this day hike. Wilderness permits are required year-round for all overnight trips. During the peak season a trailhead quota system is in effect and there is a fee; the remainder of the year permits are free. Passenger vehicles entering the park are charged a $30 admission fee, which is good for seven days.

CONTACT: Sequoia and Kings Canyon National Parks (559-565-3341 general information; 559-565-3766 wilderness permits; www.nps.gov/seki).

This popular route along the Lakes Trail offers, hands down, some of the most scenic hiking in all of Sequoia National Park. Climb through a hearty red fir forest to spectacular vistas from the Watchtower, a hulking monolith that looms over Tokopah Valley, and visit a tranquil subalpine lake festooned with heather and lodgepole pines. Though this hike culminates at picturesque Heather Lake, the first of a succession of lakes found along the trail, you have the option of continuing on to three other alpine gems (Aster, Emerald, and Pear Lakes). Strong hikers can make the challenging 12 miles round trip to Pear Lake in one day, but even better is to overnight on the northern shore where you can watch shadows dance on stark granite walls and count stars that choke the charcoal sky and color the night.

GETTING THERE

From CA 198 (General's Highway), 1.5 miles south of the Lodgepole turnoff, head east at the signed Wolverton junction. Proceed 1.4 miles to the large trailhead parking area (continue straight at the three-way stop near General Sherman Tree). Turn left into the first parking area, where you will find the trailhead and bathrooms.

THE HIKE

The trail begins at the top of a set of brick stairs at the north end of the parking area. The well-used Lakes Trail gently climbs to a junction at 0.2 mile, with a connector path leading to Lodgepole. Bear right and almost immediately you pass a second junction with Long Meadow Trail. The grade eases as you make your way along a dry ridge dominated by wolf lichen-covered red firs.

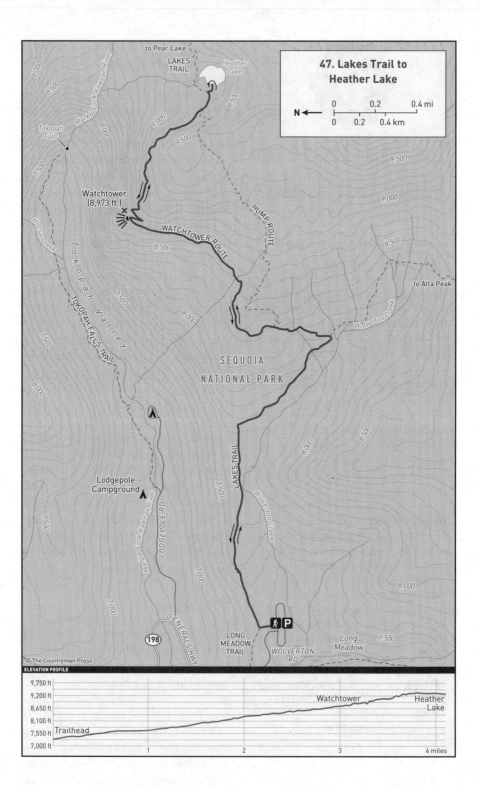

47. Lakes Trail to Heather Lake

to Pear Lake
LAKES TRAIL
Heather Lake

0   0.2   0.4 mi
N ←
0   0.2   0.4 km

9,000
8,500
8,000
Marble Fork Kaweah River
Tokopah Falls
7,500
Horse Creek
Tokopah Valley
TOKOPAH FALLS TRAIL
7,500
8,000
7,500
7,500
7,000

9,500
9,000
Watchtower (8,973 ft.)
WATCHTOWER ROUTE
8,500
8,000

HUMP ROUTE

9,500
9,000
8,500
to Alta Peak
Wolverton Creek
8,500

SEQUOIA
NATIONAL PARK

LAKES TRAIL

8,000
Wolverton Creek
8,000

7,500
Lodgepole Campground
LODGEPOLE RD
7,000

198
GENERALS HWY

LONG MEADOW TRAIL
WOLVERTON RD

Long Meadow
7,500

© The Countryman Press

ELEVATION PROFILE

| 9,750 ft |
| 9,200 ft |
| 8,650 ft |
| 8,100 ft |
| 7,550 ft |
| 7,000 ft |

Trailhead   Watchtower   Heather Lake

1   2   3   4 miles

TOKOPAH VALLEY AS VIEWED FROM THE WATCHTOWER

The neon-green-colored lichen is a combination of a fungus and an algae. The fungus, similar to a mushroom, is incapable of making its own food, and that's where the algae come in. With the ability to photosynthesize like a plant, the algae provide nutrients, which the pair use to proliferate together. Wolf lichen, which is toxic, was used in Europe to poison wolves (hence the name) and by Native American tribes to make poison arrowheads, dye, and, strangely enough, tea.

Toward the crest of the ridge, you begin to hear Wolverton Creek splashing to the right. The trail briefly drops down to its northern bank and along a verdant meadow of grasses, forbs, and sedges neatly trimmed with lodgepole pines. The ascent resumes as you parallel Wolverton Creek, occasionally utilizing tree roots for stairs. The trail alternates between open grassy clearings dotted with wildflowers and dense forest with little understory. At 1.6 miles, an easy boulder hop takes you across an aspen- and wildflower-edged feeder stream of Wolverton Creek. Arrive at the Alta Peak Trail junction not long after and veer left (north) toward Heather Lake. Climb moderately past fern-covered hillsides and recross the same small tributary, but now higher up the slope. Arrive at the Hump Route junction, 2 miles and 1,000 vertical feet from your starting point.

From here you have two options, which both ultimately get you to Heather Lake. The Watchtower Route is without question the more scenic path but isn't advised for acrophobic hikers,

TRAIL HEWN INTO THE GRANITE LANDSCAPE

as one section traverses a fantastically exposed, precipitous rock ledge. The Hump Route is steeper, rises an additional 200 vertical feet, lacks any notable views, and the concoction of twigs, pine cones, rocks, and loose sand at your feet creates a literal slippery slope (note: walking sticks come in quite handy). Its only saving grace is that it is 0.3 mile shorter. If you absolutely can't stand going the same way twice when you have the option, ascend via the Watchtower Route and return on the Hump Route. My recommendation, though, is to come and go via the Watchtower and enjoy a second helping of superb vistas.

From the junction, the trail steadily rises and the northwestward views of Tokopah Valley begin to take shape through occasional voids in the red fir forest. At 2.5 miles, the woodland briefly opens and you enter a swath of greenery surrounding a tributary of the Marble Fork of the Kaweah River. The lush area is brimming with streamside bluebells, and a lovely little waterfall tumbles upstream. Cross with the aid of steppingstones and continue onward and upward. With each advance in elevation, notice the increasing appearance of boulders and the disappearing trees.

A series of switchbacks deposits you atop the Watchtower, an enormous granite spire towering some 1,600 feet above the Marble Fork of the Kaweah River coursing below. From your perch, the views are staggering. The stark Tablelands sit in repose to the east; Tokopah Falls, cradled in the heart of the valley, careens down clefts and crevices in the polished granite; and Mount Silliman rises stoically to the north.

Leave your lofty vista point and begin the final push to the high point of the journey. The trail, initially tucked beneath the trees, eventually emerges onto an exposed ledge that was blasted from the granite cliff. Rounding the uppermost corner, the view expands to the south to include 11,204-foot Alta Peak and several of its craggy neighbors.

The rocky trail then heads gently uphill and rejoins the Hump Route at 3.9 miles. Bear left and continue 0.2 mile to the shore of Heather Lake, passing a signed path leading to an open-air toilet 200 yards from the main trail. A steep arc of granite forms the backdrop of this subalpine gem, and purple mountain heather adds a splash of color to the lodgepole pine-dotted shore. Scout out a nice boulder and spread out a picnic before returning or venturing farther.

If you extend your day hike by continuing up the Lakes Trail, you will reach Emerald Lake (9,226 feet) 0.9 mile beyond the outlet of Heather Lake. Aster Lake (9,108 feet) is accessed by turning left where Emerald Lake's outlet crosses the trail and following it 0.2 mile downstream. Pear Lake (9,548 feet) is the official culmination of the trail and is 1.9 miles past Heather. Backpackers should note that camping is forbidden at both Heather and Aster Lakes. Wilderness permit-carrying backpackers can find designated campsites near Emerald and Pear Lakes.

48

Circle Meadow

TYPE: Day hike	

TYPE: Day hike

SEASON: May to November

TOTAL DISTANCE: 4-mile loop

RATING: Easy

ELEVATION: 7,063 feet; +694 feet/-694 feet

LOCATION: Sequoia National Park

MAPS: USGS 7.5' Giant Forest, Lodgepole; Trails Illustrated Sequoia Kings Canyon National Parks No. 205

FEES AND PERMITS: A permit is not required for this day hike. Passenger vehicles entering the park are charged a $30 admission fee, which is good for seven days.

CONTACT: Sequoia and Kings Canyon National Parks (559-565-3341; www.nps .gov/seki).

The Giant Forest is by far the most heavily visited area within Sequoia National Park. This easy hike begins and ends by dodging the hordes of tourists who flock to see the General Sherman Tree, but if you can manage the masses, it's the middle of this ramble that makes it all worth the hassle. Wander off the paved pathway and skirt lush Circle Meadow, passing several notable trees in the process, minus the fences and the crowds. Start at the Giant Forest Museum, just south on General's Highway, and acquaint yourself with the natural and human history of the area before walking among the big trees.

GETTING THERE

From the Lodgepole turnoff in Sequoia National Park, drive 1.5 miles south on CA 198 (General's Highway) to Wolverton Road. Turn left and proceed 0.5 mile to a three-way stop. Turn right, following signs for Sherman Tree parking, which is 0.6 mile farther.

THE HIKE

From the parking area, make your way to the ostentatious Sherman Tree Trailhead (there are bathrooms and water here). Follow the wide paved pathway downhill, passing several interpretive plaques, and take note of the signed Congress Trail to your left. Assuming you got an early start, explore the General Sherman Tree at 0.4 mile before it gets overly crowded.

This gargantuan sequoia not only holds the distinction of being the largest tree on earth by volume (52,500 cubic feet), but also the largest living thing in the world. Named in 1879 by James Wolverton, a pioneer cattleman who served under General William

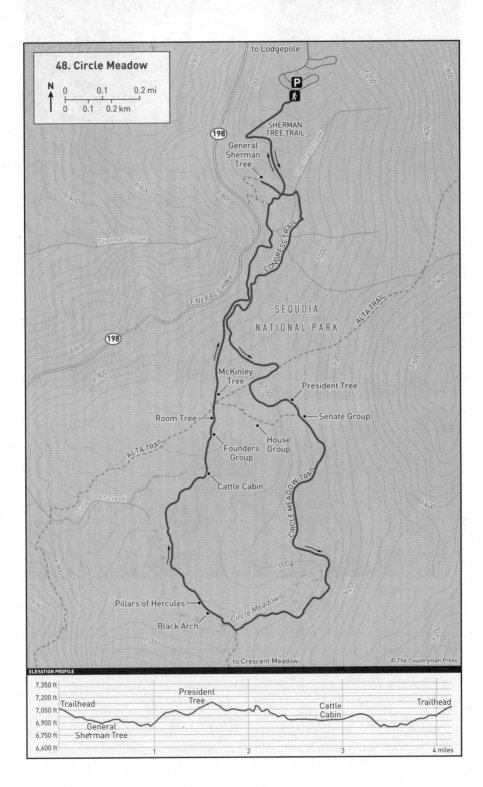

48. Circle Meadow

N
0   0.1   0.2 mi
0   0.1   0.2 km

to Lodgepole

P

SHERMAN TREE TRAIL

198

General Sherman Tree

CONGRESS TRAIL

Sherman Creek

GENERALS HWY

198

SEQUOIA NATIONAL PARK

ALTA TRAIL

McKinley Tree

President Tree

Room Tree

Senate Group

House Group

Founders Group

ALTA TRAIL

Little Deer Creek

Cattle Cabin

CIRCLE MEADOW TRAIL

Pillars of Hercules

Black Arch

Circle Meadow

to Crescent Meadow

© The Countryman Press

ELEVATION PROFILE

7,350 ft
7,200 ft
7,050 ft
6,900 ft
6,750 ft
6,600 ft

Trailhead

General Sherman Tree

President Tree

Cattle Cabin

Trailhead

1   2   3   4 miles

LUSH CIRCLE MEADOW

Tecumseh Sherman in the American Civil War, the tree stands 275 feet tall, has a trunk diameter of 36.5 feet, and is a whopping 2,200 years old. The top of the tree is dead, so instead of getting taller, General Sherman expands around the "trunk line." In optimal conditions, it adds enough wood to equal another good-size tree each year. When you're done craning your neck, wander back to the start of the Congress Trail.

The Giant Forest is crisscrossed with a multitude of well-marked paths, so it's hard to get lost. Follow the paved Congress Trail downhill to the Learning Tree and subsequently cross a pair of footbridges spanning branches of Sherman Creek. Continuing south, you pass several towering sequoias before coming to a cutoff trail on the right. Stay left (unless you want a shorter loop) and reach a junction with Alta Trail at 1 mile. Follow the pavement by bearing right on the Alta/Congress Trail and immediately come to another junction. Turn left to remain on the Congress Trail and head toward President Tree, the third largest sequoia, and later the Senate Group.

Near the cluster of sequoias named the Senate Group, find a sign directing you through the middle of this stately bunch and off the paved pathway toward Circle Meadow. The size of these trees is that much more amplified when you can actually stand next to them and gaze up their fibrous, cinnamon-colored trunks.

The trail undulates and winds through the peaceful woodland. Ferns and broadleaf lupines blanket the forest floor. At 1.9 miles, reach the southeast corner of Circle Meadow. The meadow actually forms a "C" (you are at the bottom and will follow the curve around in a clockwise direction). Ringed by majestic sequoias and other lesser conifers, the narrow clearing is filled with verdant sedges and grasses that are complemented each spring by a colorful palette of wild blossoms. Watch for bears and deer foraging in the meadow.

At 2.3 miles, come to an intersection with the Crescent Meadow Trail. Turn right and head north across the meadow. Pass through Black Arch, a fire-hollowed sequoia, and between the Pillars of Hercules, a pair of big trees flanking the trail. Continue toward Cattle Cabin, which was built by cattlemen who used the meadow for grazing prior to the establishment of the park. Past the cabin, cross the northern portion

MANICURED SHERMAN TREE TRAILHEAD

of the meadow (the top part of the "C") and stroll through the Founder's Group, a collection of sequoias dedicated to the people who helped establish Sequoia National Park. Next up is Room Tree. Climb through the low opening at the base of this giant and enter a small wooden chamber—a literal treehouse.

At 3.1 miles, you rejoin the paved Congress Trail near the McKinley Tree.

Follow the path north as it descends toward the cutoff trail and later walk through a low tunnel carved in a fallen sequoia. Cross Sherman Creek via the footbridge and ascend back to the bustling General Sherman Tree area, where you can retrace your steps uphill to the parking lot.

Crescent and Log Meadows Loop

TYPE: Day hike

SEASON: June to November

TOTAL DISTANCE: 2.5-mile loop

RATING: Easy

ELEVATION: 6,691 feet; +570 feet/-570 feet

LOCATION: Sequoia National Park

MAPS: USGS 7.5' Giant Forest, Lodgepole; Trails Illustrated Sequoia Kings Canyon National Parks No. 205

FEES AND PERMITS: A permit is not required for this day hike. Passenger vehicles entering the park are charged a $30 admission fee, which is good for seven days.

CONTACT: Sequoia and Kings Canyon National Parks (559-565-3341; www.nps .gov/seki).

There are many trails crisscrossing the popular Crescent Meadow area. This short, pleasant loop packs in a little bit of everything: splendid views, flower-filled meadows, a dose of history, and numerous giant sequoias. John Muir is said to have called sequoia-rimmed Crescent Meadow the "gem of the Sierras," and when you finish this hike you will no doubt agree with his observation.

GETTING THERE

From the Sequoia National Park Ash Mountain Entrance Station, drive 16 miles north on CA 198 (General's Highway). Just south of the Giant Forest Museum, turn east onto paved Crescent Meadow Road. Follow the narrow road 2.5 miles, past turnoffs for Auto Log and Moro Rock, to the parking area at the road's end. You will find water, pit toilets, and bears at the trailhead. Most trailheads in Sequoia provide metal bearproof lockers for visitors to store food and scented items that might attract curious bruins. Use them—they are there for a reason.

THE HIKE

This counterclockwise loop begins on the paved pathway just south of the restroom building. The first leg coincides with the 49-mile High Sierra Trail. Crescent Meadow marks the western terminus of this long-distance route traversing the Sierras from east to west. The demanding trail goes up and over the Great Western Divide, eventually intersecting the John Muir/Pacific Crest Trail, where it officially ends.

Cross fern-filled Crescent Creek via a pair of wooden footbridges and bear right at a fork to maintain course on the High Sierra Trail, trading the pavement

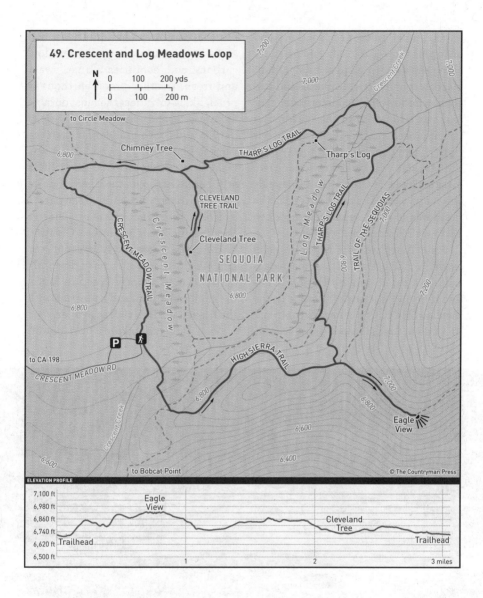

49. Crescent and Log Meadows Loop

N

| 0 | 100 | 200 yds |
| 0 | 100 | 200 m |

to Circle Meadow

Chimney Tree

THARP'S LOG TRAIL

Tharp's Log

CLEVELAND
TREE TRAIL

Cleveland Tree

SEQUOIA

NATIONAL PARK

CRESCENT MEADOW TRAIL

Crescent Meadow

Log Meadow

THARP'S LOG TRAIL

TRAIL OF THE SEQUOIAS

to CA 198

CRESCENT MEADOW RD

HIGH SIERRA TRAIL

Eagle View

Crescent Creek

to Bobcat Point

© The Countryman Press

ELEVATION PROFILE

7,100 ft		Eagle		
6,980 ft		View		
6,860 ft			Cleveland	
6,740 ft			Tree	
6,620 ft	Trailhead			Trailhead
6,500 ft		1	2	3 miles

for dirt. Immediately arrive at a second junction heading toward Bobcat Point and Moro Rock. Bear left this time and follow the easy grade uphill through a forest of red fir and scattered sequoias.

At 0.5 mile, reach a saddle and a signed three-way junction. Bear southwest toward Eagle View. You will return to this spot after a quick jaunt to the overlook. Follow the now rocky trail 0.3 mile to a lofty perch high above

the Middle Fork of the Kaweah River. Notice the dramatic shift in vegetation on the steep, south-facing slope. From here, Moro Rock is visible to the west, Castle Rocks and the Paradise Ridge sit opposite, and the snow-capped peaks of the Great Western Divide dominate the eastern horizon.

Retrace your steps to the three-way junction and follow signs toward Tharp's Log. The trail descends quickly to another junction near the southern end of Log Meadow. Turn right and meander along the eastern edge of this verdant meadow brimming with grasses and seasonal wildflowers. Watch for mule deer and bears foraging in the meadow as you approach another junction on your right, which connects with the Trail of the Sequoias. Stay straight, crossing two forks of Crescent Creek. The trail bends west as you skirt the northern end of the meadow and soon arrive at Tharp's Log and a trail junction at 1.7 miles.

Hale Tharp was the first European settler to homestead in the area, establishing a ranch among the big trees and allowing his cattle to graze in the meadow. He built a summer cabin out of a fallen, fire-hollowed giant sequoia in the 1860s that John Muir described as "a spacious log house of one log, carbon-lined, centuries old yet sweet and fresh, weather proof, earthquake proof, likely to outlast the most durable stone castle, and commanding views of garden and grove grander far than the richest king ever enjoyed." Muir was right—the sturdy arboreal domicile is still here, and holds the distinction of being the oldest structure in the park.

From the junction near Tharp's Log, briefly climb northwest. Cresting a low ridge separating Crescent and Log Meadows, you then head downhill, arriving at Chimney Tree, an erect, fire-hollowed giant, and a junction with the Cleveland Tree trail at 2 miles.

Veer left and take a short detour

BREAKING AWAY FROM THE PAVED PATHWAY AND ONTO THE HIGH SIERRA TRAIL

TRAILHEAD SIGN POINTING THE WAY AROUND THE MEADOW

(adding 0.4 mile round trip to the loop) to Cleveland Tree, one of the larger sequoias in the Giant Forest. Return to the junction near Chimney Tree and turn left, walking along the northern fringe of Crescent Meadow. Soon you'll arrive at a trail fork and turn left, following the trail as it bends south and skirts the meadow's western margin. If you hit it right, the green carpet of grass can be bursting with a cornucopia of wildflowers including shooting stars, leopard lilies, and lupines. Close the loop at 2.5 miles when you reach the picnic area and parking lot.

If you've got time to spare, head to Moro Rock and Crystal Cave. Moro Rock (you passed a sign for it on Crescent Meadow Road) is an exfoliating granite dome offering unparalleled views of the surrounding landscape. A short but steep set of stairs ascends 300 vertical feet to the summit (6,725 feet). Even though you can expect an army of people climbing alongside you, the view makes up for the dearth of solitude.

Crystal Cave, just south on General's Highway, provides a break from the granite and forests aboveground. Unbeknownst to many visitors, Sequoia and Kings Canyon include an extensive karst system. There are in fact over 200 known caves within park boundaries, Crystal Cave being the only commercialized one within Sequoia. The exquisite marble cavern is festooned with icicle-like stalactites and mounds of stalagmites that are wondrous to behold. Note that there is a separate fee required to tour the cave. Tickets can be purchased online or at the Lodgepole or Foothills Visitor Center.

50

Eagle Lake

TYPE: Day hike or overnight

SEASON: Late June to mid-October

TOTAL DISTANCE: 6.8 miles round trip

RATING: Strenuous

ELEVATION: 7,822 feet; +2,202 feet/-11 feet

LOCATION: Sequoia National Park

MAPS: USGS 7.5' Mineral King; Trails Illustrated Sequoia Kings Canyon National Parks No. 205

FEES AND PERMITS: A permit is not required for this day hike. Wilderness permits are required year-round for all overnight trips. During the peak season a trailhead quota system is in effect and there is a fee; the remainder of the year permits are free. Passenger vehicles entering the park are charged a $30 admission fee, which is good for seven days.

CONTACT: Sequoia and Kings Canyon National Parks (559-565-3341 general information; 559-565-3766 wilderness permits; www.nps.gov/seki).

A fair warning: although the hike to Eagle Lake is one of the easier treks radiating from the Mineral King area, that isn't saying much. The well-maintained trail rises swiftly more than 2,200 feet in less than 3.5 miles, but don't let that stop you. Sublime views of the metamorphic peaks surrounding the Mineral King Valley, a granite-hemmed subalpine lake, and easy brook trout fishing are just a few of the reasons to make the long journey to the seldom seen southern fringe of Sequoia National Park and venture to the tranquil shore of this high-country gem.

GETTING THERE

From CA 198, just north of the town of Three Rivers, turn onto Mineral King Road and drive 24.5 miles east along this narrow, bumpy, winding, mostly paved road to its end at the trailhead parking area (allow a minimum of 90 minutes). You will pass the Lookout Point Entrance Station approximately 10 miles into the drive. Find pit toilets across from the Mineral King Ranger Station or on the north side of the Kaweah River Bridge just prior to the trailhead. The parking area is a favorite feeding spot for marmots that like to nibble through car hoses in search of aromatic antifreeze. We didn't have any problems; however, we did see several cars wrapped with tarps or surrounded by chicken wire to keep the yellow-bellied beasties out. Check your engine compartment before driving off to make sure there are no stowaways hiding under the hood.

THE HIKE

Yes, you have to work a little to get to Mineral King. That's the downside. The upside is the chance to walk into

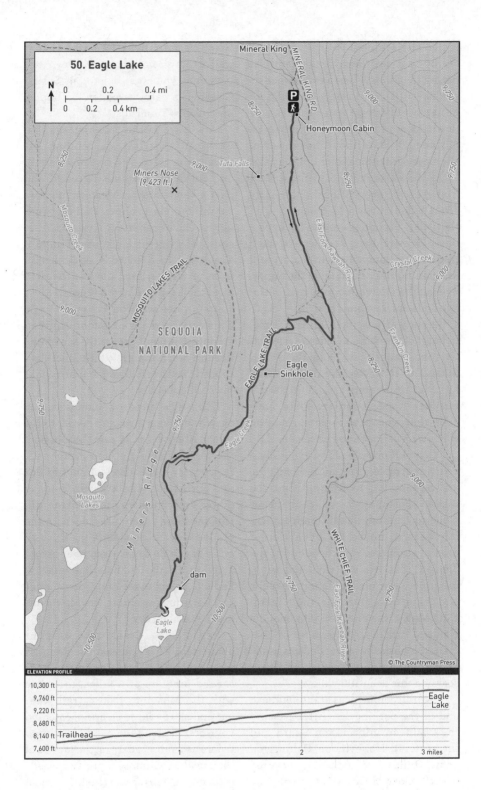

50. Eagle Lake

N

| 0 | 0.2 | 0.4 mi |
| 0 | 0.2 | 0.4 km |

Mineral King

MINERAL KING RD.

P

Honeymoon Cabin

8,250

9,000

9,750

Tufa Falls

Miners Nose
(9,423 ft.)
×

9,000

8,250

8,250

East Fork Kaweah River

Crystal Creek

9,000

Mosquito Creek

Mosquito Lakes Trail

SEQUOIA
NATIONAL PARK

9,000

EAGLE LAKE TRAIL

9,000

Eagle
Sinkhole

8,250

Franklin Creek

9,750

Eagle Creek

Miners Ridge

9,750

Mosquito
Lakes

dam

Eagle
Lake

10,500

9,750

WHITE CHIEF TRAIL

East Fork Kaweah River

9,000

9,750

10,500

© The Countryman Press

ELEVATION PROFILE

10,300 ft				Eagle Lake
9,760 ft				
9,220 ft				
8,680 ft				
8,140 ft	Trailhead			
7,600 ft		1	2	3 miles

a glacially sculpted valley framed by 11,000-foot sawtooth peaks reminiscent of the Swiss Alps, to experience its wildflower-studded meadows and gaze at narrow braids of water that course down its red-tinged mountain slopes. Oh, and all this without the crowds of the more accessible regions of the park.

As the name implies, Mineral King first gained recognition in the early 1870s when silver was discovered in the valley. Though the mines never produced, Mineral King Road, constructed by a mining company to transport mill and mining equipment up to the mines, opened the area to logging, hydroelectric development, and tourism.

As early as the 1940s, Mineral King, not part of the National Parks system at the time, was considered by the United States Forest Service as a potential site for a ski resort under its multiple-use mandate. It wasn't until the 1960s, however, that wheels were set in motion when Walt Disney Enterprises, Inc. laid out an ambitious plan for a $35 million complex of motels, restaurants, ski lifts, and parking lots to accommodate the masses. Fortunately, the resort never came to fruition, due to environmental concerns raised by a coalition of preservationists, spearheaded by the Sierra Club. After years of legal wrangling between environmental groups and commercial interests, the Mineral King Valley was annexed into Sequoia National Park in 1978 by an act of Congress, which decisively ended any plans for ski runs and hordes of visitors of ever scarring this beautiful valley.

The trail commences at the southern end of the parking lot. After passing the trailhead information board and the restored Honeymoon Cabin, you begin a mild climb up the sage-covered western slope of Farewell Canyon. The Great Western Divide forms the eastern wall of this glacially carved valley. After 0.25 mile, you cross boisterous Spring Creek via a narrow wooden footbridge; upstream is Tufa Falls.

Just beyond the crossing, pass an unsigned spur trail descending left toward the river. The trail wanders in and out of small stands of red fir and past a few contorted western junipers as you continue to climb. Your eastward view includes cascading Crystal Creek, south of Mineral Peak, and Franklin Creek, north of Tulare Peak. Both spill from headwaters high above in a rush to meet the East Fork of the Kaweah River coursing below. After crossing Eagle Creek via some conveniently placed steppingstones, the trail steepens. Reach a junction with White Chief Trail 1 mile from the trailhead and turn right toward Eagle Lake.

The single-track trail climbs steeply past the junction through a denser red fir forest. About 0.3 mile past the junction, the forest opens and you switchback up a grassy slope alive with butterflies and sprinkled with larkspur, monkey flower, and bistort. At the top of the hillside meadow, reach a ridge where the grade eases and you follow the mysteriously dry Eagle Creek streambed before arriving at Eagle Sinkhole. It is here that Eagle Creek plunges into a deep crater and flows underground, leaving its former streambed dry.

With Eagle Creek now as your chaperone, stroll pleasantly along its western bank before coming to your second junction at 2 miles, this time with the Mosquito Lakes Trail. Veer left and skirt a large clearing, catching your breath along the nearly level trail before ascending again on the far end of the meadow. Glimpse a pretty cascade through the trees as you climb a pinemat

LINGERING SNOW AT EAGLE LAKE

MARMOT PEEKING FROM ITS BOULDER-STREWN SANCTUARY

south to Walker Pass in Tehachapi to cross them.

You have undoubtedly seen several marmots scurrying about during your ascent. As you cross the talus slope, you may also spot American pikas, high-altitude relatives of the rabbit that are about the size of a large hamster. Pikas live in rocky mountain areas and boulder-covered hillsides between the timberline and subalpine forest, within reach of meadows or patches of vegetation. They have small rounded ears and peppery brown fur, and have no visible tail. They use a variety of squeaks and squeals to communicate with each other and their marmot neighbors.

Beyond the talus slope, the grade eases and you pass through a thin forest of lodgepole pines underlain with a smattering of grasses, shrubs, and slabs of granite. The trail deposits you at the north shore of Eagle Lake (10,010 feet) where a small dam, maintained by Southern California Edison, enhances the volume of the lake.

The crystalline lake is bordered by steep granite walls and decorated with lingering patches of snow well into summer. Cross the dam and explore the eastern shore, or walk farther along our trail and scout out a camping or picnic spot. If you plan on camping, the best sites are located near the midpoint of the lake on the pine-shrouded western shore.

Anglers will enjoy fishing for brook trout that I think would eat a bare hook, they are so aggressive. Though the fish are small, there is something magical about casting a line into a remote high-country lake. When you've gotten your fill, return via the same path.

manzanita-lined trail past boulders and the ever-thinning woodland.

After passing a small meadow to the east, you arrive at the base of an expansive talus slope. Begin the long trek across the exposed slope by boulder-hopping the first 100 feet. Past this small section, the trail becomes more defined. Look for red penstemon and red elderberry that sprout from rocky crevices and add splashes of color to the stark landscape.

Of course, the higher you get in this treeless terrain, the better the view. Brooding to the northeast are metamorphic Sawtooth and Mineral Peaks, and to the southeast, Franklin Pass and Florence Peak. From this vantage it's easy to understand why much of the southern Sierra is devoid of roads. In fact, Sequoia and Kings Canyon Parks form the heart of the second-largest contiguous roadless area left in the Lower 48. The southern Sierra are so rugged that you must go north to Tioga Pass in Yosemite or